Black Greek 101

Black Greek 101

The Culture, Customs,
and Challenges
of Black Fraternities and Sororities

Walter M. Kimbrough

Madison • Teaneck
Fairleigh Dickinson University Press
London: Associated University Presses

Associated University Presses
2010 Eastpark Boulevard
Cranbury, NJ 08512

The paper used in this publication meets the requirements of the American National Standard for Permanence of Paper for Printed Library Materials Z39.48-1984.

Library of Congress Cataloging-in-Publication Data

Kimbrough, Walter M., 1967–
  Black Greek 101 : the culture, customs, and challenges of Black fraternities and sororities / Walter M. Kimbrough.
       p. cm.
Includes bibliographical references and index.
  ISBN 0-8386-3977-1 (cloth) (alk. paper)
  ISBN 0-8386-4024-9 (paperback) (alk. paper)
1. African American college students.   2. Greek letter societies—United States.   I. Title.
  LC2781.7.K56 2003
  378.1'98'55—dc21   2002155863

PRINTED IN THE UNITED STATES OF AMERICA
Eighth Printing 2006

For my parents
Walter and Marjorie Kimbrough
Role models for myself, and thousands of young people.

Contents

Acknowledgments

I AM THANKFUL TO GOD FOR PROVIDING ME WITH THE DEDICATION TO complete this project, one that was long overdue. Had He not sent me to Albany, Georgia, a place where eligible women are few and far between (okay, maybe not that bad but not great either), I probably would have been out in the street instead of consistently working on this book, every day.

There were numerous people who have been involved in my development that ultimately led to this book. While I will inevitably miss some in these acknowledgments, I want them to know that they all have been helpful to me and I am truly thankful. First, I have to thank the Zeta Pi chapter of Alpha Phi Alpha Fraternity, Inc. at the University of Georgia, where I was initiated and where I was given a good foundation for my future work. Dr. Ron Binder, the advisor to fraternities at UGA while I was there, deserves special recognition for this project. Ron invited me to present with him at the 1989 Association of Fraternity Advisors convention to address Black Greek issues. That presentation, entitled "Black Greek 101," was my introduction to Student Affairs and my subsequent career path. By attending that conference, I was introduced to two significant mentors: Dr. Michael V. W. Gordon, the first executive director of the National Pan-Hellenic Council (NPHC) and one of my dearest friends, and Dr. Tyrone Bledsoe, my "big brother," who has served as a great role model in my profession. Special thanks go out to historian extraordinaire, Bro. Skip Mason, who has been a great mentor for conducting historical research.

Numerous faculty have provided guidance along the way, including Dr. Marcia Baxter-Magolda, Dr. Judy Rogers, and Dr. Gary Knock of Miami University; and Bro. Dr. Alfred McWilliams and Dr. Philo Hutcheson of Georgia State University. Thanks to my supervisors and colleagues in Student Affairs at Emory University, Georgia State University, Old Dominion University, and Albany State University. They have all been supportive of my efforts to be involved professionally, especially allowing me the opportunity to travel the country and share with undergraduates. Special thanks goes out to Dr. Todd Schill, Dr. Bridget Guernsey-Riordan, Camellia Flanigan (my second mother), Dr. Jim Scott, Dr. Kurt Keppler, Kevin Propst, Dr. Lori Hart-Ebert, Dr. Dana Burnett, Dr. Maggi Curry-Williams, Carretta Cooke, Lesa Clark, my whole Student Activities staff at Old Dominion University, Dr. Portia Holmes Shields (Madame President), the Cabinet, Reginald Christian, and my division of Student Affairs at Albany State University.

Colleagues in the Association of Fraternity Advisors (AFA), Southern Association for College Student Affairs (SACSA), National Association of Latino Fraternal Organizations (NALFO), North American Interfraternity Conference (NIC), National Panhellenic Conference (NPC), and the National Association of Student Personnel Administrators (NASPA) have been a tremendous support over the duration of my career. Thanks so much for your support. Special thanks goes to Bro. Dr. Michael Sutton (my faculty mentor and partner in crime), Bro. Dr. Ralph Johnson (father of the Alpha Leadership Academy), Bro. Dr. Brian Hemphill, Shaun Harper, Mike Hayes, Rick Barnes (second best looking man in AFA), Greg Singleton, Maureen Syring, Dr. Will Keim, Dr. Kent Gardner, Dave Westol, Mary Peterson, Monica Miranda, Dr. Ed King, and Jonathan Brandt.

Thanks to my good friends of the NPHC and the National Black Greek Leadership Conference (BGLC). Y'all always invite me to speak to the students, and I always try to deliver. Much love to Cassandra Black, Virginia LeBlanc, Candice Wicks, Jennifer Jones, Bro. Darryl Peal, Bro. Brett Waterfield, Charles Talbert, Fran Davis, Dr. Jason De Sousa, and the late Gloria Duncan. From the BGLC, special shouts to Bro. Robert Page (founder of the BGLC), Pam Reese, Kevin Jones, Zakiya Smith, Bryant Smith, Lori Patton, and Dr. Ishmail Conway. Most importantly, I have to thank the STUDENTS who have attended these numerous conferences and invited me to speak on their campuses. Over the years you have taken great care of me and we've had a good time. I look forward to more campus visits in the future!

Bro. Lawrence Ross Jr. deserves a special word of thanks. Lawrence convinced me that I could write the book, and was a good mentor throughout the process. But more importantly, he opened the door for more books on the Black fraternal experience by writing "The Divine Nine." Now it is my turn to help someone.

I have spent several years rummaging through many university archives along the way. Everyone was very helpful, but I'd like to especially thank Susan Pevar at Lincoln University (Pennsylvania), Jacqueline Brown at Wilberforce University, and Shelia Darrow at Central State University.

Finally, special thanks to the congregations of Cascade United Methodist Church in Atlanta (my dad's church), and the Mt. Zion Baptist Church in Albany, for helping me stay grounded. Thanks to all of my family and friends for all their love and support, and most importantly, thanks to my sweetheart and best friend, Adria, whom has been a tremendous blessing to me.

Introduction

IN THE FALL OF 1985, I WAS PREPARING TO VENTURE OFF TO THE University of Georgia as a freshman. Of course, much of my thoughts were on the challenges I expected academically. However, having been an involved high school student, including student body president, I knew that I would continue to seek opportunities for development outside of the classroom.

I clearly remember a conversation with my father before I left. He reiterated that my major goal at Georgia was to do well academically. Of course, that was a given for me. He did offer his "advice" on joining a fraternity. "If you decide to join a fraternity, you'd better join the right one," he indicated. "Otherwise, you will become a work-study student."

The rebel in me was not to be intimidated by his threats, and so I entered school that fall ready to take on the challenges of college life. Part of the challenge was navigating the Greek life scene. I was determined to have an open mind when it came to fraternities as far as possible, so I convinced myself that I would explore my options. Since I attended an overwhelmingly Black high school, the thought of joining a White fraternity never seriously entered my mind. Any Black freshman at UGA abruptly learned that segregation and racism still existed in the mid-1980s. In fact, my naïveté quickly ended during an intramural game of football as my residence hall floor team beat a White team, and one of the losers (in retrospect, in more ways than one) called us "niggers." I had never been called that to my face, and fully expected that we were about to come to blows. But a levelheaded sophomore told us that he just wanted to call us that, and we left.

So, my realistic options for fraternalism were found in historically Black Greek–lettered organizations. Only three groups were active my freshman year, and I thought there were two I might consider joining. I attended each of their smokers, trying to learn more about the organizations and the men who made up their chapters. In fact, after attending the first smoker, that of my father's fraternity, some of the brothers actually encouraged me to view another smoker so that I could be sure I knew which organization was the best fit for me.

In my eighteen-year-old mind, there was only one choice for me, and that spring of 1986, I pledged Alpha Phi Alpha Fraternity, Inc. With all the challenges of pledging, I actually enjoyed the process and the experiences. Having two parents who are Greek, my father also an Alpha, and my

11

mother a member of Delta Sigma Theta, I couldn't call home and get any sympathy. My mom would calmly say, "If all those other boys could do it, you can too." And that was about it for compassion!

On 18 May 1986, I was initiated into the fraternity. This was an important day for me not only because it signified the accomplishment of completing pledging, and in a larger sense, of gaining social competence that the developmental theorist Arthur Chickering described, but also it was the beginning. It began an intense curiosity about this new community I joined—not just Alpha Phi Alpha, but Black Greek life as a whole.

I tried to get the most out of my undergraduate experience: the programs, the service projects, the parties, and the step shows. I was a part of an informal group in the chapter that we called the "social bros."—brothers who attended every Black Greek event, and maintained GPAs above 3.0. So I found a way to go to all the parties, no matter who served as host, and on many occasions I came home at about 2 A.M. and proceeded to study for a few hours. After all, I was a biology major.

My involvement caused my undergraduate chapter to nominate me for Brother of the Year during the 1987–88 school year. This was quite an honor as my chapter had produced the previous two national College Brothers of the Year. Within the fraternity, undergraduates are able to compete on several levels for awards. And so I was named the College Brother of the Year for the state of Georgia, and then for the Southern Region. I didn't prevail at the general convention that summer, but at the regional convention I was also elected Southern Assistant Vice President. I was now a board member for my fraternity, representing what arguably was and is the most influential region in Alpha (at least that's what we say in Alpha South).

These experiences did nothing but intensify my curiosity about the fraternity and the Black fraternal experience. I was able to attend meetings where we discussed the development of national projects, the innovations of chapters, and yes, the cases of hazing that plagued the fraternity. I personally had a chance to interact with past General Presidents of the fraternity, several of whom were university presidents, who planted a seed in my mind that I too would become a president of an institution.

In fact, one of these men played an integral role in my future as it would unfold. During my term as Southern Region Assistant Vice President, I began my first year in veterinary school at the University of Georgia. I was accepted after three years of undergraduate study, and as far back as I could remember I knew I wanted to become a vet. That was, until, I began taking classes. My studying increased at least fourfold, but my grades were atrocious for my standards. I had never been used to consistently making "Cs," and those occasional "Ds" were a shock to my system. Also, being one of two Black students (the other a good Kappa friend), we felt left out on the many study groups that developed.

I tried to bail after the first quarter, but they convinced me to give it that good college try. But halfway through a neuroanatomy course where 75 percent of the final grade was based on the final exam, I knew that it was time for me to go. So I threw in the towel, knowing full well that I had no idea what I would do next. That was a scary feeling for a twenty-one year old who thought he had done everything in sequence as he had planned.

So at the summer general convention in 1989, a new direction was revealed to me through the late Walter Washington. Dr. Washington was a past president of Alpha Phi Alpha as well as president of Alcorn State University, a post he held for over twenty years. I told him that I thought I'd like to become a college president one day, but was unsure of my next move. He indicated that I should obtain a master's degree in college student personnel. Of course, I had no idea what this was, but started to investigate this course of study and determine where I could attend that following January, as I was to graduate from Georgia in December 1989.

Around the same time, the fraternity adviser at Georgia, Ron Binder, approached me with a unique opportunity. He indicated that he annually attends a meeting of Greek advisers from all across the country, and he noticed that there were very few if any programs that addressed the Black Greek experience. He indicated that he felt comfortable speaking as a White adviser working with Black Greeks, but wanted to add a portion of the presentation that discussed the history, traditions, and practices of Black Greek–lettered organizations. My chapter always thought that Ron was cool. He reached out to us and to the Black Greeks on numerous occasions, whether attending one of our smokers or working with the Interfraternity Council (IFC) and Panhellenic Council to provide funds that helped us secure the coliseum for the annual Greek show. So I thought this was a great opportunity.

In fact, I think it was an epiphany for me. There in Dearborn, Michigan, in December 1989, as an undergraduate student preparing to graduate and go to Miami University (Ohio) to pursue a master's in college student personnel services, I gave my first presentation on Black Greek–lettered organizations. We called our program "Black Greek 101." I was a little intimidated as I saw some of the national officers of the Black Greek organizations enter the room, and I worried if I had accurately researched the organizations sufficiently so I wouldn't have to face their wrath. But just the opposite occurred. The "elders" provided me with great support and encouragement, and I thought to myself, "I really like doing this. I should do this more often."

And so it was. By entering Miami, I gained a foundation in higher education and student development. I realized that I was learning how to study and make sense out of my Black Greek experience, and the more I learned, the more excited I became about the prospects. I was able to begin writing papers for class on my area of interest, and I quickly learned that there wasn't a great deal for me to read. Most of the information appeared to be anecdotal, provided through newspaper and magazine articles. I saw an unmet need, and I decided to become an expert on Black fraternal life.

My experience in Dearborn was a springboard for this goal. As a graduate student, I was invited to participate in the International Greek Life Teleconference in 1990, hosted by Dr. Will Keim, a renowned speaker in the interfraternal world. This conference exposed me to some of the leading experts and speakers on Greek life, many of whom I continue to see today as we travel around the country. Soon I would gain some notoriety and was being asked to come to various campuses to lecture on Black Greek life.

And as I traveled and interacted with students, I became curious about their curiosity. I found that the Black Greek experience was perpetuated through stories, myths, and legends outside of the history books. Even some of the "history" of the organizations had been distorted so that the truth was fuzzy at best. So I decided to spend time each summer investigating some aspect of the Black fraternal experience. Shortly after the ban on pledging, I decided to figure out what went wrong with the process. Later I decided to really research the entire concept known as pledging, and share with people exactly how it came to be.

My notion of the breadth of the Black fraternal experience was narrowed to eight groups, which made up the National Pan-Hellenic Council (NPHC) for so many years. Through my research I later realized that this was seriously deficient. I began to figure out exactly how many Black Greek–lettered organizations existed or had existed, and what other manifestations of Black fraternalism existed as well. Indeed, I learned that there was an untapped mine of information on numerous groups outside of the eight mainstays of the NPHC.

My quest to learn more and more became insatiable, and the hundreds of students I met along the way fueled it. I became excited in their excitement to learn, and I continued to become motivated to seek new areas of scholarship. I decided along the way that the Black Greek culture was rich, filled with numerous customs and traditions that give it a flavor unlike any other student culture. And I learned that practically no one had any solid understanding as to how these traditions came to be. So I spent several summers digging through archives trying to develop a historical perspective on the development of Black Greek customs.

In addition, I tried to continue empirical research that could quantify the Black Greek experience. Through my doctoral studies at Georgia State University, I tried to determine if undergraduate membership in Black Greek–lettered organizations provided Black students with involvement and leadership skill development. After a decade of membership intake, I decided to investigate the effectiveness of a program that has been and continues to be controversial at best.

All of these experiences led me to this point in time. After spending over a decade studying the Black Greek experience, and continuing to learn so much about groups that continue to maintain a high level of visibility and popularity, I am convinced that what is needed is a text that would fully describe and explain Black fraternalism. To this point, very little has been written that provides new knowledge on the Black Greek experience. The literature is primarily dominated by news articles (which most often cover heinous acts of hazing) and magazine articles. Less than twelve dissertations have been written that explore aspects of Black Greek life, and a handful of empirical research articles explore this vibrant culture.

In a breakthrough effort, Lawrence Ross published *The Divine Nine* in 1999. This text provided a history of the now nine members of the National Pan-Hellenic Council, augmented with interviews of undergraduate and graduate chapters of each organization as well as interviews of famous members of all organizations to describe their experiences and thoughts on Black Greek life. This book has had a powerful impact on the Black Greek world by giving all members an opportunity to learn basic historical information about other groups, and hopefully, develop a newfound respect and appreciation for each organization. But the real power of this book is that now prospective members can fairly learn about the organizations and make informed decisions. In essence, the secrecy of history as maintained by members who challenged potential members to do their research when so little was available has now been revealed to a mass audience.

And so, *The Divine Nine* was the needed foundation for any subsequent works on Black Greek Life. Thanks to the dedication of Brother Ross for completing his book, the time for a text that furthers the understanding of Black fraternalism has come. The goal of this book is to do just that—to bring together over ten years of research into a volume that gives all who are members of the Black fraternal community, as well as those who aspire for membership and those who work with these organizations on campuses, a thorough understanding of historical events, customs, practices, different organizations, and additional areas for inquiry and research.

Chapter 1 discusses the foundations for the Black fraternal experience in America. In conventional thought, most think of Alpha Phi Alpha as the beginning of the Black Greek movement. But this chapter reveals that a few organizations existed prior to the founding of Alpha Phi Alpha, and that their limited successes are an important part of Black Greek history. Chapter 2 provides a detailed history of pledging while describing the growth of Black Greek–lettered organizations. This chapter is important in that it provides a complete understanding of how pledging evolved, and a realistic view of the challenges that caused the "end" of pledging. Chapter

3 continues to discuss pledging under the guise of membership intake and how it has affected Black Greek life. An apparent sense of lawlessness emerged in the 1990s as undergraduates defied the policies that forbade pledging, and developed a new culture of pledging that was semisecret and often abusive. Countless news reports are reviewed in this chapter, along with research that assessed the first decade of the membership intake era.

Chapter 4 asks the question, "Was Eight Enough?" While most have a limited view of the number of Black fraternal organizations, over eighty groups have or presently exist as of the writing of this book. And these organizations are not just the ones with Greek letters, but those that embrace the philosophy of African fraternalism, or more directly, African fraternities. Chapter 5 is an exploration into the culture of Black Greek–lettered organizations. Black Greek–lettered organizations have created a lexicon of their own: plots, stepping, handsigns, calls, etc. All of these actions, activities, or objects have been inextricably linked to our understanding of Black Greek life in this country. But sadly, too few have any real understanding of how these cultural icons came to be, and what their significance is in Black Greek life.

Chapter 6 poses some questions for the future of Black Greek life. As times change, these conservative organizations are facing new challenges. In the future, Black Greeks will have to address non-Black membership, homosexuality, and the pledging/intake dilemma. This chapter poses some thoughts for the future as well as covers areas that are in need of further research.

Black Greek 101

1

The Foundation Era of Black Fraternalism

You mean your mama didn't tell you 'bout, A Phi A
She didn't tell you 'bout our smooth and sexy ways
She didn't tell you how we slide to the side so sweet?
She didn't tell you we're the first among all the Black Greeks.
'Cause we're the Alpha Bros. for heaven's sake
We're the granddaddies makin' no mistakes
We're the first, the first, we're never late
From us all others originate.
—Alpha Phi Alpha chant

THIS INFAMOUS CHANT SUMS UP THE ATTITUDE OF THE BLACK GREEK experience when it comes to the founding of fraternities and sororities. In essence, Alpha Phi Alpha in conventional wisdom has always been viewed as the first Black Greek–lettered organization. And because of most of the literature available to the masses, this assumption made sense. For the average person, including members of Black Greek–lettered organizations, Alpha Phi Alpha marks the beginning of the Black Greek movement in the United States.

But upon closer inspection, there were actually several attempts at forming Black fraternal organizations prior to the organization of Alpha Phi Alpha at Cornell University beginning in the fall of 1905. Some of those organizations were short-lived, doomed to fail because of the challenges that faced the students on those campuses. At least one organization perpetuates its existence today, and rightfully deserves the distinction as being the oldest Black Greek–lettered organization currently in existence.

In the debate over the founding of Black fraternal orders, the issue of Masons appears now and then. Freemasonry in the larger context was organized in the fourteenth century by persons who were actual masons—an itinerant profession of skilled laborers. They were involved in building cathedrals, bridges, palaces, and other structures. The Masons established lodges in the areas where they worked to serve a dual purpose. The first was a place for shelter, as Masons typically rented rooms or even purchased property if their work would require significant time. The second purpose was as a place for meetings. Alan Axelrod indicates that the lodges served as a form of trade union, where impostors could be screened and identified by Masons who employed secret grips and passwords.[1] Both of these tools

19

have been employed through the modern-day Black Greek system as well—a definitive link to Masonic influences.

These original Freemasons are also known as Operative Masons due to the fact that they were skilled stone workers. Succinctly, they performed the art of masonry. As early as 1600, some were granted honorary membership in Masonry. These Masons were then known as Speculative Masons, a group that grew in numbers in the seventeenth-century.[2] W. L. Wilmshurst concurred that Masonry grew in popularity. He described Masonry as "a semi-secret, semi-public institution . . . with its doors open to any applicant for admission who is of ordinary good character and repute."[3]

As Masonry expanded during the seventeenth and eighteenth centuries, issues of race became important in determining membership. It is estimated that as early as 1775, during the era of revolution in America, Prince Hall, a Black Methodist minister born in Barbados, and fourteen others were initiated into Military Lodge Number 441, under the jurisdiction of the Grand Lodge of Ireland.[4] Yet, the new Masons experienced racism. Lawrence Graham writes

> When he and the other blacks felt they were not received as well as they had hoped, he asked permission to start an all-black lodge of the same organization. After repeated requests, the British Grand Lodge gave him permission to begin what becomes a "black version" of the organization.[5]

In 1787, with a charter from the Grand Lodge of England, Prince Hall founded African Lodge No. 459, inaugurating an era of Black lodges, more commonly referred to as Prince Hall lodges.[6] With African Lodge No. 459 being considered a regular lodge of Free and Accepted Masons, the organization expanded with the second Black lodge, Hiram Lodge No. 4 being established in Providence, Rhode Island, in 1797, and a third lodge established in 1798 by Absalom Jones and Richard Allen, founders of the African Methodist Episcopal (AME) Church. By 1977 there were forty grand lodges made up of over fifty-five hundred lodges and over half a million members.[7]

It is clear that there is an undeniable kinship between Masonry and fraternities as a whole. According to Frederick Rudolph, "aided by the disclosure of the practices and terminology of Freemasonry . . . fraternities incorporated much of the Masonic spirit into their movement."[8] Masons founded some college fraternal organizations, such as the Acacia Fraternity. The ritual of the Beta Theta Pi Fraternity was patterned after Freemasonry, and groups such as Kappa Alpha Order and Chi Psi Fraternity refer to their chapter houses as "lodges," as are Masonic chapter houses. While many fraternal practices such as grips, passwords, and challenges have origins in Masonry, the fact remains that Masonry began primarily as a secret society. Axelrod contends that "Freemasonry is unquestionably the largest, oldest, and most influential of all secret societies."[9] But it has been primarily just that, a secret society.

Ironically, in the past decade Masonry has taken on a more public appearance. Those unfamiliar with the craft, as it is known, now are able to view members wearing paraphernalia, or see it being sold at many Greek-related events. On some campuses Masons have formed active organizations that operate as do Greek-lettered organizations. This isn't a completely new phenomenon, as the Masonic Club of Alabama A&M University posed for a picture in the 1961 yearbook, *The Heritage*. However, there is a marked increase in visibility of these organizations and their members.

So in order to present an accurate picture of Black fraternal development in the United States, Freemasonry must be mentioned for the sake of historical accuracy. But arguably, a number of differences prevent a concrete linkage between the two entities. And for the purpose of this volume, the Black fraternal movement as described focuses on Black fraternal organizations primarily centered on the college campus. A college education historically has not been a requirement of membership as a Mason. The history clearly indicates that masons (operative) were working-class, skilled laborers. For the purposes of this work, the focus on Black fraternalism will be related to, but not exclusive to, the college experience.

With that foundation being established, it would be over one hundred years before Blacks made an attempt to initiate a fraternal organization. But unlike the movement started by Prince Hall and his associates, the next wave would be spearheaded by collegians. As with the case of Masonry, Whites began the introduction of collegiate fraternal organizations with the establishment of Phi Beta Kappa at the College of William and Mary in 1776. This organization, which evolved over time to become a standard for excellence in collegiate academics, spurred the formation of the Kappa Alpha Society at the University of North Carolina, Chapel Hill, in 1812, a group founded by four Phi Beta Kappas.

Soon the "social" Greek-letter movement began sweeping the country. In many instances fraternities rooted out the established literary societies as college men began challenging the strict codes of the faculty. Horowitz indicated in the text, *Campus Life,*

> The fraternity had great appeal. For those undergraduates with the wealth, inclination, and leisure to join, the new Greek-letter organizations gave an arena of privacy away from college eyes. In colleges founded by Protestant denominations that demanded abstinence and self-denial, members could break the official codes among trusted brothers. Fraternities provided the economic and social basis for feasts, strong drink, loose talk about women, cardplaying and gambling.[10]

With women entering higher education in the early 1800s, after a period of time they too sought the benefits of membership in a single-sex organization. Particularly for women, the need to bond was great given their small numbers and the heavily paternalistic environment of the American college campus. Much of the course of study for these women students focused on activities that were considered suitable for women, while some courses of study were deemed inappropriate for women.

And so in the mid-1800s, collegiate sororities evolved on college campuses. And soon, these organizations grew as a compliment to the burgeoning fraternity system that established a culture of student leadership and involvement as well as one of recklessness and frivolity. But Greek life, by the turn of the century, had created an indelible mark on college life. This mark would serve as an impetus for Black students to make an entrée into the world of collegiate fraternalism.

ALPHA KAPPA NU: PRECURSOR TO BLACK FRATERNALISM AT INDIANA UNIVERSITY

As indicated from the outset, conventional wisdom for most bestows the honor of the first Black Greek–lettered organization to Alpha Phi Alpha. To an extent, the founders of Alpha Phi Alpha felt they were the first. In an article written for *The Sphinx* magazine in 1946, Alpha founder Henry Arthur Callis indicated that the fraternity believed itself to be the first group of collegians united under a brotherhood and designed to advance the causes of Black people.[11]

In actuality the Black fraternal movement for collegians was attempted first in Bloomington, Indiana, which would eventually become the birthplace of Kappa Alpha Psi Fraternity. Indiana University was founded in 1820. Students were actively involved in student life practically from the inception through literary organizations, the first being the Henondelphisterian Society. By 1830 this organization had ceased to exist, and in its place were the Athenian and Philomathean Societies, the latter formed by remaining members of the Henondelphisterian Society. But these early organizations were for men, and it would not be until 1870 that the Hesperian Society was organized for women to serve the same functions. Literary societies were central to student life for almost seventy-five years.[12]

The literary societies were forerunners of the fraternity movement, providing a social outlet for students. But the fraternal organizations would begin making their presence known by the mid-1800s. The first Indiana University student was initiated into a fraternity in 1845, but the first chapter, that of Phi Delta Theta, was established in 1849. By the year 1870 there were four fraternities on campus.[13]

Around the time that fraternities became present on the campus, the town of Bloomington began to acknowledge the presence of Blacks, although not always in positive ways. In 1867 the editor of the student newspaper wrote about an encounter with a Black man who walked by him without speaking after the editor greeted him by the name "Sambo." The editor was incensed at being ignored and wrote that he was "in favor of the 'nigger' in his right place," but warned that if they were to come within a square-mile radius, they would be subject to the wrath of like-minded students.[14] The same student paper in fact reported that the Ku Klux Klan had a strong presence within the university by 1872. Yet, Black students did enter Indiana University. The recorded history is unsure as to when the first Black students enrolled, but there is evidence that three Black students entered in 1890. The climate was still hostile at that time.

Just fourteen years after these students enrolled, there was a racial incident involving a Northwestern University shortstop. A local hotel refused to allow the Black player to stay because his presence would be upsetting to the White guests. The student newspaper had changed somewhat by that time, and complained about the mistreatment of the player. In the previous year, 1903, the Alpha Kappa Nu Greek society was formed. The existence of this organization is documented in two sources. In the *Story of Kappa Alpha Psi,* William Crump indicates that the organization existed for only a short time, roughly fourteen months. In the house history of Indiana University, Thomas Clark discusses the existence of the fraternity in 1903, and indicates through town records that the fraternity purchased a house by October 1911.[15]

That group was in actuality Kappa Alpha Nu, the original name of Kappa Alpha Psi. Clark continues to discuss the fraternity by indicating that in 1914, Kappa Alpha Nu (not Alpha Kappa Nu) had formed chapters in a couple of additional states and was a strong organization. Clark continues by indicating that the fraternity changed its name on 15 April 1915 to Kappa Alpha Psi.[16] Kappa Alpha Psi historian William Crump provides a variation in the history. He indicates that the Alpha Kappa Nu Greek society was formed in 1903, but that it lasted for only a short time. After it disappeared, the next group was Kappa Alpha Nu founded in 1911. Crump writes, "The new Fraternity was designated Kappa Alpha Nu, perhaps as a tribute to the black students of 1903 who organized the Alpha Kappa Nu club to foster a better life on the Indiana campus."[17] But Clark does correctly list when the name of the fraternity changed to Kappa Alpha Psi, probably due to comments made by Indiana undergraduates who on at least one occasion referred to it as Kappa Alpha Nig.

Sigma Pi Phi: The First Black Greek–Lettered Organization

While the attempt to form Alpha Kappa Nu was a short-lived venture, a more substantive effort began in Philadelphia under the leadership of Henry M. Minton. Minton, born in South Carolina in 1871, graduated from

Philips Exeter Academy in 1891, and then the Philadelphia College of
Pharmacy in 1895. He would later complete the Jefferson Medical College
in Philadelphia in 1906. According to Charles H. Wesley in a history of the
organization, "Minton's career as a student and professional worker had
been enriched by experiences with members of fraternities, both collegiate
and professional. He had been considered for such memberships but had
not been successful in attaining approval."[18]

So similar to the experiences of Prince Hall, Minton had also been spurned
for membership in some fraternal organization. Therefore, Minton aspired to
create an organization that would provide the benefits of a fraternity for Black
men, benefits he saw from his White counterparts. Therefore he began to
conceptualize the beginnings of a Greek-lettered organization. After sharing
the idea of a fraternity, Minton met at the home of Dr. E. C. Howard on 15
May 1904 with Dr. A. B. Jackson and Dr. R. J. Warwick to discuss the formation of a fraternity in Philadelphia. The foursome knew that they were
embarking upon a major task. Carrington Davis wrote

> Now it must be imagined that this meeting marked the first stirrings in the
> minds of these men with reference to the need of organizing such a frater-
> nity. For some time prior to this date there had been earnest and frequent dis-
> cussion amongst them the serious lack of a brotherhood of the type that
> provided for groups of men of similar training and like tastes on the other
> side of the color line, so many imponderable values that figure greatly in
> rounding out a complete life. Dr. Minton had presented to a selected num-
> ber of his professional friends and intimate associates the benefits that might
> be derived from such an organization.[19]

While the idea was expounded upon at the first meeting, the organization did not truly take form until the second meeting. At the second meeting, Dr. E. T. Hinson and Dr. Robert J. Abele were invited to participate in
the formation of the organization. These two men are considered founders
of the organization, as they were present when the permanent organization
was formed, and officers were selected. It is also noted that five of the six
founders were physicians, and the sixth a dentist. It is clear from the outset that Sigma Pi Phi was to be an organization composed of an elite class
of Black citizens.

As evident by the names Sigma Pi Phi and Boulé (the alternative name
of the organization), and usage of terms such as archon, the organization
patterned itself heavily on ancient Greek society. The organization was
established as a graduate fraternity. In only two instances were undergraduates offered membership. In a short-lived program, the fraternity decided
to admit undergraduates under a class of membership known as Thetes.
Incidentally, both men died shortly after being initiated into the fraternity,
and the organization decided at that point in time to confine its ranks to col-

lege graduates.[20] Thus, the only true linkage between The Boulé and under-graduates ended at that time.

Lawrence Graham further identified The Boulé as the first elite Black men's club. He indicated that "it is considered by many the elite men's club, and its membership has included the most accomplished, affluent, and influential black men in every city for the last ninety years."[21] The organization developed from the outset in a manner that would perpetuate high standards. Graham further indicated

> The Boulé selects its national membership strictly on the basis of professional accomplishments rather than popularity among a certain local social group. Conducting all of their official activities and social gatherings in black-tie attire with formal ceremonies, Boulé members are men who are attracted to the fraternity because of its intellectual discussions and its interest in promoting scholarship among a group of accomplished black professional men.[22]

Yet the organization, as viewed by those in the broader community who knew of it, was a means for the Black bourgeoisie to hold power and recognition. E. Franklin Frazier, in a landmark treatise on the Black bourgeoisie wrote, "Although the original aim of the society was to bring together the 'aristocracy of talent,' it has become one of the main expressions of social snobbishness on the part of the black bourgeoisie."[23]

Efforts were made by the founders of the organization to cautiously move toward expansion for fear of developing a mediocre and average membership. In fact, it would be over three years before the second chapter, the Beta Boulé, would be established in Chicago in 1907. Subsequent Boulés were established in Baltimore (1908), Memphis (1910), Washington, DC (1911), New York (1912), St. Louis (1912), Kansas City (1915), Detroit (1917), and Atlanta (1920). By 1950, only twenty-eight Boulés were established nationally by the organization. This is in contrast to the rapid expansion of undergraduate Greek-letter organizations during the same period of time.

Throughout the years, the Boulé remained very secretive in its existence. In a very practical sense, only within the last ten years has a wider audience become aware of the organization. So the purpose of the organization was questioned by the broader community, especially because of the veil of secrecy for decades. But there is evidence that the purpose of the organization was questioned internally as early as 1948. In "The Talented Tenth Memorial Address" given by Archon (title given to all members) W. E. B. Du Bois, delivered at the Nineteenth Grand Boulé Conclave of Sigma Pi Phi, he declared, "What the guiding idea of Sigma Pi Phi was, I have never been able to learn. I believe it was rooted in a certain exclusiveness and snobbery, for which we all have a yearning, even if unconfessed."[24]

Du Bois wanted to challenge the organization to become more active in addressing the needs of Black America (as Du Bois referred to American Negroes). Specifically, he wanted the organization to support his new conceptualization of the Talented Tenth, which he termed "Guiding Hundredth." In his address, Du Bois painted a picture of the organization to put it in proper perspective. Du Bois indicated that the membership represented 440 families, which equated to one ten-thousandth of Negro families. Almost half of the Boulé at that time were physicians, dentists, and pharmacists, with the next largest group being educators, clergy, and social workers. Du Bois was concerned that the group did not represent "typical America," and that the Boulé was "an old, timid, conservative group."[25]

Du Bois, in a speech that has to have ruffled many feathers in this elite organization, declared that the Boulé in its form at that time was not the ideal type of organization to further his theory of a "Guiding Hundredth." Because the group was inclined not to question the past but accept the values of America at that time, a belief within the membership that they were "unusual and exceptional colored folk," and a general feeling of helplessness in a White world, Du Bois raised doubts about his idea working through The Boulé. One primary reason was because the membership was old. Du Bois claimed in his speech, "Unless we begin to recruit this fraternity membership with young men and large numbers of them, our biennial conclaves will be increasingly devoted to obituaries."[26] Concluding this point, Du Bois stated

> It is inconceivable that we should even for a moment dream that with a membership of 440 we have scratched even the tip of the top of the surface of a group representative of potential Negro leadership in America. Nothing but congenital laziness should keep us from a membership of 3,000 by the next biennium without lowering of quality; and a membership of 30,000 by 1960. This would be an actual numerical one hundredth of our race: a body large enough really to represent all.[27]

The vision that Du Bois shared with the membership of Sigma Pi Phi has not become reality. One of the few newspaper articles on The Boulé appeared in the *Los Angeles Times* in 1990 surrounding their biennial meeting in Los Angeles. The article quoted a membership of three thousand and consisting of ninety-six chapters. The incoming Grand Sire Archon (similar to national president) Dr. Benjamin Major, acknowledged that until the early 1980s, the group remained what it wanted to be, as the rest of society (those who knew of the organization) claimed it to be a group more interested in social activities and celebrating its exclusiveness rather than contributing to Black America as a whole.[28]

In fact, in volume 2 of the *History of Sigma Pi Phi,* Sidney Jarrett indicated that as of 1989, the fraternity was unknown by its official name or the name used by its members (The Boulé). Only since 1980 had a sincere effort begun to publicize the existence of this organization that was the oldest Black Greek–lettered fraternity still in existence. With the inauguration of Theodore Jones as the Grand Sire Archon of the fraternity, he implemented a two-year term designed to expand membership, leadership, and service. Part of this initiative included the establishment of a functional public relations board, an idea recommended in 1968 but not acted upon.[29]

So in the early eighties the organization launched a plan designed to inform the public about the fraternity, especially young Black professionals, to serve as role models for Black youth, to investigate underwriting of programs by business communities, and to provide information about selected fraternity activities. To that end the first press conference in the history of the organization was held at their thirty-sixth Grand Boulé, held in Detroit on 16 August 1982. An article appeared in *Jet* magazine about the Grand Boulé that October.[30] It would be in the 1990s before the highest officer, the Grand Sire Archon, would be listed in *Ebony*'s annual "Most Influential Black Americans" issue.

Since that time the few articles that have appeared about the organization tend to underscore the issues raised by Du Bois in 1948. The *Los Angeles Times* story indicated that the average age of the members was sixty. In the interview, Dr. Major commented that the group was getting old and dying, and there was an emphasis on recruiting some younger men. Major indicated that the younger men wanted social activism to become a part of the organization. In addition, the organization began to become less secretive. So approximately forty years after Du Bois challenged the organization, change was just becoming a reality in terms of emphasizing a youth movement, and addressing the social concerns of the day, as Du Bois had hoped in 1948. In addition, a 1990 questionnaire of the membership found that the majority of Archons were in two broad professions: medicine and education.[31] Again, the pleas of Du Bois appear not to have been heeded immediately by the membership.

Almost a decade later, Lawrence Graham, thirty-three years old when he was invited to join Sigma Pi Phi, writes in the book *Our Kind of People* that the membership was 3,700, organized into 105 subordinate Boulés. He noted that the Grand Sire Archon, Anthony Hall Jr., who joined in 1977, estimated the average age of new members to be fifty-two, mainly due to the fact that the organization accepted men who were established in their fields. Graham notes that many chapters still will not accept men younger than forty-five years of age.[32]

Yet the idea of admissions standards still appears to be a major point of contention for members. Many of the conservative older members, according to Graham, are concerned that the standards for admission have been lowered. Some believe that the organization accepts men because of their wealth or fame. Volume 2 of the *History of Sigma Pi Phi* clearly states, "It cannot be overemphasized that the Fraternity's policy has persisted in guarding against any lowering of standards."[33] But many still believe that the group is still the most selective Black men's fraternal organization.

And in almost one hundred years of existence, The Boulé's membership was and is the Who's Who of Black men in America. Men such as James Weldon Johnson, Carter G. Woodson, John Hope, Charles Drew, Percy Julian, Martin Luther King Jr., and Benjamin E. Mays can be counted as initiates of the organization. Contemporary figures such as Louis Sullivan, Benjamin Hooks, Vernon Jordan, John H. Johnson, and Earl Graves along with the vast majority of Black mayors and college presidents, represent the current ranks of the organization. Many of these men also hold membership in the Black fraternities that make up the National Pan-Hellenic Council as well.

Which leads to a final word on The Boulé. In the 1990s, several conspiracy theorists provided commentary on the newly discovered Boulé by the masses. With The Boulé practically being introduced to Black America during the late eighties and early nineties, many wondered what this organization was that rightfully asserted itself as the oldest Black Greek–lettered organization in the country. It would be accurate to describe the attitude toward the organization as skeptical.

Through the development of the Internet during this period of time, thousands of persons began to understand that Sigma Pi Phi had existed for almost one hundred years. In particular, during the mid-1990s a web-based magazine devoted several articles to The Boulé. The inspiration for the articles were lectures presented by Steve Cokely, an influential speaker known for challenging the Black establishment. The articles assert that the eight Black fraternities and sororities (excluding Iota Phi Theta Fraternity) were subordinates of The Boulé, that the members had taken oaths to maintain the state of White supremacy, and implied that founders of Alpha Phi Alpha were members of The Boulé before creating the organization, therefore providing a direct link to the two. In essence, The Boulé began to be portrayed as the group that supports a White power structure by controlling eight Black Greek–lettered organizations.

But a reading of Du Bois's speech to The Boulé in 1948 clearly challenges the conspiracy notions. As indicated, Du Bois told the members in that speech that he felt they were afraid to challenge White America, but that was what the organization needed to do. Conspiracy theories placed Du Bois as a central figure in The Boulé, when in actuality (like much of the work of Du Bois), he was more of an outsider unable to effect change. One of the main points of the speech was to espouse a new concept, that of a "Guiding Hundredth." Du Bois pondered the use of college fraternities to achieve this goal. But he believed that their membership, even with graduate members, was too young or too busy trying to earn a living. He further felt that collegians were caught up in youthful activities.[34] Du Bois espoused this sentiment as early as 1930 at a Howard University commencement address, where he chastised Black male students who sought membership in athletics and Greek organizations, and where the greatest meetings "have become vulgar exhibitions of liquor, extravagance, and fur coats. We have in our colleges a growing mass of stupidity and indifference."[35]

In reviewing Wesley's history of Sigma Pi Phi, there are no references to any founders of Alpha Phi Alpha fraternity holding membership in the organization at any point at the time the book was published (1954). With the Beta Boulé not being established until 1907, Alpha Phi Alpha was organized and founded before the second chapter of the organization. There appear to be no links between any of the founders of Sigma Pi Phi and Alpha Phi Alpha between the founding of The Boulé and the organization of the literary organization that evolved into the first collegiate fraternity in the fall of 1905. But there is one historical link between The Boulé and a Black fraternity. The Epsilon Boulé was organized in Washington, DC, in February 1911. Nineteen men were initiated at that time, one of whom was Dr. Ernest E. Just, professor of biology at Howard University. In November of that year, Dr. Just worked with three students to organize Omega Psi Phi Fraternity on the campus of Howard University. While this is the only clear link between a Black college fraternity and The Boulé, it is not clear what impact Dr. Just's membership in Sigma Pi Phi had on the founding of Omega Psi Phi, if any.

THE BLACK FRATERNALISM EXPERIMENTS IN OHIO:
PI GAMMA OMICRON AND GAMMA PHI

During the social study stages of Alpha Phi Alpha Fraternity in the 1905–6 academic year, Robert Harold Ogle, who would become one of the fraternity founders, discovered a news item in the *Chicago Defender* that indicated that a Black fraternity, Pi Gamma Omicron, had been established at Ohio State University. Ogle wrote a letter to the registrar of the university to inquire about the status of the fraternity. The registrar responded that there was no recognition of such an organization. While relieved, it is quite possible that the thought of another group establishing such a fraternity before the men at Cornell were able to do so may have nudged the group to seriously consider the formation of the fraternity.

However, in the state of Ohio there was in fact a collegiate fraternity founded prior to Alpha Phi Alpha. That organization was called Gamma Phi Fraternity and was founded 1 March 1905 at Wilberforce University. This is significant since the next fraternal organization, the Xi Chapter of Alpha Phi

Alpha, was founded in 1912, followed by the Beta Chapter of Delta Sigma Theta founded in 1914, and the Delta Chapter of Kappa Alpha Psi in 1915. First pictured in *The Forcean* yearbook of 1923, Charles F. Potter, chapter historian for Gamma Phi, offered this description of the organization:

> The "Gamma Phi" has the enjoyable distinction of being the oldest organization of its kind on the campus; it was founded at Wilberforce University, in 1905, by Gus. Williams, Dr. Lackey, and Edw. Clark. Notwithstanding the tremendous difficulties it has often encountered, the fraternity has, since the beginning, had an enviable record and has grown with leaps and extended bounds. Until a few years ago the activities of the organization were merely local; but there are now other Chapters doing splendid work, but the Alpha chapter at Wilberforce is the leader.[36]

The 1923 yearbook listed seven men as officers, five honorary members in the faculty, eight honorary student members, and twenty-two active members. They also listed three "Honorary In Urbe," two of whom lived in Dayton and one in Wilberforce. The assumption is that these were graduates, a form of alumni member. It is noted here that during this time period is was quite common for the fraternities and sororities at Wilberforce to list members who were in the faculty under the headings "Fratres In Facultate" and "Sorores In Facultate."

The 1924 *Forcean* yearbook indicated a total membership of thirty-five men, with six faculty members. The colors of the organization were blue and white, and the flower was the white carnation. At that time four chapters of the organization existed. Gamma Phi had a consistent presence in yearbooks until 1930, when it was not pictured. However, the organization was pictured off and on until roughly 1947, but it isn't clear exactly when or why Gamma Phi ceased to exist. However, unlike Alpha Kappa Nu whose lifespan at Indiana University was insignificant in terms of campus impact, Gamma Phi existed at least three decades at Wilberforce and established at least three additional chapters for some point in time. Therefore, any discussion of the history of Black fraternal organizations must include this organization that has essentially been missing from any conversations up until this point in time.

THE FOUNDING OF THE MAJOR
BLACK GREEK ORGANIZATIONS, 1905–30

The period of 1905 to 1930 can be considered the foundational period for Black fraternities and sororities on college campuses. Sigma Pi Phi Fraternity was just formed, but its focus on graduates of colleges really did

G.G.C. CLUB

GAMMA PHI

R.C.C. CLUB

Gamma Phi fraternity, 1923 (Courtesy Wilberforce University Archives)

nothing to address the needs for closer associations between college men and women through a brotherly or sisterly bond. And during this period of time, four campuses served as the birthplaces for Black collegiate fraternalism. Three of these campuses, Cornell University, Indiana University, and Butler University, were predominantly White institutions. This seems reasonable due to the conditions that Black students experienced on these campuses, even though they were more open for diverse students to attend, with Cornell even being founded on that principle.

But Howard University could be referred to as the "cradle of Black Greek civilization," in that five of the first eight collegiate organizations that went on to exist continuously were founded on that campus. In addition, the second chapter of Alpha Phi Alpha, Beta, was founded at Howard in December 1907 and became the first Black fraternal organization on the campus. An exploration of the culture of student life at Howard revealed one that was very strict and disciplined, so the formation of fraternities and sororities also represented a means for student expression and escape.

As indicated, Alpha Phi Alpha was the first continuous intercollegiate Black Greek–lettered organization, founded at Cornell University. As at Indiana, fraternities evolved into major forces on campus in a relatively short period of time. Andrew White, one of the key figures in the founding of the institution, was himself a member of three fraternities. In the first year of the university, founded in 1865, students formed seven fraternities. By 1878, one of the organizations had built a fraternity house that served as a lodging for members.[37]

In the fall of 1905, forty years after the fraternity movement began at Cornell, a group of Black students formed a social studies club. The group sought to have some kind of organization that would support their desire to interact positively with their peers, given that there would be few, if any, in the larger campus community. As the group met during the 1905–6 school year, they struggled with the concept of a fraternity versus a literary society. While the undergraduates were interested in the fraternity, the graduate student who was a part of the initial group felt that Blacks did not have the cultural foundation to start such organizations. So when the group decided to become a fraternity, the graduate student, C. C. Poindexter, removed himself from the organization.[38]

Howard University opened its Normal Department in 1867, with the first four students being White females. Within months there were over sixty students who varied in age from thirteen to thirty, and who had great variations in academic preparedness. Like most Black schools opened during this time, Howard really could not truly be classified as a university. In the next year a preparatory department was developed in order to meet the needs of the students, some of whom were former slaves.

And with many Black institutions, there was a great deal of paternalism in working with the students. Regulations in 1880s indicated that students were forbidden to ride, take walks, or even correspond with the opposite sex without proper permission.[39] These rules were even stricter for woman students. Strict rules forced upon the women also included severe sanctions if they were caught smoking or drinking, or if evidence was found that they had engaged in either of the two activities. So the environment for the woman students at Howard was somewhat similar to their peers at White institutions.

Some of the earliest student activities in the early 1890s included athletic games, generally limited to three to four hours a day, every day except Sunday. In 1891 the students began holding nightly military drills after study hours or on Sunday afternoons. But the drills disturbed people living in the neighborhood, so they were limited to one day for two hours. Continuing to seek outlets, students also began to develop literary, musical, art, and dramatic clubs, such as the Howard Players, founded in 1907.

But none of these organizations took hold of student interest like Greek life. Once Alpha Phi Alpha started a chapter in 1907, five completely new organizations followed on the campus in the next thirteen years. During the 1907–8 year, Ethel Hedgeman, a junior, worked to organize her peers in forming a sorority. Few women were on campus—eight who were in the class of 1908 and two in the class of 1909. So the formation of the sorority was "simply structuring a relationship that already existed."[40] So on 15 January 1908, nine women met and organized Alpha Kappa Alpha Sorority at Howard University. In February of that year, seven sophomore students were invited to join the organization without initiation, and the sorority recognizes all sixteen as founders of the organization.

Three years later, three students and a professor at Howard founded the Omega Psi Phi Fraternity. The founding at Howard appears to be different from the previous two in that there appeared to be administrative opposition to the group being a national organization. There is no discussion about the challenges, if any, the members of Alpha Phi Alpha had in establishing a chapter at Howard. The founders of Alpha Kappa Alpha secured university approval within a week after forming the organization, but it was later clarified to be only for the local group. But the history of Omega Psi Phi, as recorded by Robert Gill, indicated administrative opposition to the group forming a national fraternity, and their recognition was on the condition that the group not expand beyond the campus. He indicated:

But intense efforts of the founders to win University approval for organization as a national fraternity persisted. When University consideration of the matter appeared to the young organizers to be too slow, they proceeded to announce the national organization of the Omega Psi Phi Fraternity. The announcement was met with a public statement in Rankin Chapel by President Thirkield that no such organization existed together with a rebuke of the founders for their precipitate action.[41]

But after a series of meetings, the organization was granted recognition as a national fraternity.

One of the major historical points of contention during the foundation era of collegiate Black Greek–lettered organizations was the founding of Delta Sigma Theta Sorority. As Alpha Kappa Alpha Sorority evolved, the newer initiates began questioning some of the group's practices and ideology. According to Paula Giddings, some members thought that the name had no original meaning of its own, but was rather a derivation of Alpha Phi Alpha. This theory probably is given consideration since the key founder of Alpha Kappa Alpha was friends with the president of the newly established Alpha Phi Alpha chapter, George Lyle, whom she later married. In addition, according to Giddings, some thought that the use of Greek titles was "unnecessarily pompous."[42]

The AKA chapter of 1912 planned to change the name and colors of the organization after contacting some women who had graduated for their input. This stirred at least one dissenter, who fought the changes of the organization and forced the hand of the twenty-two undergraduates. Eventually the undergraduates continued with their plan and formed Delta Sigma Theta, prior to university approval. But at the 6 February 1913 board of trustees meeting, both sororities were recognized by Howard with the provision that they too remain local. Once again both groups maneuvered around this provision in later years.[43]

In 1910, student A. Langston Taylor enrolled at Howard with an idea for a fraternity after speaking with a recent alumnus who spoke about fraternity life there. By 1914 he spearheaded the founding of Phi Beta Sigma Fraternity. The founding of Phi Beta Sigma has additional importance in that the group worked with female students, most notably Arizona Cleaver, to form a sorority that would be the sister organization to the fraternity. After securing permission for this sorority and forming a constitution for it based on Phi Beta Sigma's, Zeta Phi Beta Sorority was organized in 1920 and the two became the first official brother and sister organizations.[44]

The organization of Kappa Alpha Psi, as explained, closely ties to the short-lived existence of the Alpha Kappa Nu society at Indiana University eight years prior. But the group expanded well and finally established a chapter in 1920 at Howard. The final group founded during this era was Sigma Gamma Rho Sorority. During the 1920s the state of Indiana was a stronghold for the Ku Klux Klan. Yet at Butler University, then a teacher's college, seven Black women sought to form a sorority, probably as much for survival as for the need to bond in a sisterhood. On 12 November 1922, Sigma Gamma Rho Sorority was born.[45]

With these eight groups formed, the foundation was laid for Black fraternalism on college campuses. By the 1920s the power of these groups was realized on campuses. For example, non-Greek students at Howard began to complain about how Greeks chose members, about the hazing occurring in the groups, and the coalitions they formed that helped Greeks perpetually hold high level student positions, including homecoming queen.[46] It was also a time when the groups realized that they needed some type of organization that would work to benefit all.

As early as 1922 at Howard, representatives of the Greek organizations met to try to establish some sort of all-Greek conference. However, that meeting did not prove fruitful. But the need for such an organization was reinforced. In the March 1927 Kappa Alpha Psi *Journal,* Rufus Kuykendall, an IU student, challenged the university because the school fraternity council did not recognize any of the three Black Greek–lettered organizations. On 28 December 1928, representatives from Alpha Kappa Alpha, Delta Sigma Theta, Sigma Gamma Rho, Alpha Phi Alpha, and Omega Psi Phi met again, this time in Indianapolis during the Kappa Alpha Psi Grand Chapter meeting, to establish the Pan-Hellenic Council. The idea was set but the representatives were not able to take official action at that time, so they set another meeting for 1929.[47]

During the 1929 meeting, the National Pan-Hellenic Council was officially organized. By that time, each of the national organizations had formally discussed and approved membership in the council. Wesley noted in the Alpha Phi Alpha history book that the fraternity approved membership during their December 1929 national meeting. The completed constitution was approved at Howard University on 10 May 1930.[48] The national organization of the National Pan-Hellenic Council does officially recognize that date as the founding of the organization.

There is some slight discrepancy as to when the organization actually began, as Giddings indicated that it formed in 1930, evolving from an earlier National Interfraternal Council. No solid records exist with the present NPHC that verify or refute the existence of this earlier-named organization. Crump indicates 1922 as the year of the first attempted meeting. This is confirmed in the 1922 Howard yearbook, *Initium,* which explained on the Delta Sigma Theta page "a meeting of the Inter-Fraternal Council, held in Washington April 17, 18 and 19, inclusive, Dr. Sadie Tanner Mossell . . . was elected chairman of the Executive Committee."[49]

So it appears that the 1922 group, the Inter-Fraternal Council, was a prototype of the present NPHC. However, it took years to take root, as even at Howard University in 1931 the local undergraduates called their council the "Inter-Fraternity Council." It was as late as 1945 before Howard University students began calling their group the Panhellenic Council, organized by Ernest Oppman, a non-Greek student.[50] On many other campuses during the 1930s through 1960s, interfraternity councils were the names given to the organized bodies of Black Greek–lettered organizations.

In 1930 the group listed as its initial purpose "to consider questions and problems of mutual interest to its members and to make such recommendations as the Council may deem necessary."[51] These concerns included collegiate matters, including scholastics and discrimination on White campuses, as well as broader community issues such as the Joint Committee of the National Recovery Association.[52] The students at Howard indicated that its primary purpose

> was to unite the Greek letter fraternities and sororities into one cooperative body dedicated to benefiting the campus as a whole. The aim of the Council is to promote the Greek-letter ideas of scholarship and character, and to develop those ideals through concerted effort, friendly rivalry, and a full-orbed recognition of over-all, fundamental purposes to which each of the organizations is individually committed.[53]

In any event, the establishment of the Pan-Hellenic Council signaled the end of a foundational period, with eight national groups taking ground on college campuses and in major cities as well as the establishment of an umbrella body which would work to further the interests of the collective group.

2
The History of Pledging

MORE THAN ANY OTHER FACET OF THE BLACK GREEK EXPERIENCE, pledging has been and continues to be a defining characteristic of the organizations. The concept of pledging has been a way for members to identify themselves. As a part of any introduction of members, both within and between organizations, the conversation centers on when a person pledged, and where they pledged. In some instances further discussions sought to ascertain how long a person pledged, and what kinds of activities constituted pledging. In fact, Greek members generally introduce themselves by their name, chapter, and term of pledging (i.e., Walter, Zeta Pi, spring '86).

The pledge period was viewed as the rite of passage for Black fraternal organizations. The badge of honor gained by students who completed a pledge program and were initiated elevated their status on their respective campuses. Pledging in essence was the event that gave Greeks a sort of mystique with their peers. They were seen with an admiration in many instances because they completed a difficult process and achieved a goal that many, whether they verbalized it or not, sought to accomplish as well to become a member of a fraternity or sorority.

Yet, a process so central to the identity of Greek lettered organizations and their members remains vaguely understood. The espoused importance, the origins, and the significance of pledging probably has as many variations as there are members of Black fraternal organizations, which, based on statistics touted by the National Pan-Hellenic Council, include over 1.5 million people. Pledging has evolved in that sense as a mystical process that has affected everyone differently, each making meaning of the experience differently. However, time revealed that the concept of pledging was very flawed. Not only were members not making lifelong commitments through pledging as they have continued to espouse for decades, but the process was responsible for countless injuries and a number of deaths. But pledging was easily justified at least in the minds of members because it was thought to have existed since the inception of the organizations.

A thorough study of pledging reveals a process that evolved for decades, making it difficult to determine which aspects of pledging originated at what points in time. In the broadest sense, pledging is best described as a culture within a culture. More specifically, it could be defined as a cultural appendage that has taken on a life of its own. It has evolved over time into a complex culture that has birthed numerous customs and traditions associated with Black Greek life. In that regard it is an integral part of the Black fraternal experience. On the other hand, it also evolved into a culture that is self-destructive, constantly threatening the very existence of these organizations. In this chapter, pledging will be deeply explored and chronicled since it has played a major role in the evolution of Black Greek life.

BEFORE PLEDGING, THERE WAS HAZING

Hank Nuwer, an author who is an expert on hazing in fraternities, sororities, high schools, and athletic teams, chronicles the history of hazing in the book *Wrongs of Passage*. He indicates that for centuries there have been activities that could be described as hazing. Many were probably viewed as rites of passage for boys and may have been violent and physical. But the vestiges of hazing as it relates to higher education began in the twelfth century, according to Nuwer.[1]

This was during a developmental phase for higher education as well. One of the earliest European universities was the University of Bologna, founded in 1000. It was a student-run institution formed by students who had left the University of Padua, which was under Catholic control. Students there hired professors, and determined what they taught and how much they would be paid. The students there organized into guilds, which were formal organizations used to preserve a craft or trade. In some regards these organizations were like early examples of fraternities. In that same regard the guilds began competing against each other and lost control of the university to the Catholics after about four hundred years.

According to Nuwer, a ritualization of practices now better termed hazing occurred in the medieval universities. He indicates:

> In the thirteenth through fifteenth centuries, it was understood that boys who wished to gain the status afforded by attending a school of learning would have to submit to brutal hazing by older students, just as they had to pay for university fees and to buy books. As older students began routinely hazing newcomers, such practices became ritualized.[2]

These practices soon developed identities. In some European institutions, freshmen wore caps with yellow bills during the mid to late 1400s. They were called *bejauni* in some instances, and later a *beanus* (which later evolved into the beanies characteristic of American freshmen).[3] As early as 1400, but clearly evident by the 1700s, a process known as "pennalism" existed. The term developed from freshmen at German universities who carried their pen cases with them for use at lectures. The freshmen were called *pennals*. The process was built on the notion that freshmen were untutored and uncivilized. During this time of pennalism, freshmen were subject to having to don weird articles of clothing, physical abuse, coarse jokes, and extortion of money or dinners.[4] Pennalism was more of a one-time event that lasted only a short period.

As the practice of pennalism evolved, in Great Britain it became known as fagging around 1770. Fagging included personal, menial service and drudgery, characteristics that were not a part of pennalism. As a part of fagging, each upperclassman had his personal fag. The system was justified, under the same ideology of pennalism—that freshmen were uncivilized—as a means to teach humility and proper behavior. This process lasted for a year and was an around-the-clock activity. According to some accounts, fagging ended in 1798 due to persuasion by a first-year student, but other accounts indicate that it continued readily into the nineteenth century.[5]

During the mid-1800s the word "hazing" emerged in reference to American higher education. Nuwer noted that although the word hazing "would not be commonly used on college campuses until after the Civil War, acts of servitude similar to European fagging bedeviled new students at Harvard as early as 1657."[6] Hazing stressed perpetrating crude pranks rather than the personal servitude of fagging, and included running errands for upperclassmen and obeying their orders. Some accounts described hazing as a much more violent activity. Sophomores would fight freshmen in activities called either freshman-sophomore rushes, or class battle royals. These fights were responsible for deaths at several universities. In addition, sophomores were known to steal the personal effects of freshmen and humiliate them. Humiliation could include being tarred and feathered in the town square.

Some incidents revealed the brutal nature of hazing. At Cornell, freshmen and sophomores were engaged in hazing, described by Bishop as "an ancient and dear college tradition."[7] And as early as 1873 at Cornell, a pledge to the Kappa Alpha Society died after being blindfolded and told to find his way home, only to be assisted by his brothers who removed the blindfold but became lost as well, and all three fell over a cliff. Only the pledge died in the accident.[8] In the early 1900s at Indiana University, freshmen and sophomores battled in bloody student scraps. Sophomores also engaged in the scalping of freshmen, but this form of hazing was also reciprocal. Clark, in volume 2 of the history of Indiana University, indicates that on one occasion a sophomore held freshmen at bay with a shotgun as they returned to his room to finish the job they had started the week before.[9]

For over seven hundred years in higher education, and over two hundred years in American higher education, some form of hazing has existed, a systematic means of indoctrinating new members of the university community through a rite of passage. It is within this culture of hazing that fraternities and sororities were born. This includes historically Black organizations as well. Between 1906 and 1922, when the eight largest Black collegiate Greek-lettered organizations were founded, higher education perpetuated a culture of hazing. The hazing in higher education occurred at all types of institutions, including historically Black colleges. Andre McKenzie, in a dissertation that examined Black fraternities at four historically Black colleges and universities (HBCUs), indicated that "at some of the institutions, the hazing of freshmen by upperclassmen had been a standing tradition that preceded fraternity involvement in the practice."[10]

FROM FRESHMAN HAZING TO PLEDGING

During the 1920s, students began challenging the process of freshman hazing. At Howard and Fisk, students sought to end the process, especially in light of the lynchings occurring in the South. The parallel was fairly accurate. Freshman hazing at Lincoln included nightly paddlings that lasted from the opening of classes until the holidays. As a part of freshman hazing, the freshmen were called "dogs," were made to roll pens with their noses, were responsible for cleaning the rooms of sophomores, and even had their heads shaved prior to the Thanksgiving football game.[11] In the evolution from pennalism to fagging and then to hazing, the characteristics of servitude and physical abuse remained fairly constant, even in light of the differences between European schools and historically Black American ones.

During this time period there was no discussion of pledging within Greek-lettered organizations. This is a key point because one of the major issues today is distinguishing between pledging and hazing. Pledging is generally justified as something entirely different from hazing, which is difficult to explain given the fact that pledging (especially within the Black Greek context) did not evolve until after higher education began to move toward abolishing the hazing of freshmen. This movement to end hazing of freshmen took root in the 1920s, and according to Nuwer, noticeable decreases in the practice did not appear until around 1930.[12] Vestiges of freshman hazing remained in isolated instances through the 1970s, and furthermore, even today some benign freshman traditions still carry on the notion of an untutored freshman class through certain ceremonies and activities.

The period of the 1920s is critical in the development of pledging in Black fraternal organizations. With opposition to freshman hazing proving effective in ending the practice, the culture of hazing that had grown for over two hundred years in American higher education needed a new vehicle for its manifestation. That vehicle became to be known as pledging. In fact, there were some signs in the years prior to the end of freshman hazing that some principles of hazing were visible in the Greek-lettered organizations. The 1914 *Howardiana* yearbook introduced Greek life in a section entitled "Secrets," which implied a clandestine initiation process. By that year there were five fraternities at Howard, including one, Xi Delta Mu, which was established in 1913 for medical, dental, and pharmaceutical students.

In the Howard yearbook of 1916, the sectional divider for fraternities pictures a student on his knees in front of a petrified log with two beasts behind the log. The log has arms that are extended toward the student, who is shrieking in fear as his hat flies off his head. Etched on the log are the Greek letters of the five Pan-Hellenic Council organizations (fraternities and sororities) present on campus at that time.

This mysterious and scary image of Greek life was continued into the 1920s. The 1920 Howard yearbook sectional divider for fraternities shows a man in a hooded robe with a cross on the front of it, holding a skull in his left hand. A candle burns at his right, and a serpent hisses on a stack of books to his left. This image is similar to pictures of upperclass students in the early 1900s who wore robes and hoods as a part of the intimidation of first-year students. At Wilberforce University the 1920 yearbook introduces fraternities through two skulls, one engraved with the letters ΑΦΑ, the other ΚΑΨ—the two fraternities on the campus that year. Similarly, sororities were introduced through skulls similarly engraved, but with ΔΣΘ and AKA. However, the skulls were pictured in front of a witch riding a broom. These pictures show a link in the practices used to scare freshmen, and those used in the 1920s to intimidate new initiates.

As indicated, the movement to end freshman hazing began during this time as well. Freshmen at Howard around 1920 were called "paenies," a word similar to beanies, and they wore "paenie caps."[13] At Howard, freshman hazing was specifically "tabooed" by 1924.[14] At the same time, the idea of pledging had emerged. The idea of pledging actually emerged as early as 1919 at Ohio State University. During that year, Kappa Alpha Psi began the Scrollers Club. In the 1939 edition of *The Ayeni,* the yearbook for Tennessee A&I College, the Kappa Alpha Psi page gave a brief history of the Scrollers Club:

The Scrollers Club which is an integral part of Kappa Alpha Psi Fraternity, was founded on the campus of Ohio State University, May 19, 1919 for the purpose of unifying the men who aspire to the achievements that Kappa Alpha Psi offers. Since that time each undergraduate chapter of Kappa Alpha Psi has had its own Scrollers Club.[15]

Fraternity introduction, 1923 (Courtesy Lincoln University Archives)

Two years later, Alpha Phi Alpha created the Sphinx Club at Howard University. It was described as "a brief stopping place where the members of the fraternity in theory attempt to study a man's character, to get acquainted with him, and to let him get acquainted with them in order that both the fraternity and the sphinxman may decide intelligently whether or not either wishes to continue the friendship and cement it into brotherhood."[16] At Wilberforce in 1923, Delta Sigma Theta defined the Pyramid Club as "a group of Freshman girls who are aspirants to the Delta Sigma Theta Sorority. The club has for its aims the highest in scholarship, ideals and womanhood."[17]

By 1922 the word "pledges" was used as it appeared in reference to the Ivy Leaf Club. In fact, in 1922 three organizations at Wilberforce organized pledge clubs. The 1924 Wilberforce yearbook went further to attempt a historical listing of the creation of pledge clubs. The information listed included a date of founding, a location, and colors of the pledge club, several of the dates in question but nonetheless an interesting attempt to document this aspect of Black Greek life (Table 1).

The Bison (now the name of the Howard yearbook) of 1924 verified through the Greek section that pledging was in full swing. The word "pledgee" appeared under the calendar of events for Greeks, as the record indicated that Kappa Alpha Psi had a pledgee dance.[18] During the same edition, under the section for Delta Sigma Theta, an interesting text appears to describe an early pledge process to some degree:

> We took with us a few "nuns" to show them a little of the outside world. Across a sea, up mountains and down valleys we took them, and finally when we realized that the poor things were so cold that they could scarcely walk or talk, we brought them back over the same rough road. But "all is well that ends well"; so they found themselves in the secret places of our sisterhood.[19]

In less than ten years from the beginnings of pledging in Black fraternities and sororities, the signs of hazing emerged. McKenzie theorized that

TABLE 1

Establishment of Pledge Clubs

Name of club	Date established	Place established	Colors
Sphinx Club	1916	None listed	Orange and black
Pyramid Club	1920	Philadelphia	Green and white
Scrollers Club	1921	Ohio State	Gold and blue
Ivy Leaf Club	1922	Wilberforce	Pink and blue

Source: The Forcean Yearbook, Wilberforce University, 1924.

"the social norms that had dictated the acceptance of hazing made it relatively easy for the fraternities to incorporate the practice into their pledge
activities."[20] By 1925 the Howard University newspaper chronicled a
period known as "Hell Week" where pledges marched around the campus
in odd attire while singing. Some may also view this as the genesis of stepping, but the descriptions of the attire link more closely to the practices
used with first-year students who endured pennalism, fagging, or hazing.
And this practice also produced painful results. In a 1928 article for the
Lincoln (PA) University newspaper, a fraternity member challenged the
brutal hazing he witnessed, hazing that left wounds he described as raw as
"fresh beef steak."[21]

PLEDGING MATURES: 1930–60

The challenges of pledging and hazing were evident in the mid to late
1920s, and continued into the 1930s. By 1930 it was clear that the pledge
classes were second-class citizens in their pursuit of membership. In the mid-
1920s at Wilberforce, both Sigma Gamma Rho and Alpha Kappa Alpha called
their pledge classes "barbarians," a practice that became more entrenched in
later years. The concept of pledge clubs became more entrenched by 1930.
Zeta Phi Beta had established a group for "those young ladies who wish to
become Zeta members and have expressed that desire are 'Archonians,'
pledge members."[22] By 1931 the separation between members and aspirants
was couched in familial terms, as noted at Howard with the Ivy Leaf Club
members describing themselves as "ten of us freshmen are building new
hope on the first step of the ladder of a nation-wide sisterhood. We are the little sisters 'of the Alpha Kappa Alpha Sorority.'"[23]
    By 1934, fraternity pledging and sorority pledging were challenged
much like freshman hazing, and for the same reasons—the process was
violent and abusive. McKenzie noted, "The swarms of protest against 'Hell
Week' activities, like the 'probation' periods themselves, surfaced nearly
every autumn and spring. Fraternities would pass resolutions to make
future initiations less severe, while condemnations of the groups would be
spouted across the nation."[24] During that year a group of former pledges
from the various fraternities formed Gamma Tau Fraternity at Howard. It
developed an alternative to Hell Week that included a week of lectures and
informal discussions, but there is little evidence that Gamma Tau had any
lasting impact on Greek life at Howard or elsewhere.
    By the end of the 1930s, some of the documented pledging activities
were as brutal if not more so than the freshman-sophomore class rushes. At
Lincoln University, the paddling of pledges could be heard throughout the
dormitories. Those pledging, called probates because the period was seen

as probation from the rest of campus, were seen limping around campus. They were forced to clean the rooms of "big brothers," wash their clothes, and run errands. Due to sheer exhaustion, probates often fell asleep in class. These activities serve as continued proof that freshman hazing was alive and well through the guise of fraternity and sorority pledging, although at this time most accounts of hazing were in the fraternities.

The 1940s became, in a sense, a decade of acknowledgment by the Greek-letter organizations that hazing was a problem. This acknowledgment came in the form of actions by the colleges, by the specific hazing acts on the campuses, and by the implementation of policies by the various organizations. In 1942, Lincoln University instituted a "no hitting" law in an effort to end the violence being perpetrated on students pledging the fraternities in particular. University officials met with fraternity representatives in an effort to set guidelines for probation activities that were free of brutality. Likewise at Fisk, the executive committee of the faculty suspended all probation activities due to brutality.[25]

The student media at various campuses captured this dominant characteristic of Greek activities through their college annuals. The Clark College yearbook in 1946 used as a sectional divider for fraternities a drawing of a man with a paddle preparing to strike another man who was bent over. The irony of sectional dividers such as this one was that in the following pages, each chapter was pictured. They were normally in formal attire, clean cut or made up, and giving an air of culture and sophistication. But the reality was that these same students were in many cases perpetuating brutal acts of hazing. Accordingly, the national organizations began to create policies that specifically outlawed brutality. In the 1940s, three national fraternities passed laws forbidding hazing and brutality.

The 1940s also became a time of great expansion for Greek-lettered organizations. Much of the expansion took place in the South at historically Black colleges and universities.[26] Much of this coincided with the accreditation of these schools, a criteria set by many national organizations at the time. But some schools were skeptical of Black fraternal organizations and moved cautiously to establish chapters. Hampton University was one school in particular. A faculty-and-student committee in 1946 was formed to study fraternities at Black schools. The committee felt that the organizations would benefit the interests of the college. One of the issues mentioned was the lack of incentive students generally had about school, and that Greek organizations, with their high scholastic standards, would cause students to seek better grades as required for membership in the Greek-lettered organizations.

The school, Hampton Institute at that time, had some local clubs that served similar purposes to fraternities and sororities. The Phyllis Wheatley Literary Society conducted probation or pledging activities including public performances in the cafeteria by their probates. The probates of the Olympic Club could be seen lapping milk out of bowls like dogs. But these organizations, according to the committee, did not maintain students' time or money once they left school because these groups had no national recognition. So, after approval by the board of trustees in 1947, fraternities and sororities were chartered on the campus with the full recognition that while these organizations had obvious benefits, there were some potential pitfalls as witnessed on other campuses.

In the minutes of the semiannual board of trustees meeting on 27 April 1951, the issue of fraternities and sororities was reassessed due to the initial caveat that the groups would be chartered during a five-year probationary period. A portion of the report indicated the following:

> They recognize that the existence of fraternities and sororities on a college campus creates certain problems. At Hampton Institute these problems have centered on:
>
>   1. Increase in cost to students.
>   2. Some petty rivalries.
>   3. Some unnecessary extremes in connection with rushing and initiation.
>   4. An excessive number of activities of a promotional and social nature.
>
> The officers of the college, including the President, have been deeply concerned with these problems. We do not consider, however, that the problems are of sufficient gravity to justify the denying of the students the right to have fraternities and sororities.[27]

In the end, the board voted to continue fraternities and sororities at Hampton, noting the obligation of the administration to work with the organizations to produce the "best possible results in student life and to require the adherence of these chapters to standards that will prove beneficial to Hampton Institute."[28]

The challenges noted at Hampton Institute in the late 1940s coincided with a culture of pledging that was developing a life of its own. During this decade, major innovations in pledging became noticeable. One of the additions to pledging was the dressing alike of pledges, also called pledgees or probates on some campuses. The similarities were fairly generic, as male pledges would wear suits and female pledges may have worn similar dresses or skirts and blouses. In some cases a male pledge class could be seen wearing tuxedos. In addition to the dressing alike, some pledge clubs could be seen carrying similar objects. Photos from the Clark College yearbook of 1948 picture Phi Beta Sigma pledges (called Crescents) who had similar paddles, and Omega Psi Phi pledges (called Lampados) holding lamps. This time period marks the beginning of a sophistication of pledging as a culture in and of itself.

But the brutality witnessed in the 1940s was still a major point of contention for campuses and national organizations. By 1948, Lincoln University, an

Hell Week, 1949 (Courtesy Lincoln University Archives)

institution that battled hazing from sanctioned activities with freshmen to more secretive hazing of pledges, suspended all probation and initiation activities. Both universities and organizations sought ways to change this behavior. One initial effort made by the organizations was to change the period known as "Hell Week" since the late 1920s, and replace it with "Help Week." This was no small task, as Hell Week had become a major component in the culture of pledging. At Central State, a full spread in the 1950 yearbook under the caption "Hell Week" showed numerous images of pledges being hazed. As a part of Hell Week during the early 1950s, pledges at Clark could be found participating in numerous stunts and antics as well as eating together, dressing alike, and attending chapel and university functions together as a group.[29]

Help Week essentially resembled the activities that the Gamma Tau Fraternity at Hampton tried to accomplish during the 1930s. During this week the pledges would participate in discussions on proper eating habits at formal events and on current events, and undertake special service projects.[30] A 1954 *Tennessean* yearbook pictured Alpha Kappa Alpha pledges from Tennessee State College in smocks labeled "AKA Help Week." The students appeared to be involved in some sort of service activity as a part of their final week of pledging. Help Week activities were also prevalent at Central State during 1954 as well.

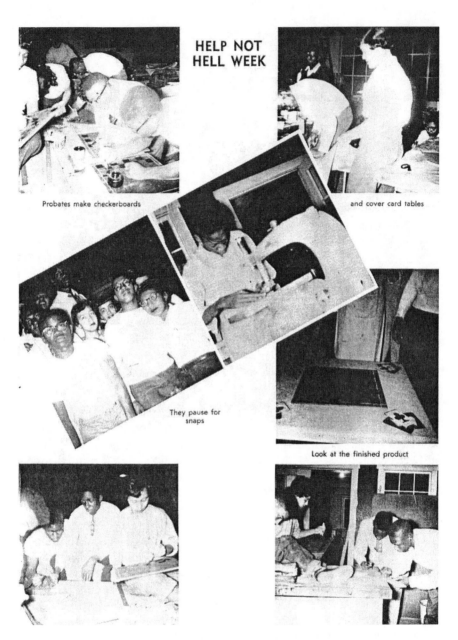

HELP NOT HELL WEEK

Probates make checkerboards

and cover card tables

They pause for snaps

Look at the finished product

Help Week activities, 1954 (Courtesy Central State University Archives)

The rest of the 1950s served as a time for the new culture of pledging to become more refined and defined. Pledge classes now were seen dressed alike in specific uniforms. The men wore suits that were nearly identical, and may have been accessorized with matching ties or hats. The more extravagant pledge classes, and in some cases now called "lines," wore flashy capes, turbans, or carried nice walking canes. One of the most creative pledge uniforms was worn by members of an Omega Psi Phi line at Clark College in the early 1950s, who held lamps in their left hands while wearing Scottish kilts and regalia. Sorority pledges wore identical dresses or skirt-and-blouse combinations, and in some cases, matching hair bows, hats, handbags, or other items. All of these lines also carried objects that held some type of significance for their specific organization. A prominent item was the paddle, which was usually decorated and painted. Some lines carried decorated shields that normally had the Greek letters of the group on them, and maybe some symbol for the organization.

But some interesting items appeared during this time as well. Many of these objects were unofficial symbols of the organizations. As indicated, Omega Psi Phi pledges began carrying lamps in the late 1940s, but by the 1950s some of the pledges also donned dog collars and leashes. In subsequent years the canine image would become a controversial part of the Omega Psi Phi culture. Delta Sigma Theta lines could be seen either with a pyramid affixed to their clothing, or to a bag, as a symbol that they were members of the Pyramid Club. During the 1950s, Pyramids could also be seen in some instances carrying rubber ducks. An interesting break from the duck symbolism occurred at Howard during the early fifties as the Pyramids carried stuffed panda bears. The Sigma Gamma Rho line from Jackson State in 1954 carried baby bottles and baby dolls.

And the 1950s was also a time when students began to try to describe the impact the Greek experience could have on a student, despite the extravagances associated with pledging. It was a time when Greeks made sincere attempts to sell the experience to potential members. The Central State College newspaper, *The Gold Torch,* ran a story in 1954 that explained Greek life's benefits. For extroverted students there was the opportunity to "question his actions and that of others in order to strike a happy medium for which everyone longs."[31] For introverts, Greek life was also portrayed as having advantages.

> Most times this is your first time to live and mingle with those other than your family or neighboring friends. You don't have the initiative to make friends readily therefore pledging first and becoming a part of a small organization offers many challenges. You have a chance to get closer to individuals, study them, and study yourself thus making for a fond sisterly or brotherly love to be cherished throughout your lifespan.[32]

Probates of
Alpha Kappa Alpha

Probates of
Delta Sigma Theta

Probates of
Kappa Alpha Psi

Probates of
Omega Psi Phi

Howard probates, 1956 (Courtesy Howard University Archives)

This became a decade that tried to help students navigate the often tenuous pledging process as it continued to evolve.

CIVIL RIGHTS AND PLEDGING WRONGS

While pledging entered a creative phase during the 1950s, the organizations struggled to remain relevant during the early 1960s. The Civil Rights movement reached America's colleges and universities, and students were turning their attentions away from Greek life and toward the goals of the movement. An *Ebony* magazine article, discussing the rebound the organizations made in the 1980s, indicated

> During the turbulent '60s, they often were viewed as irrelevant social clubs. Black fraternities and sororities, despite a history of support for scholarship and community service, just seemed out of touch with the times—times when many Black students were rushing to sign up for the front lines of campus activism. Enthusiasm was for picket lines, not pledge lines.[33]

And while Greek life was being challenged within the Black community, Iota Phi Theta Fraternity emerged as a force that would gain national status within the next two decades. The twelve men starting Iota Phi Theta differed from founders of the eight national groups at that time, in that they were nontraditional students—generally three to five years older than average collegians, some married, some veterans, and some with full-time jobs. The founding of this organization can be seen as a symbol of the 1960s— a new approach to address the concerns of Black America.

Also during the 1960s the effects of the Brown vs. Board of Education decision of 1954 were being felt. Black students were now integrating the major state universities of the South, including the University of Mississippi, the University of Alabama, and the University of Georgia. And interestingly, Black fraternity and sorority members in some cases were the ones on the front lines of these integration battles. The University of Georgia's first two Black students were Charlayne Hunter, a member of Delta Sigma Theta initiated at Wayne State, and Hamilton Holmes, a member of Alpha Phi Alpha initiated at Morehouse. While now they were members of the larger Greek community, they knew they were unwelcome as the Kappa Alpha Fraternity members lowered the Confederate flag to half mast to welcome them to Athens.[34] But when asked during that time how she withstood racial abuse, Charlayne Hunter indicated that "she kept remembering the words of her Delta Sigma Theta sorority oath: 'Keep a calm mind, courageous spirit, bar bitterness from my heart.'"[35] Their treatment may have eased fears of Black fraternity and sorority officials who in the 1950s feared that the Brown decision may have caused a situation where "groups which had traditionally excluded members of minority groups began to eliminate their racial restrictions and recruit Black women students," thus threatening their growth.[36]

Yet, it was also acknowledged during the 1960s that many of the key figures in Civil Rights were members of Black Greek–lettered organizations. A famous Associated Press photo shows, on the balcony of the Lorraine Motel in Memphis prior to the assassination of Dr. King, four Black Greek men who were key figures in the Civil Rights movement: Martin Luther King Jr. (Alpha Phi Alpha), Jesse Jackson (Omega Psi Phi), Hosea Williams (Phi Beta Sigma), and Ralph Abernathy (Kappa Alpha Psi). Many of those leaders indicated that their experience pledging made it easier for them to handle the brutal treatment they received while fighting for equal rights. Andrew Young, in an acceptance speech after being given an award at the Alpha Phi Alpha General Convention in Washington, DC, in 1997, joked that after the hazing he endured as a pledge at the Beta chapter on the campus of Howard University, the beatings the Klan gave him were nothing.

So pledging continued to evolve during the 1960s. The dressing alike became even more sophisticated, along with a strategic placement of pledges that arranged them in height generally from the shortest to the tallest, although sometimes done in reverse. Some male pledges had their heads shaved, or they may have had their hair cut into a Mohawk. The more formal dress of the 1950s started to subside as lines wore shorts or other casual clothes. One of the most interesting yearbook spreads was found in the 1961 *Brownite* for Morris Brown College. The pictures and captions attempted to provide a description of "Pledge Club Life." Pledges are described cleaning paddles of a big brother, or polishing the shoes of a big brother. One pledge had the task of cleaning the fraternity penlight that was used for chapter programs. These elements of personal servitude were visible remnants of the acts of pennalism, fagging, and hazing.

And the 1960s were also a time when there was evidence that freshman hazing was still around in varying forms, meaning that some students had to in essence pledge twice if they chose to join a sorority or fraternity. In the early 1920s, freshmen may have been called "dogs" on the campus as a symbol of their place in student life. The freshmen entering Morris Brown in 1960 were also called dogs and wore beanies as well. They endured their second-class citizenship just prior to Thanksgiving, when they participated in Hobo Day, when they dressed as hobos and were led on a processional by the upperclassmen. This was their final rite before becoming true "Brownites."[37]

These activities appeared at numerous other institutions. At Mississippi Valley State, freshmen in the early 1960s engaged in subservient behavior to upperclassmen, often bowing in their presence. In other instances, upperclass students quizzed freshmen. They were made to wear beanies and called "crabs." Freshmen at Hampton were also called crabs during this time period. At Wilberforce, the act of giving freshmen their beanies was called "capping." And in 1965, freshman week at Howard was described as "beanies on heads, papers in hands; inundated with welcoming speeches, ill treated by medical examiners, suffering in endless lines, they were, nevertheless, anxious to go to class."[38]

But the criticism of pledging on the respective campuses intensified during the 1960s. The aura of the Civil Rights era cast a shadow on the importance of pledging, and with the sophistication of campus media, more students openly criticized the Greeks and their activities. In the late 1960s at Central State, a student group called "Unity for Unity," a Black power group, was suspected of providing rumors about hazing abuses. In an article filled with hard points and sarcasm, the Central State College newspaper asked the question "Hell Week or Plain 'Hell'" in regard to pledging. In describing what students would witness during a "probate show," the article indicated:

> When the spectators witness the tired, beat, lifeless beings going through their daily routines during Hell Week like mechanized elements, their hearts will go out to the pledges. They will think of how terrible these persons have been treated—they will never know for certain until they have pledged in an attempt to seek membership to the realm of sisterhood or brotherhood. It is true that pledges do things they do not particularly care to do. Of course, everyone knows that Ivies, Lampadoes, Pyramids, Scrollers, and Sphinx are never on restrictions. It is just that they prefer talking to their Greek and Greek-to-be sisters and brothers. Other nice things about pledging are that you never HAVE to do anything you do not want to do, you can say what you want and go where you want and with whom you want.[39]

The 1970s did not offer much new in terms of the development of pledging. This period is most notable for having a mass expansion of Greek-letter organizations across the country. For example, Alpha Kappa Alpha Sorority never added more than five new undergraduate chapters in any given year prior to 1969. Yet, with rapid integration of Black students on predominantly White college campuses, chapters of Greek organizations were soon springing up. Between 1969 and 1979, AKA added at least ten new undergraduate chapters per year, with at least twenty chapters in three of those years.[40] Similar patterns of growth were experienced by other organizations during this period.

So, much of the look of pledging continued the trend set in the 1960s, with the lines dressed alike, carrying objects that had significance to the organization, and moving together in a single file line. The cultural additions, which will be discussed in greater detail later in this volume, included

Hell-Week
And
Rabble

Hell week activities, 1968 (Courtesy Lincoln University Archives)

giving each pledge a number (called a line number), and a name (line name). In addition, the entire pledge club would be given a collective line name as well. Pledges also began to wear some form of lavaliere that may have had a symbol that represented their group, such as Phi Beta Sigma pledges, called Crescents, who may have worn a lavaliere shaped like a crescent moon.

Ebony magazine's article on Greek life in 1983 emphasized that interest in these organizations, despite elaborate pledge programs that subjected students "to a variety of embarrassing and sometimes belittling situations," was on the rise.[41] The article pictured a Phi Beta Sigma line marching across campus wearing dark coats and pants with combat boots that appear to be linked together while carrying numbered bricks in their right hands. Yet, one national president interviewed said that numerous worthy applicants came forward, in fact, too many to be accommodated.

And this sophisticated pledge program continued to flourish as more affluent Black students, many second-generation college students, put more money into this process so that the look of pledging was more contemporary. The uniforms of the pledges were nicer, with every accessory matching. Fraternity pledges could be seen in some instances wearing khaki pants and blazers while wearing matching shirts, ties, and even socks. They might even carry with them matching book bags or briefcases. Others adopted a more rugged look, as pledges might wear fatigues and boots, or jeans and jerseys that would be in the fraternity colors but without the letters. Variations of the jersey usage appeared as early as the 1950s as pledges wore caps that had two Greek letters but missed the middle letter of the fraternity name. Sorority pledges wore matching skirts and blouses, with intentional emphasis for the hair to be made plain, and no makeup. The sorority pledges in the 1950s and 1960s as pictured in yearbooks always were neatly made up, but that could have been for the purposes of the photo only. There were cases as well when sorority pledges would wear jeans and T-shirts or sweatshirts that might indicate what organization they were pledging.

The 1970s and 1980s were also years when pledging was intellectualized. The elaborate practices were given newfound meanings, especially since chapters were now on predominantly White campuses that were confused by the actions of the pledges. Paula Giddings indicated:

> There is a special emphasis on the line of initiates acting in unison, whether through the dance steps that they perform, dressing alike, or even walking across campus in a kind of lockstep. As in many such organizations where group action must supercede individual ones, many of the pledging activities were of conscious design. The stripping away of individuality is achieved through activities that are designed to "humble" a pledgee (some would,

accurately, characterize it as humiliation). A "one for all, and all for one" mentality is further developed through the knowledge that if one pledgee does something "wrong" the whole "line is punished; if one is unable to perform a certain task, someone on the line will have to perform it twice.[42]

Yet Giddings, writing about Delta Sigma Theta when Lillian Benbow was national president from 1971–75, indicated that complaints of abuse were more numerous during this period. Benbow reiterated that brutality and harassment could not be tolerated, and would not be tolerated. She instituted new policies that intensified penalties for hazing, and by 1979, thirty-eight chapters were disciplined, with four suspended.[43]

POP CULTURE EXPOSES BLACK GREEK ATROCITIES: THE SPIKE LEE EFFECT

This culture of pledging within the larger Black Greek lifestyle was for all practical purposes invisible to the general population. It was a facet of Black college life known primarily by Black America, especially with alumni members being very active in their communities. But that changed in 1988 with the release of the movie *School Daze* by Spike Lee. The film addressed numerous issues within Black America as played out on the fictional campus of Mission College, but a central story line was that of the fictional fraternity, Gamma Phi Gamma, and its activities, which included the parties, the step shows, and the antics of the pledge club known as the "Gammites." One description of some of the pledge activities explained

> It's Homecoming week at Mission College, and the Gamma Phi Gamma pledges, sans hair, are about to cross over into the fraternity brotherhood. This is make-or-break night for the young pledges. During their six-week pledge period, they have had to wolf down Alpo dog food and walk chain-gang fashion on dog leashes. Now, under a full moon, they must hold an iron torch for hours while their fraternity brothers scream obscenities at them.[44]

In an interview, Spike Lee suggested that the fraternities and sororities had lost their original purpose and instead were engaged in foolishness and name-calling. He felt that his portrayal was mild, not showing "the really sick stuff they do, like tying guys to chairs or pushing them down stairs."[45] In Lee's book *Uplift the Race: The Construction of School Daze,* he indicated that he created Gamma Phi Gamma by rolling "the worst elements of the Qs, Alphas, Sigmas, Grooves, and Kappas into one."[46]

Yet many criticized the film that had sequences showing pledges being paddled by their big brothers. They were concerned that the film did not show any of the positive aspects of Greek life. But Lee's book revealed some secrets about the movie. In particular, cast member Roger Smith described the creation of the Gammite sequences, as Lee placed him in charge of that group. He discussed the choreography of the marching and greetings, and the difficulty some cast members had with understanding pledging. They benefited from a real-life example, as Smith shared.

> My nephew was on line at Morehouse at the same time I was on line [as a Gammite for the movie]. He'd come to me every Tuesday and Thursday, hiding out from his big brothers, and crash in my hotel room. I picked up a lot from him: the fatigue, the persecution, the whole head trip they put you through. His going over coincided with the Gammites', it was practically simultaneous.[47]

Furthermore, Lee hired his Morehouse friend Zelmer "Z-Dog" Bothic to serve as the technical adviser for the fraternity scenes. Lee recalled Bothic, who pledged at Morehouse, could not sit down in class due to the paddlings he received while pledging.[48]

The movie did in fact capture some aspects of Black Greek life in regard to pledging, whether members wanted to acknowledge it or not. The ugly side of pledging became very visible in the 1980s due to this movie, and despite positive actions of fraternities and sororities, it was clear that pledging had become the defining event of the Black fraternal experience. In an interview, Michael Price, then assistant executive director of Alpha Phi Alpha, said, "The public sees eight to twelve weeks of foolishness and two or three days of community service. Which do you think they remember?"[49]

The mid-1980s were almost a repeat of the mid-1940s in terms of national organizations trying to address the renewed emergence of hazing issues. Since organizations banned brutality and hazing in the 1940s, the next step was to modify the pledging process. Much of this had been occurring since the 1960s as pledge periods were shortened over time. Programs that would last a semester or more became standardized eight to twelve-week periods, and into the 1980s were whittled down to a fairly standard six-week pledge program. Along with this change in time, organizations attempted to change the whole idea of pledging. In 1984, Delta Sigma Theta officially adopted the term "membership intake" to describe pledging. In 1985, Omega Psi Phi changed its pledge program to move away from the brutality associated with pledging. This movement continued in 1986 as Alpha Phi Alpha instituted a risk management program. Members of the fraternity were required to pass a test on fraternity structure and workings as well as policies related to pledging and hazing. After all members were tested, all pledges after spring of 1986 were required to pass the exam prior to initiation.

Phi Beta Sigma Fraternity instituted the most radical change in 1987. At that point in time, Phi Beta Sigma announced that it banned pledging. In a letter to the undergraduate chapters, the executive director of Phi Beta Sigma, Gerald Smith, wrote, "Mark it on your calendars. Pledging is dead."[50] An article in the *Atlanta Constitution* described the new process, and how the Georgia State University chapter of Phi Beta Sigma was executing it. The new initiates did not walk in line, participate in stepping, or any activities that had become to be known as a part of pledging. Instead, the potential members had to "meet rigid academic standards, demonstrate leadership abilities and complete a series of civic projects while learning the history of the organization."[51]

Many undergraduates did not approve of these new processes. They feared getting the same reactions that the members of Phi Beta Sigma at Georgia State received—a lack of acceptance and ostracism for not pledging. In the process a new term emerged in the pledging culture. "Paper" became the term for persons who were initiated into an organization without pledging, or simply by completing the necessary paperwork for membership.[52] Most undergraduates, in response to this program and shortened pledge programs in all other organizations, began to institute a counterculture by continuing to pledge "underground," a semisecret process designed to be invisible to administrators and fraternity or sorority officials while known to undergraduates on campus. This concept, emerging in the late 1980s, became much more dominant by the early 1990s.

THE END OF PLEDGING

While Gerald Smith of Phi Beta Sigma communicated that pledging was dead to undergraduate members of his fraternity in the late 1980s, the final straw actually occurred in October 1989. At Morehouse College, the members of Alpha Phi Alpha Fraternity were preparing to begin another line, the next group of men to enter the fraternity through that chapter. Joel Harris and other young men had begun pledging Alpha Phi Alpha "underground," meaning that this process had not been sanctioned by any fraternity officials nor officials from the college. In an off-campus apartment, thirty students, both brothers and would-be brothers, participated in a pledge session, sometimes referred to as "sets." The pledges were being quizzed on fraternity history, not of the national fraternity, but of the Morehouse chapter.

Informal accounts of the evening revealed that hazing was occurring at the apartment, as brothers punched and slapped prospective members as means to correct behavior or to prevent future mistakes.[53] The hazing was described as "extremely violent" by the medical examiner who interviewed several of the students. Joel Harris, a Morehouse sophomore, was in the apartment. The brothers knew that he had a congenital heart defect that required surgery when Joel was two.[54] So Joel was spared any of the physical abuses while his line brothers absorbed his share. Yet the intensity of the session caused Joel to go into cardiac dysrhythmia, and despite ten minutes of attempted resuscitation, he died.

Members of the chapter interviewed by the *Atlanta Journal-Constitution* expressed disbelief that they, honor students without any disciplinary records, were being charged with violating school policies and the law. They noted that Joel had won a wrestling match with a brother a few weeks before his October 17 death (an activity that was common with pledging and hazing), and that he was a karate red belt. Succinctly, student Randy Richardson said, "We didn't expect it to happen to us."[55] And while the brothers interviewed indicated that the October 17 meeting was only an informal meeting with aspirants having an opportunity to learn more about the fraternity, the evidence pointed to underground pledging that ironically left the one person dead who was not physically hazed that evening, a sign that the mental toll of hazing could be just as deadly.

But the interview revealed that the culture of pledging was strong, and that those who perpetuated it honestly felt that it was a beneficial process. Their words revealed a process that was laden with acts of hazing. The brothers defined pledging as a time when the pledges shaved their heads, dressed alike, and remained on a period of probation where they could not speak to anyone except the other pledges, the fraternity members, and professors. The pledges in effect take on childlike qualities, but by the end of the process, the brothers indicated that the pledges' hair grows back, and they are able to talk again—that they have returned to manhood. Student Merion Stewart described it as "a humbling process. There's a breaking down and a building-up process, and by the time you become an Alpha Phi Alpha, you become a man of distinction."[56]

In the end, the breaking-down process was irreversible with Joel Harris dying. This death capped a decade of abuses that began garnering local and national media attention—alcohol poisonings, ruptured eardrums, broken limbs, burnings, and even assaults using two-by-fours.[57] The characteristics that defined pennalism, fagging, and freshman hazing were all very visible in Black Greek life on college campuses, and beginning in the 1970s, newsworthy items. With the heightened awareness of Black fraternities and sororities after the Spike Lee movie *School Daze,* along with increasing numbers of visible hazing incidents culminating with the death of Joel Harris, the hand of national organizations was forced to go in a direction that was completely uncharted, one that would produce an entirely new set of challenges and headaches. In a sense, pledging died along with Joel Harris. But it was resurrected through a new vehicle—membership intake.

3

The Membership Intake Movement

This was a long-overdue decision. It was time to say enough is enough. Pledging just presented opportunities for abuses to occur and it was time to close the window.[1]

It is a courageous stance that these organizations united for the purpose of making sure that hazing is not involved in the membership process. This continues to build a certain momentum. Fraternities are moving in a similar direction.[2]

The only thing giving us a black eye is pledging. The colleges and universities have said to us, "If you can't clean up your act, we will do it for you. . . . If it's such a good policy, why do we have to spend so much time in court defending ourselves against lawsuits?"[3]

Those traditions developed over time. Pledging doesn't call for walking in line, shaving your head, or being someone's personal slave.[4]

Too many people have been conditioned by pledging. They say, "It was done to me, so I'm going to do it to you." It's going to meet with a lot of opposition from the undergraduates and the alumni.[5]

IN FEBRUARY 1990, THE EIGHT PRESIDENTS WHO REPRESENTED THE GROUPS holding membership in the National Pan-Hellenic Council met in St. Louis to discuss the state of pledging. All had experienced numerous hazing incidents, and started to notice increases in lawsuits as well. They decided that, at that time, the only logical way to protect their organizations was to ban the process of pledging, the event viewed as the source of all their problems. They agreed that by the fall of 1990, no one would continue the practice of pledging.[6]

The death of Joel Harris at Morehouse College in October 1989 did prove to be the final straw, as some national officers acknowledged.[7] After that highly publicized death, it appeared as if these organizations reached a point of dissonance where they could not justify continuing pledging while students were being injured and even killed. Critics accused the national organizations of even looking the other way while hazing went on, even though the media began indicating, based on the Harris case, that pledges endured "a gamut of pledging sessions—in which they are screamed at, taunted, paddled, punched, etc."[8] After that death, the call became clear in 1989 for each group to rearrange the way that new members entered its organization.

The accounts of pledging during this time all painted a new and insightful view of the experience. While little was written about pledging as a whole prior to the mid-1980s, with most of the writings attempting to describe the process and intellectualize its worth, more accurate accounts provided a different picture. These new accounts of pledging seemed to support the radical change from the pledging that existed prior to that time to a membership intake process thought to focus more on educating new members.

But once the change to membership intake was announced, the history written in the newspapers painted a picture that should have prompted those unfamiliar with pledging to ask why the process hadn't changed years ago. The atrocities associated with pledging were now described as "hazing rituals that have ranged from practical jokes and minor humiliations to forced intoxication and beatings."[9] A *Washington Post* article declared, "On college campuses, black fraternities have a reputation for distinctively violent hazing."[10] Other accounts indicated that the major Black fraternities and sororities

> Have developed a reputation for permitting their pledge practices to become peculiarly abusive, crossing a line into what is commonly referred to as hazing. For decades, violence and humiliation have been part of pledging, for fraternities and sororities of all colors. . . . In the last 20 years, pledging for thousands of black college students has come to mean voluntarily being kicked, slapped or struck with oversized wooden paddles painted in the fraternity's colors and coat of arms. Along the way, there have been broken bones and teeth, torn flesh and bruises of body and spirit. . . . For weeks, sometimes almost an entire semester, black pledge periods have required that prospective members shave their heads, eat dog food, walk through campuses in regimented lines and carry painted bricks, boxes and wooden shields.[11]

Some were concerned that the media would use the opportunity to bash Black fraternities and sororities. The numerous articles written about the end of pledging graphically described the process unlike before. But the entrance into the membership intake era also was also an opportunity for some Black Greeks to express a sense of sorrow for participating in hazing. In an extremely candid interview with the *Washington Post* in June 1990, a fraternity man who pledged in 1986 at a southern, predominantly White university told of the horrors of his process. Speaking under the guarantee of anonymity, he acknowledged that he had been hazed, and had hazed, noting that he had a three-inch scar on his buttocks. His pledge process was one as described in other accounts—dressing alike in fatigues, not speaking to anyone outside of class, marching in line, and memorization of special greetings for big brothers (his favorite being a thirty-five-word greeting for the chapter president).[12]

This anonymous member then gave a very detailed account of pledging, one that fully described the hazing he endured. The man explained that the chapter imposed harsh discipline when pledges, for example, incorrectly presented the greetings, with their preferred method of punishment being paddling. In his description, the man indicated that paddling (also called swinging the wood) occurred all the time.

> Nighttime, daytime, anytime. Mainly at night, mainly on weekends. Three whacks ain't that bad after about 10 of them. After you get your first 10 in life, you can take three good ones. . . . It gets to a point where you can't sleep on your back anymore because your butt gets surprisingly hard. It gets swollen and black.[13]

His story of paddling ends when he discovered blood in his underwear, readily acknowledging that he did not feel any pain because of his numb buttocks. Fortunately, the violence ended then as well.[14]

Based on incidents such as this one, the decision in February 1990 was viewed as the logical means to protect the organizations. The national officials began to disclose openly that the organizations had been subject to numerous lawsuits due to hazing. They also indicated that they had been placed on notice by college presidents, especially those on historically Black campuses (and many, ironically, were also members of these organizations), that if they did not address the issues associated with hazing, their chapters would no longer be recognized.[15] But the organization presidents also realized that a great segment of their members, both undergraduate and graduate, were skeptical of the proposed process. They tried to ease their fears by indicating that membership intake would not just be a walk into the organizations. Prospective members would have to interview and then attend educational seminars, and in some cases, pass tests.

So each national president, after the February meeting, began the process of lobbying for the new process. Most had to return to national meetings that summer and have the new membership intake policy adopted. In essence, many presidents began politicking for the new process as a means of saving the organizations from themselves. In an article for the summer 1990 issue of *Sphinx* magazine, official organ of the Alpha Phi Alpha Fraternity, Napoleon Moses, then chair of the fraternity's committee on membership, standards, and extension, wrote:

> The question Alpha must address is a relatively simple one: What do we intend to do about the question mark which has been attached to our fraternity. . . . Each of you can see the crisis—the impending disaster. The time is here that Alpha must prove, conclusively and for all time, that we are of value

to higher education, that we can and will continue to make a unique contribution to the modern college and university. . . . However, the traditions which sustain us are not those destructive ones found in the rigours [*sic*] and rituals of pledging. Pledging is like a cancer eating away at the marrow of Alpha. Its tradition is not connected to the idealism and commitment of our founders, but instead, to the tribal mentality of members long ago outlawed by our General Organization.[16]

Other groups, such as Phi Beta Sigma and Kappa Alpha Psi Fraternities, made the decision to ban pledging through their national boards.[17] In both situations, the entrance into membership intake was to be shaky at best.

UNDERGROUND PLEDGING: THE BEAT GOES ON

During this time of transition the opposition was very vocal. Many indicated that pledging was a tradition that had to be continued, and one that students (and alumni) were committed to continuing. Some in the interfraternal world questioned, "Does taking away the pledging process eliminate hazing—or put it at another level? If we assume we're going to pass policy and it's going away, we're kidding ourselves."[18] Just that happened, and students began to endorse a new concept that was informally implemented in the late 1970s and early 1980s. As the result of shortened pledging periods, students created ways to extend pledging. The phenomenon as a whole became known as "underground pledging."[19]

With the advent of membership intake, underground pledging became viewed as a legitimate means to continue the culture of pledging. Members threatened openly that the end of pledging would cause underground pledging to emerge as the vehicle to keep pledging alive. But more interestingly, potential members wanted pledging to continue underground. One student at Clark Atlanta University, interviewed in 1990 after the ban on pledging was in effect, indicated, "I hope pledging goes underground. It's unfortunate it has to be done, but at the same time I want to do the same things the people before me did to create that bond."[20]

So first, a "pre-pledge" phase was instituted—an unofficial start to the pledge period that was not sanctioned by the national organization.[21] Essentially, though a national organization sanctioned a two-week pledge program, a local chapter could continue a six to eight-week program through prepledging. Once the new intake process was instituted, prepledging was augmented with the concept of "post-pledging." In this instance a chapter could give the appearance of following all of the national guidelines as prescribed for membership intake, and after all the official ceremonies were conducted, and chapter advisers, state, or regional directors had returned to their domains, the underground pledging began.[22] In essence, fully initiated members, with all rights and privileges thereto, subjected themselves to pledging and hazing in order to be fully "respected" as a member, a term that took on a new meaning in the Black Greek lingo after 1990. The decision to end pledging in 1990 and replace it with membership intake would have consequences unforeseen, inaugurating a turbulent decade.

CONFIRMATION OF UNDERGROUND PLEDGING: THE WILLIAMS STUDY

In 1992, John A. Williams completed doctoral studies at Kansas State University. His dissertation sought to study the perceptions of the new policy, known as membership intake, by the current undergraduate members of Black fraternities and sororities. Within the first two years of membership intake, questions still lingered about its purpose and effectiveness. Williams sought to determine if the elimination of pledging would end hazing, what input undergraduates had on the implementation of the new process, what the impact, if any, the absence of pledging would have on membership quality, and if the new process hindered the establishment of bonds and a lifelong commitment to the organizations.[23]

So in the spring of 1992, Williams conducted a national study in which 227 undergraduates participated, representing all of the regions as defined by the National Pan-Hellenic Council (NPHC). The students also represented historically Black and predominantly White institutions. Well over half of the participants were then, or had been chapter officers, and almost half of them had attended a national meeting of their organization. It is presumed then that this sample was one that was current with the policies and procedures associated with membership intake. The first segment of the survey included a scale designed to determine how familiar the students were with the policies regarding membership intake.[24]

One of the major instruments created for the study was a Hazing Tolerance Scale. This showed a list of ten activities that students had to determine whether or not they considered hazing (see Table 2). The research study determined that differences in views on hazing, based on the scale, were present based on the type of school attended (with students attending White public schools the most tolerant), if they were initiated prior to 1990 (with those students more tolerant), and by region of the country (with students from the West and East being the most tolerant). This set of data indicated that potential troubles with hazing could have been expected at public White institutions in the East and West, perpetuated by students initiated prior to membership intake. There were no significant differences by gender.[25]

The final section of the instrument determined the extent to which students endorsed the no-pledge policy. The students appeared to give very candid responses to the questions. Williams learned that only 40 percent of the respondents believed undergraduate members had an opportunity to

TABLE 2
Williams' Hazing Tolerance Scale

Walking in line
Carrying bricks (or other symbolic objects)
Intensive history study sessions
Saluting (speaking up to) big brothers/sisters
Dressing alike with other pledges
Calisthenics
Practicing steps
Speaking in unison with other pledges
Running errands for big brothers/sisters
Buying or making gifts for the chapter

Source: Williams, John A. "Perceptions of the No-Pledge Policy For New Member Intake By Undergraduate Members of Predominantly Black Fraternities and Sororities." Ph.D. diss., Kansas State University, 1992.

Note: Students were asked to indicate whether they felt each of these items was hazing or not hazing.

give input before implementation of the new process. Seventy-six percent believed that the new process would prevent bonding opportunities for future members, and 73 percent felt the new policy would reduce the life-long commitment that members would have for their organizations. Most strikingly, only 22 percent of the students felt that membership intake would eliminate hazing in Black fraternities and sororities.[26]

The students had an opportunity to provide an open-ended response to express themselves on the issue of membership intake. Williams was able to note several themes. Among these themes, he determined

1. Undergraduates felt the new process was enacted too quickly and without their input;
2. The national definitions of hazing were so broad that they excluded the traditional activities that undergraduates did not consider to be hazing;
3. Bonding opportunities were lost due to membership intake; and
4. "The issue of *gaining 'respect'* by pledging *is important* enough for undergraduates to risk sanctions by engaging in underground or illicit pledging."[27]

The last point was prophetic, although unheeded at that time. One respondent indicated that she had been caught in an illegal pledge process, but felt that it was worth it, simply because she would not have been respected had she not pledged. Williams, in discussing the implications of the study, clearly determined:

This research points out the apparent gap between the expectations of national leaders of black fraternities and sororities and the perceptions of undergraduates to a no-pledge policy for new member intake. The effective promulgation of a policy to eliminate pledging and hazing is not insuring effective implementation of that policy. . . . The overall low level of endorsement of the impact statements associated with the no-pledge policy by predominantly black undergraduate fraternity and sorority members suggests that the national leaders have not made a clear case for the no-pledge policy.[28]

The importance of this study in determining the climate on campuses through undergraduate attitudes about the membership intake process was not readily seen by the national organizations. In fact, during a conversation I had with Dr. Williams a few years after the study was done, he indicated that none of the organizations were interested in his results. This included his own fraternity. The study offered numerous suggestions designed to meet the challenge head-on, but the response was nonexistent. And yet, the study proved to be prophetic. The students clearly indicated intentions to continue pledging despite the potential consequences. They determined that the consequences of not pledging, by losing respect "on the yard," would be greater than being suspended for participating in or conducting illegal pledge activities.[29] This ethos became the dominant pattern of operation during the first decade of membership intake.

Of Moratoriums and Madness

Many national organizations were unsure as to how to proceed in this new era of intake. Ending pledging was a bold risk by presidents who felt that they had no other option. The problem was that the decision to end pledging was in part a reaction to the Morehouse incident, and each organization agreed to this new process without fully investigating how to operationalize membership intake. Furthermore, no organization studied how this cultural change (the formal end of pledging) might manifest itself on the college campus, even with the hints and suggestions that the counterculture of underground pledging had already begun and was about to move into full swing. And because of the lack of interest in the research, which signaled a long, difficult road in changing the culture of pledging, organizations sought some type of plan to tackle the new era.

So, many national organizations instituted "moratoriums," a new catchphrase in the lingo of the membership intake era signifying a period of time when all membership intake activities for a national organization were suspended while the organization worked on a plan, or a better plan, for implementing the program. Moratoriums were very common during the early 1990s—a signal that the decision to implement membership intake had not been thought out, and this became the time to strategize after the decision had been made.

By 1993 most organizations had completed their moratoriums and rolled out brand-new plans for implementing membership intake. Presumably, many of the persons who had participated in sanctioned pledge activities had graduated by then, so there was great optimism that the new process would begin without much difficulty. Williams foreshadowed the problems through his study. But an interesting interview in 1990 proved to be a preview for a major hazing event. In the *Washington Post* article, "The wrongs of the rites of brotherhood," Marlow Martin, the former Omega Psi Phi president at the University of Maryland, commented on the need for a rigorous process to ensure bonding. Martin told the paper, "The physical aspect makes you want it more. . . . And without that physically and mentally challenging aspect, I don't see how you could put the pressure on people where they would have to lean on each other and develop that bond."[30]

Ironically, the first highly publicized hazing case of the membership intake era involved Omega Psi Phi at the University of Maryland, where Martin once was president. In this case, twenty-four members of the fraternity were charged with hazing six pledges in an underground process. The paper reported,

> Police allege that the six would-be members were punched, kicked, whipped and beaten with paddles, brushes and belts over a two-month period. All of the recruits sustained serious injuries, some of which required hospitalization. . . . The most severely injured pledge had a ruptured spleen and a collapsed lung, and another was treated for a ruptured eardrum and cracked ribs. One received a concussion and another a fractured ankle, the documents state.[31]

Another account indicated that the pledges were dripped with hot wax and asked to eat vomit and drink from toilets. They were also to attend classes for big brothers and write their papers.[32] Another account indicated that several of those charged were not even students, but members of the fraternity in their late twenties who hung around campus, attempting to impress freshman female students.[33]

The initial investigation was instituted because, according to reports, police and university officials received a letter in early April from an anonymous female student who reported the hazing. The fraternity members targeted one pledge, Joseph Snell, because he was seen as a potential source of the investigation. In fact, the 5 May 1993 *Washington Post* editorial contained an interview from a pledge who revealed he wanted to join the fraternity that his uncle was a member of in the 1930s.

The Omegas were in fact correct. During his testimony in a civil suit years later, Snell indicated that he first attempted to call the fraternity national headquarters in Washington, pretending to be the father of a pledge, after spending a week in the hospital. When he received no response, he wrote the letter as a female student, which ended up being the impetus for the investigation leading to the arrests. Just prior to the criminal trial in June 1994, Snell dropped the charges, partially due to harassment and threats received by Omega members. The agreement was that the fraternity would pay for medical expenses and lost tuition.[34]

Even after the settlement, Snell was harassed and threatened when he attempted to return to the University of Maryland. He transferred, and in 1995 initiated a civil suit against the fraternity because the members failed to pay the bills as promised. In 1997 he was awarded $375,000. Lawyers for the fraternity argued that Snell could and should have walked away. But Snell's father, a police officer himself, in an interview with the *Washington City Paper* explained:

> The pledge process Joe went through closely parallels tactics described by people who have later been deprogrammed from religious cults. . . . Joe and the other pledges were always told that the point of the hazing was to see if they could become the kind of leaders black folks need, the kind who could live up to Omega's ideals of perseverance and manhood.[35]

This high-profile incident began to raise doubts publicly, and some officials asked whether or not the membership intake program was effective.[36]

This doubt was justified that same semester, as the Kappa Alpha Psi Fraternity at the University of Georgia was temporarily suspended for hazing after a prospective member was hospitalized. The student, Christopher Powell, needed surgery for an infection in his buttocks caused by paddling because he did not seek immediate medical treatment.[37] These cases in the era of membership intake (and presumably no pledging) started to raise suspicions. In an article that circulated numerous times via the Internet, *Ebony Male* magazine documented the hazing cases of the late 1980s and early 1990s while asking the question, are Black Greek fraternities still culturally relevant. "Why any organization that seeks to align itself with Black culture would mimic so closely the institution of American slavery, down to details including whippings, beatings, verbal humiliation, forced servitude, sleep deprivation, and even the branding of the flesh, is anyone's guess," the article rightfully asked.[38]

The Failure of Membership Intake: The Death of Michael Davis

February 1994 marked the four-year anniversary of the decision made by eight major Black fraternities and sororities to end the practice of pledging. Membership intake was now four years old. The first two years were mostly spent in moratorium—time to strategize how best to implement a process that did not include the decades-old custom of pledging. Year three could best be described as a year of awakening, as the hazing cases at Maryland and UGA (and additionally at Norfolk State University in 1992) provided evidence that everyone was not following the new program. Although Williams discovered in 1992 that undergraduates had little intention of adopting the new policy, these cases were some of the first disconcerting data about the status of membership intake.

Yet, the fourth anniversary of the decision to end pledging was marked in the most ominous of ways. In Cape Girardeau, Missouri, at Southeast Missouri State University, seven men were charged with involuntary manslaughter in relation to the death of Michael Davis. An additional six men were charged with hazing, a misdemeanor. All were the result of the death of SEMO student Michael Davis, twenty-five, who died on Tuesday, 15 February 1994 as the result of serious injuries he received during hazing at the hands of members of the Kappa Alpha Psi Fraternity there. Michael was one of five men engaged in underground pledging on the campus.[39]

As the story unfolded, the nation learned that Davis had "pledged" once before this attempt, in 1991. The underground line was halted when the national office began investigating tips about hazing. But he attempted again in 1994. His girlfriend reported that he had been subjected to verbal abuse, demands for money, and beatings. His mother reported that she saw him the previous weekend when he returned home, getting money to buy presents for fraternity members. During their conversation he indicated that he had been beaten, but that he had to take it in order to become a member.[40] After being beaten late on February 14 into the morning of February 15, he was returned to his apartment, where later in the afternoon, a brother of the fraternity called paramedics because Davis was not breathing.[41]

The aftermath was immense. Once the dust settled, seven undergraduate members of the fraternity were charged with involuntary manslaughter, four additional undergraduates were charged with hazing, and four alumni members of the chapter were charged with hazing. The news accounts reiterated the point that just four years prior, a few hours away in St. Louis, the national presidents had decided to end pledging. The numerous editorials penned were scathing indictments of Black Greek life as a whole. Kappa brother William Cox, president of *Black Issues in Higher Education*, declared

> Deaths and injuries are becoming all too common among Black fraternities on college and university campuses of late. When will these organizations learn that the tradition of initiation is no excuse for violence. . . . What amazes me is the failure of the national organizations to respond forthrightly to these atrocious criminal acts. Don't tell me about policies that "outlaw"

all forms of hazing and abuse. We all know them. The national headquarters of these organizations must also share and accept blame for the monsters we have created. . . . If the national organizations cannot provide leadership for this critical task, let them hand the responsibility to someone who can.[42]

And in an editorial in the St. Louis newspaper by a Black sorority member, she compared the actions to those of gang members. She wrote that Kappa Alpha Psi's "initiation activities were no different from those of the hoodlums on the street—if you want to wear our colors, you'll have to show us you're tough, show us how much you want it, how much you can take. Michael could have stayed home and joined a gang. . . . Michael Davis escaped the dangers of street gangs only to fall victim to one on a college campus."[43]

And the experts in the field also provided analysis as to what was happening with underground pledging. Jason DeSousa, as a part of a cover story for *Black Issues in Higher Education*, declared, "The death of Michael Davis shows that the New Member Intake Process has been a failure. We just didn't get enough students to buy into the new process at the chapter level. As a result, hazing has been driven underground where it becomes even more dangerous."[44] John Williams weighed in his scholarly "I told you so," after predicting through his dissertation that hazing would continue. "I said then [that continued hazing] was predictable because students never bought into the intake process. The organizations chose to ignore an underlying theme that students wanted a process with rites of passage."[45]

This case is especially of note because of the electronic media accounts of the hazing death. Michael Davis's mother appeared on both the *Oprah Winfrey Show* and the *Leeza Gibbons Show*. Those two daytime programs probably reached a great deal of households, especially on the strength of Oprah Winfrey. But it would be *Dateline NBC,* a newsmagazine airing numerous times a week and always scoring high marks in the weekly Nielsen ratings, that would spend roughly half of its hour program on the case at Southeast Missouri State. The description of the hazing of Michael Davis, along with the words of the perpetrators of the crime, make up what is undoubtedly the most vivid picture of hazing, underground pledging, and the mentality that perpetuates this culture.

In a story entitled "Blood Brothers," *Dateline* indicated that in his letter of application, Davis said he was impressed by the positive image of the fraternity and their community service projects. But he knew he would be subjected to hazing, confirmed by John Davis, a student who was pledging with Michael Davis. John Davis, in an on-camera interview, said they were punched in the stomach, slapped, and caned on the bottom of their feet. Once they were hit in the back with a frying pan. After four nights of hazing, John Davis "dropped," or quit pledging. His body told him that he could not take it, and he didn't know how Michael Davis could, being over one hundred pounds lighter.[46]

The abuse continued. Michael even told a professor, Ben Bates, that pledging was rough. After being hazed by six fraternity members from the St. Louis chapter on a Saturday night, that following Monday, February 14, he and two other pledges were taken to an isolated field. The men were sent through different stations, where each brother either slapped, kicked, or body slammed the pledges. A final kick knocked him unconscious. At that point two other pledges and two brothers took Davis home. The *Dateline* piece revealed that instead of caring for the unconscious Davis, the group made a trip to Taco Bell because one brother was hungry.[47]

Somewhere after midnight, Davis was placed in bed, with two pledges assigned to watch him. By 1 P.M. the next day one pledge tried to wake Davis, but panicked when he saw a greenish-black liquid coming from his mouth. He called a brother, Carlos Turner, who came over and immediately called 911. *Dateline* obtained the 911 tapes, and it revealed Turner saying, "One of the guys we were playing football with last night . . . he was hit real hard, and right now I don't think he's breathing." While paramedics were on their way, a neighbor walked in on Turner and others who were trying to remove papers and anything associated with Kappa Alpha Psi. The documents were later found hidden in a dumpster. Edith Davis, Michael's mother, told *Dateline* about the call she received from the doctor. He indicated that Michael was injured playing football, and she immediately corrected him, saying, "They're lying. My baby was pledging a fraternity." The doctor further explained that Michael was dead.[48]

One of the men present during the hazing, Carlos Turner, provided insight into the mindset of the students and their activities the night of Davis's death. In an on-camera interview with Deborah Roberts, he said he participated in the hazing and acknowledged that he gave Michael "a light kick to the chest. Not a kick I felt would do serious damage." He later admitted that he had on boots. When asked directly why he kicked Davis, Turner paused and finally said, "I don't even know." Turner, who indicated that he too was hazed, said that pledging was torture. But when asked why he and others go through it, he said, "It's a respect thing. Basically, it's like you wanna be recognized for achieving this."[49]

The chapter president at that time, Lamar Taylor, seconded that sentiment. "To be accepted, fully accepted, you have to do it," he told Deborah Roberts during the interview. He "bragged" that he was known for hitting the hardest in the chapter. He explained that the hard punching by the brothers was almost like a competition, where they tried to see who could make the loudest sound with a punch or slap. Taylor said the hazing was essentially something that was going to take place—there was no formal decision to do it or not.[50]

Dr. Michael Zaricor, a forensic pathologist, described the intensity of the hazing as something typically seen in car wrecks and other sudden decelerations. Michael Davis had tears to his liver, lung, and brain. Carlos Turner felt that the national fraternity leaders knew about the pledging and hazing. Davis's mother, Edith, shared an interesting exchange with Deborah Roberts about her interactions with the national leaders:

> *Roberts.* "What have you heard from the fraternity since Michael died?"
> *E. Davis.* "Nothing."
> *Roberts.* "Nothing?"
> *E. Davis.* "Nothing."
> *Roberts.* "No apology?"
> *E. Davis.* "Nothing. And these are professional, educated men. Nothing. Not
>   even a card."

Carlos Turner, when asked by Roberts about what the lesson should be from the case, said, "It's really not worth it—at all."[51]

LESSON UNLEARNED: HAZING CONTINUES

During the *Dateline NBC* program, Carlos Turner and Lamar Taylor reiterated the philosophy of undergraduates during the beginning of the membership intake era. Turner said it was about respect. Taylor said that they had to do it to be accepted. Two years after Williams's study, one of his key points, that the issue of respect was important enough to continue pledging underground, proved to be all too true at Southeast Missouri State. The death of Michael Davis, at that point in time, became the most highly publicized Black fraternity or sorority hazing case in history. Many felt that this case would be a wake-up call for undergraduates who sometimes could not see the danger associated with underground pledging. Others felt that this would be a wake-up call for national organizations and universities that may have been slow to acknowledge that membership intake had not been accepted by students, and pledging was alive and well in a new, underground form.

But the impact of Davis's death lasted roughly two weeks. It was revealed on 2 March 1994 that in Atlanta, a Southern Tech student was hospitalized in late January due to a hazing incident. He was hazed by six Georgia Tech and Southern Tech students (and one former Southern Tech student) who were members of Kappa Alpha Psi Fraternity. The victim, Stephen Otey, was struck in the chest, beaten on the buttocks, and slapped while pledging, and was eventually hospitalized with abdominal injuries after some brothers stood on his stomach.[52] The incident, along with the

Davis death, occurred less than six months after the Kappa Alpha Psi Grand Polemarch's (national president's) executive order, reiterating that pledging was outlawed. Not only were the students pledging, but the chapter, seated at Georgia Tech, was on probation, which prevented non–Georgia Tech students from being initiated. The chapter was suspended from 1992 to 1993.[53]

But the first after-Davis hazing was at Indiana University, where Kevin Nash was hazed while pledging Omega Psi Phi Fraternity. He was hospitalized following a hazing incident, which later led to the arrest of the chapter president, Curtis Whittaker, along with two other Omegas, including a law school student and a former IU student.[54] On March 4, Nash held a press conference at the university. He described pledging in detail that included paddling, slapping, beatings with a folding chair, and having cigarette ashes dropped in his mouth. His descriptions provided the general public with terms associated with hazing, including "giving neck" and preparing to be paddled by getting in the "cut." The members were smoking marijuana through the February 26 incident that proved to be the final straw, a hazing session attended by the chapter adviser, IU law student Ozie Davis III.[55]

The continued hazing by Black Greeks, and specifically, Black fraternities, was enough to cause additional debate. *The Chronicle of Higher Education* reported that four hazing cases (including Georgia Tech and Indiana) occurred between the death of Michael Davis and their late June news story. Dr. Michael V. W. Gordon, executive director of the NPHC, indicated that the recent abuses raised questions about the effectiveness of the new initiatives.[56] Even the *Wall Street Journal* weighed in, noting, "Hazing abuses have prompted calls at national and regional black fraternity conferences to either abolish undergraduate chapters or take away the students' ability to choose new members, giving the responsibility to alumni."[57]

Halfway through the first decade of membership intake, one student was dead and at least two more had been hospitalized. Despite all of the press coverage of these incidents, the abuse did not cease. In 1995, twelve members of Alpha Phi Alpha Fraternity at Purdue University were arrested for hazing after a student was hospitalized. The student, Luis Algarin, told police about hazing that included rough football games where his shoulder was dislocated, paddling, and even an instance where a brother showed a gun, threatening to use it. Algarin was beaten to the point that blood was passed in his urine.[58] The news reports indicated that the fraternity had just been reactivated in 1992 after serving a three-year suspension for hazing.

And yet, national leaders still defended intake. In an article about the Purdue hazing, Richard Smith, assistant executive director of Omega Psi Phi at the time, indicated that intake was a new program with a limited educational period "so there would be no time for hazing . . . It has worked so well that any hazing that goes on is not a part of the official system."[59] This statement was an admission that for some, the national organization's hands were clean because any pledging or hazing was definitely outside of the system. Therefore, membership intake was a success because hazing had to occur either as a part of prepledging or postpledging.

In 1996 numerous hazing cases surfaced. At the University of Pittsburgh a student was placed on kidney dialysis due to severe kidney damage received when he was hit with a cane and a wooden paddle. Five members of Kappa Alpha Psi were arrested and charged with aggravated assault, causing their exasperated executive director, Ted Smith, to declare, "The organization cannot assume total responsibility for the behavior of people who are renegades and hoodlums."[60] Also that spring, ten members of Omega Psi Phi were arrested at West Virginia University after hazing a freshman student, possibly causing permanent hearing loss.

The high-profile case for 1996 occurred at the University of Georgia, as a varsity football player was treated at the hospital for deep bruises and broken blood vessels in his buttocks. The athlete, Roderick Perrymond, told police that three members of Phi Beta Sigma Fraternity paddled him about seventy times.[61] Three men—two students and a former student—were officially charged with hazing and battery. The former student, Thomas Stevens, twenty-nine, was the chapter adviser. During the magistrate hearing, Perrymond and two other pledges described how they were paddled, or got "wood" as a form of punishment. When Perrymond was hit in the hamstrings, after telling members he normally received treatment for sore legs, an altercation ensued where Perrymond collapsed. He was taken to the hospital the next day.[62]

The fraternity was found guilty by a university hearing board and suspended for five years, with the opportunity for reinstatement in two years. Yet, the national organization planned to appeal the sanction, citing that there may have been some biases among members of the hearing panel. The executive director, Lawrence Miller, indicated that he did not believe the national fraternity should be held responsible for the actions of its members.[63] Six years into membership intake, national organizations continued to deny any culpability for the by-product of the new program—underground pledging.

THE PRICE OF MEMBERSHIP INTAKE

1997 began with news that the civil suit filed by the parents of Michael Davis had been settled out of court. Kappa Alpha Psi Fraternity agreed to pay a total of $2.25 million dollars to settle the wrongful death suit. The attorney for the family noted that Kappa Alpha Psi had experienced similar problems with other chapters, and that, hopefully, the settlement would end hazing.[64] The fraternity was concerned about the lawsuit and had even petitioned graduate members to contribute to their legal defense fund.[65]

The first death during the membership intake era produced the largest single settlement ever for a hazing case. For the death of Joel Harris in 1989, both Alpha Phi Alpha and Morehouse College settled for about five hundred thousand dollars each. The family then sued each member of the chapter there, approximately thirty students. The thirteen-million-dollar suit was projected to cost each man 20 to 25 percent of his earnings for a period of twenty to twenty-five years. They too settled, for the maximum value of their parents' homeowners insurance policies. But the results of this case were not highly publicized.

The hazing case in 1994 at Indiana University produced a lawsuit that, after a jury trial in 1997, cost Omega Psi Phi $774,500. As previously mentioned, the Omega Psi Phi Fraternity settled for $375,000 in July 1997 for the hazing of Joseph Snell at the University of Maryland. But just months before the Snell case was settled, another case of hazing would eventually produce a suit that would be costlier than either of the first two to the fraternity. On 7 April 1997, Shawn Blackston, a student at the University of Louisville, was admitted to the hospital for injuries to his spleen and kidneys. He indicated to police that he voluntarily submitted to the beatings of Omega Psi Phi Fraternity members there.[66]

In 1999 a Kentucky jury awarded the student $931,428 in his case against the fraternity. The award included $750,000 in punitive damages and $181,428 for medical and related expenses. The fraternity's lawyer, William Peale, indicated that they would appeal, citing that the hazing was kept secret from the national officials, thereby making the national organization unaccountable. He further said that the fraternity planned to sue the brothers who were directly involved, and potentially, the pledges. Peale, in an interview, proclaimed, "I am confident that we will never have to pay a penny of this verdict."[67]

But less than a year later, Omega Psi Phi dropped the appeal and agreed to pay the penalty. Of the almost one million dollars, Blackston was paid six hundred thousand dollars at the time of settlement, with the additional money to be paid over a four-year period. Sheryl Snyder, the attorney who handled the fraternity's appeal, said the verdict included interest of 12 percent a year, therefore, a loss at the appeal could have potentially cost the fraternity an additional one million dollars.[68] The fraternity did make good on its promise to go after its own members who inflicted the damage, and in 2000 the fraternity sued the members of the University of Louisville. The outcome of this case will set a new precedent for how national organizations respond to hazing in the membership intake era.[69]

SORORITY HAZING IN THE INTAKE ERA: THEY'VE GOT NEXT

Prior to this point, Black Greek hazing almost exclusively meant fraternities. There had been isolated cases of sorority hazing that made the news, but most incidents did not. It was not that sororities did not and were not hazing. The difference was that the sorority members had not inflicted the kind of punishment that normally landed pledges in the hospital. But it has been noted that Black sororities also experienced their share of hazing in the 1970s and 1980s, which caused them to reform their pledge programs.

Only three years into the membership intake era, members of Alpha Kappa Alpha Sorority at the University of North Texas engaged in a publicized hazing case. The five members, all alumni, hazed pledges by paddling them, forcing them to eat hot peppers, and breaking eggs over their heads. The five women received a probated sentence of ninety days in jail along with five-hundred-dollar fines for two of them, and the chapter was suspended for five years.[70] In 1996 at the University of Georgia, three Delta Sigma Theta pledges indicated that they were physically and verbally harassed, hazing that ultimately caused the sorority to be suspended for two years. One of the hazed students later made an appearance on Geraldo Rivera's talk show.

But brutality entered sorority life in the late 1990s. In the spring of 1997 at Georgia State University in Atlanta, Kimberly Kelly was treated at a hospital for bruises suffered as a part of a hazing incident. This was not the usual hazing incident though. Kelly was hazed by her five fellow pledges, or "line sisters" in the pledging lingo. The pledges were to participate in an activity during "Freaknik," the Black college student spring break that was popular in Atlanta during the 1990s. Kelly did not attend due to out of town guests in town for the event, but was subsequently hazed as a punishment.[71]

Four of the five were issued summonses to appear in court. The fifth was not listed as a student at the institution. The Georgia State students were eventually suspended from school due to the event, but the chapter remained active. After a close call, it would appear that the sorority members would have ceased the hazing activities. But this was not the case. Having worked at Georgia State from March 1995 to December 1996, I had a chance to interact with numerous students through the orientation program. One student I often interacted with was charged in the April 1997 beating, much to my dismay as we had talked in depth about not participating in illegal activities.

But another student decided to attempt to join the sorority that fall, and began participating in an illegal pledge program. However, she became concerned about the hazing that was occurring, and sent me an e-mail, as I had moved to Virginia. On 20 November 1997, I read the following message:

THIS IS BETWEEN YOU AND ME, OK!!!!

We are all about ready to drop line. It is only three [of] us. One of the girls is about 120 and then the other girls is about my size. The other night this ho [sic] beat us with a damn Kappa Cane. My LS was hurting so bad, that she nearly passed out. . . . My whole thing is this, ARE WE KAPPAS? And ARE WE MEN? I don't know why this ho was trying to show out in front of her man (he's a Kappa). It was not like she hit us one time, it was repeatedly and then she is suppose [sic] to be our DP. I thought the DP was suppose to protect you. I'm having surgery in about three weeks. I'm constantly going back and forth to the doctor. If my doctor see [sic] all of these bruises on my ass, of course he is going to ask me what happened. . . . I'm just stuck in a bad predicament. I don't know what I'm going to do, any suggestions?

DEPRESSED
p.s. and don't start fussing at me.

With only a moment of thought, I forwarded the message to the dean of students at Georgia State. In the end the members of the sorority involved in the hazing were suspended from the organization while the pledges were initiated. But it was a sign to me that brutality was now a part of sorority hazing as well.

This trend continued through the end of the decade. In 1998, Delta Sigma Theta Sorority was suspended from the University of Kentucky after an investigation found the chapter guilty of physical and mental abuse. Not long after, Delta sorority members hazed a student at Western Illinois University, but Litesha Wallace, the student, sued the organization in 1999 due to hazing that included sit-ups, drinking hot sauce and vinegar, swallowing her own vomit, and grinding her knees and elbows until they bled.[72] At Bennett College, the Alpha Kappa Alpha chapter was suspended for four years following hazing there. Two members of the sorority were almost prevented from graduating, but a judge forced the college to allow them to graduate.[73]

In 1999 members of Delta Sigma Theta at Norfolk State University in Virginia were expelled just weeks before graduation due to a hazing case that left a student hospitalized and in intensive care. Details of the case were never released, but the university president, also a member of the sorority, sought to send a tough message about hazing on the campus. While the expelled students attempted to have the action overturned, a judge upheld the ruling.[74] Around the same time of the expulsion, members of Zeta Phi Beta at the University of South Florida were accused of paddling ten pledges from late February until late March, after one of the ten reported the hazing. As with many of the cases, former students also participated in the hazing. Not only was membership intake losing to underground pledging as the method for introducing new members into Black fraternities and sororities, the violence associated with underground pledging was now a regular by-product of sorority pledging.

BROKEN PLEDGES

As the first decade of membership intake came to an end, it was clear that membership intake did not replace pledging but rather gave it a new look. The new version of pledging was a semisecret, underground process virtually invisible to national, regional, and graduate level officials as well as college and university staff members. But students who were aware of Black fraternities and sororities knew when people were pledging. As noted by numerous students, underground pledging was done to gain respect; therefore their peers must know that they have participated in the process. The balance between who should know and who shouldn't made and continues to make underground pledging a risky proposition for those who perpetuate it.

And, based on the news reports of the late 1990s, many students chose to take the risk. In an alleged hazing incident at Georgia State University, Phi Beta Sigma Fraternity was suspended after a non–Georgia State student's mother contacted the national organization because her son was hospitalized. The injured student attended Emory University, as did three other pledges. Another casualty was the student government president at Georgia State, who resigned from office and from his bid for reelection, as he was a member of the fraternity.[75] He later attempted to return to office, but that bid was not approved by the university administration.

As incidents continued to pile up, more began to weigh in on the hazing in Black fraternities and sororities. *Black Issues in Higher Education* began to take a lead in this regard. Two substantial articles were printed, one in the summer of 1997 and another in the summer of 1998 to address hazing. What might have seemed like overkill to some was just a reflection of the times. Between the two articles, more hazing cases were reported at the University of Maryland-Eastern Shore (UMES), Kansas State University, and Southern Illinois University. While the summer 1997 piece talked about "Broken Pledges," the next year the realization was that underground pledging and hazing were continuing without reason. The magazine sought out psychologists to understand "The Persistent Madness of Greek Hazing" through a range of theories from homoeroticism to a simple need to belong.[76]

That year the electronic media would again focus on Black Greek pledging in the membership intake era. In April 1998, after the hazing involving Kappa Alpha Psi at the University of Maryland-Eastern Shore, five students who were fully initiated members found themselves in the hospital after enduring two months of paddling. Some of the men had surgery due to cuts and infections on their buttocks.[77] *BET Tonight,* a weeknight news program hosted by Tavis Smiley, addressed the issue within weeks after the hazing at UMES as well as another incident at Kansas State University. Smiley (a member of Kappa Alpha Psi) was joined by Richard Snow, executive director of the fraternity, Dr. Michael V. W. Gordon, executive director of the National Pan-Hellenic Council, and Dr. John A. Williams, author of the previously referenced dissertation on new member intake.[78]

Smiley initially attempted to determine what difference there was between pledging that students supported, versus the hazing that led to the recent incidents. Gordon indicated that in essence, undergraduates have made the two phrases synonymous. It was hard for the panel to place blame for these kinds of incidents, whether fault was with members who hazed or aspirants who were hazed. Mr. Snow clearly indicated that, "There is no pledging," and that the Maryland incident was perpetrated against students who had been fully initiated into the fraternity. But Smiley challenged that notion and felt that membership intake was not working. Williams countered Snow's statement by indicating that through his research, students indicated that there was pledging, and it was in an effort to be considered real members and not "paper."[79]

Several callers supported pledging for various reasons. One student from Oklahoma indicated that the process taught how to deal with adversity and trouble as well as how to become a "true man." A woman indicated that it was necessary for respect on campus, and that was why it persisted. In the end of the hour-long conversation, both Snow and Gordon were optimistic about the future for Black Greek–lettered organizations. But John Williams pointedly gave all nine NPHC organizations a grade of "F" for documenting how and if membership intake was effective, and that their future was dim without a willingness to conduct more research and to host open dialogues on the topic.[80]

Membership Intake at Ten

After the teleconference, I decided it was time to replicate John Williams's study in order to fully understand, from an empirical point of view, what was occurring with membership intake. A great number of hazing incidents made some form of news medium during the first decade of intake (Table 3). After a decade of membership intake as well as several generations of college students experiencing the changes associated with this new process, an assessment of membership intake would provide some sense—beyond the news reports and anecdotal information provided by student affairs professionals and national officials—of current undergrad-

TABLE 3
Summary of Media Reported Hazing Cases, 1990–99

Variable	f
By Year	
1990	1
1991	1
1992	1
1993	3
1994	4
1995	1
1996	3
1997	4
1998	3
1999	11
By Gender	
Fraternity	26
Sorority	6
By Institution Type	
Public, Predominantly White	26
Public, Historically Black	4
Private, Historically Black	2
Private, Predominantly White	0
By NPHC Region	
South	14
East	8
North Central	8
Southwest	2
West	0

uates' awareness of the membership intake policies, their hazing tolerance, and their level of endorsement for membership intake.

The methodology followed the design implemented by Williams (1992) with slight modifications. A target sample of 540 undergraduate Black Greek members was sought. This national sample was divided into five regions based on the structure of the NPHC, as changed at their 1999 convention from six regions. In each region, six institutions were selected to participate in the study. Target institutions with active NPHC chapters were chosen, and all institutions had advisers who consented in advance to assist in the facilitation of the study. The institutions were also selected to provide students who attended public and private, historically Black (HBCUs), and predominantly White institutions (PWIs). No private, historically Black institutions participated in the first study.

Of the thirty institutions targeted to participate, twenty-six (86.7 percent) actually participated. Several institutions returned uncompleted instruments, and subsequently the total number of instruments actually disseminated was 405. 185 completed instruments were returned, for a return rate of 45.7 percent. All of the returned instruments were usable. It is noted here that the somewhat low return rate may be due to the nature of the instrument, described below, which sought students' comments on prohibited activities in which they may have taken part as a condition for membership. As indicated recently by Sweet, the study of "fraternity hazing is methodologically problematic."[81] The secretive nature of the organizations (and in this case, the perpetuation of a banned process) undoubtedly affected the return.

Of those who participated, 61 percent were female, a figure consistent with trends for Black students in higher education (see Table 4). The vast majority of the sample was of traditional age, at least of junior standing, attended predominantly White institutions, and were initiated in 1997 or after. Of particular interest, 51.3 percent admitted that they had participated in a pledge program.

For the purpose of this study, the survey questionnaire designed by Williams was utilized with slight modifications. This instrument tested three scales, as described by Williams:

(1) The *Policy Awareness Scale* measured student awareness of actions taken by their fraternity or sorority to inform, educate, and involve undergraduate members on the no-pledge policy.
(2) The *Hazing Tolerance Scale* measured student attitudes on hazing by asking them if a list of activities should or should not be considered hazing.
(3) The *Policy Endorsement Scale* used a five-point Likert scale to assess the level of agreement/disagreement expressed by respondents on ten impact statements associated with the no-pledge policy (p. 51).

Some of the wording for the Policy Endorsement Scale was modified to fit the present tense. In addition, each respondent had the opportunity to complete an open-ended question to express his/her opinion on the process. The first two scales do not lend themselves readily to tests for validity, but Williams reported a correlation coefficient of .84 for the eight paired items on the Policy Endorsement Scale.

TABLE 4

Demographic Characteristics of Respondents

Variable	f	%
GENDER		
Male	70	37.8%
Female	115	62.2
CLASSIFICATION		
Freshman	3	1.6%
Sophomore	22	11.9
Junior	59	31.9
Senior	99	53.5
Other	2	1.1
NPHC REGION		
East	32	17.2%
North Central	49	26.3
South	34	12.9
Southwest	39	21.0
West	42	22.6
INSTITUTIONAL TYPE		
Public, Predominantly White	114	61.3%
Public, Historically Black	27	14.5
Private, Predominantly White	25	13.4
Private, Historically Black	20	10.8
YEAR INITIATED		
1995 or earlier	11	6.2%
1996	29	16.2
1997	55	30.7
1998	63	35.2
1999	21	11.7
DID YOU PLEDGE?		
Yes	91	53.2%

The respondents also provided demographic data for purposes of comparison among several independent variables. These variables included gender, age, classification, present chapter officer status, past chapter officer
status, year initiated, participation in a pledge process, and legacy status.

Advisers directly or indirectly working with Black Greek chapters were
contacted about their interest in the replicated study. Those who agreed to
serve as facilitators were mailed a packet containing eighteen instruction
letters, informed consent forms, and questionnaires. The number of targeted participants theoretically would allow two participants from each
NPHC organization to participate in the study. The adviser was instructed
to disseminate two per organization if all nine NPHC organizations were
represented on the campus, and in cases where there were fewer than nine
(which was the prevalent situation), they were asked to solicit volunteers
to complete the remaining instruments.

The packets were mailed to the advisers during the spring of 1999
around the various schools' spring break schedules. The packets included
self-addressed, stamped envelopes so the students could return the instruments directly to the researcher for an added sense of confidentiality. After
the packets were mailed, follow-up e-mails and phone calls were made to
the advisers to improve the return rate.

The data collected from the instruments were analyzed using the SAS
statistical program. For the demographic data items, the data were reported
in the form of frequencies and percentages. For the first two scales, simple
frequency counts were totaled (e.g., the number of times the respondent
answered "yes") to provide a score for that scale, which was compared to
the selected independent variables using an analysis of variance. For the
policy endorsement scale, the Likert scores were totaled and divided by the
total number of responses for a mean score, and the mean scores were compared to selected independent variables utilizing an analysis of variance.

Table 5 compares key questions asked to determine undergraduate perceptions of membership intake based on data obtained from the original
and the present studies. In every instance, present undergraduates were
more optimistic about the new process. In 1992, 69.4 percent of the respondents agreed to some degree that chapter members would have less of a
voice in the selection of new members, while 60 percent of the 1999 sample felt they had less of a voice in selection. Only 33.6 percent of the 1992
sample felt that postinitiation education could instill new members with a
sense of history and tradition, while 54.9 percent of the 1999 sample
believed that postinitiation education was effective.

Just over a majority (55.9 percent) of the 1999 sample believed that the
new policy reduced lifelong commitment, which was down from over two-
thirds of the previous sample who feared a reduction in lifelong commit-

ment. Finally, there was the smallest amount of change for the four selected variables with regard to the ability of the new process to screen out uncommitted applicants. While 84.8 percent of the 1992 sample believed members were not able to screen aspirants with the new process, roughly 80 percent of the 1999 sample felt this was indeed the case.

For several selected variables, an analysis of variance test was conducted to determine any statistical differences in the three scales (see Table 6). In comparing fraternity members versus sorority members, there were no statistically significant differences in any of the three scales. However, fraternity members were less aware of the policies concerning membership intake and had a higher tolerance for hazing. Fraternity members also were slightly less supportive of the membership intake selection process than were sorority members.

There were no statistically significant differences based on geographic region of the country for any of the scales. In general, the North Central region students had the greatest policy awareness ($x = 4.47$), and students in the East had the least ($x = 4.03$). In terms of hazing tolerance, students in the East had the highest tolerance for hazing ($x = 2.81$), and those in the South had the least tolerance ($x = 4.79$). Finally, for policy endorsement, students in the North Central region had the highest level of endorsement for the policy ($x = 2.90$), while students in the South supported the policy the least ($x = 2.40$).

There also were no statistically significant differences based on the type of institution the students attended. All types were very similar in their level of policy awareness. Students attending private PWIs had the highest tolerance for hazing ($x = 2.96$) while students attending private HBCUs had the lowest tolerance ($x = 4.30$). Students attending the private HBCUs, while having the lowest tolerance for hazing, supported the policy the least ($x = 2.50$) while their peers at public HBCUs supported the policy the most ($x = 2.83$).

The only variable that provided any level of significant difference was the acknowledgment of participation in an illegal pledge process. Students who admitted to pledging had a significantly lower awareness of the membership intake policy, a significantly higher level of tolerance for hazing, and a significantly lower level of endorsement of the intake policy. The level of significance for all three scales was below the .01 level.

The major goal of this study was to assess the progress made since membership intake was instituted in 1990. The use of Williams's instrument provided a means to compare the sample of 227 students used in the original study, versus the 186 students in the 1999 study. Table 7 compares the means for several of the key groups during the seven years between each study. In general, for each of the variables selected, there was a trend

TABLE 5

*A Comparison of Likert Scores of Respondents (Expressed as Percentages)
on Selected Policy Endorsement Statements*

Statement	SA	A	AS	D	SD
1992 Chapter members will have less of a voice in new member selection	32.3	21.2	15.9	20.4	10.2
1999 Chapter members have less of a voice in new member selection	24.2	20.6	15.2	29.7	10.3
1992 Post initiation education will instill new members with history and tradition	16.8	6.2	10.6	25.7	40.7
1999 Post initiation education is adequate to instill new members with history and tradition	25.0	16.5	13.4	18.3	26.8
1992 New policy reduces lifelong commitment of new members	27.8	23.3	22.0	21.1	5.7
1999 New policy has reduced lifelong commitment of new members	12.3	18.4	25.2	29.4	14.7
1992 Members cannot screen out uncommitted applicants	48.2	23.2	13.4	7.1	8.0
1999 Members cannot screen out uncommitted applicants	40.9	20.7	18.3	12.8	7.3

Note: SA = strongly agree; A = agree; AS = agree slightly; D = disagree; SD = strongly disagree.

toward more awareness of the policy, a lower tolerance for hazing, and a higher level of endorsement for the policy.

Fraternity and sorority members progressed in all three categories, while not significantly differing from each other. Fraternity members made the greatest gains for two of the scales, but still were lower in their policy awareness, higher in their level of hazing tolerance, and lower in their endorsement of the policy. In the 1999 study, as with the former study, significant differences existed on the pledge variable. There was a small increase by students who pledged in terms of awareness, a gain less than that by those who did not pledge. The level of tolerance for hazing was much lower for students who did not pledge in 1999 versus those in 1992,

TABLE 6
ANOVA Results for the Three Scales by Selected Independent Variables

| | Scale | | | | | |
| | Policy Awareness | | Hazing Tolerance | | Policy Endorsement | |
Variables	M	SD	M	SD	M	SD
GENDER						
Fraternity member	4.41	.94	3.18	3.30	2.66	.78
Sorority member	4.26	.82	3.38	2.98	2.76	.79
PLEDGE STATUS						
Pledged	4.11	.99*	2.41	2.63*	2.41	.70*
Did not pledge	4.60	.63*	4.16	3.28*	3.11	.72*
REGION						
East	4.03	1.03	2.81	3.00	2.69	.86
North Central	4.47	.74	3.00	3.04	2.90	.78
South	4.42	.65	4.79	3.66	2.40	.62
Southwest	4.20	1.08	3.54	2.47	2.72	.80
West	4.43	.70	3.10	3.33	2.49	.74
INSTITUTION TYPE						
PWI Public	4.34	.90	3.23	3.03	2.66	.76
PWI Private	4.32	.75	2.96	2.68	2.68	.89
HBCU Public	4.22	.97	3.41	3.35	2.83	.85
HBCU Private	4.35	.67	4.30	3.69	2.50	.74

Note: M = mean; SD = standard deviation; PWI = predominantly White institution; HBCU = historically Black college or university; $p < .01$

while those who pledged also reported a noticeable decrease in tolerance. Both groups increased in their level of endorsement for the policy, but the group that pledged reported a very small (.18) increase compared to those who did not pledge (.54).

Differences were based on the region in which the student resided. Most notable for awareness, students in the Southwest were less knowledgeable of the policy, while in every other region awareness increased. There were varying decreases in the level of tolerance for hazing. Students in the South lowered their tolerance by over 2.3 points, whereas students in the North Central area lowered their tolerance by one-tenth of that

TABLE 7
Mean Comparisons for Selected Variables, 1992 and 1999

	Scale					
	Policy Awareness		Hazing Tolerance		Policy Endorsement	
Variables	1999	1992	1999	1992	1999	1992
GENDER						
Fraternity member	4.41	3.97	3.18	1.92	2.66	2.35
Sorority member	4.26	4.04	3.38	2.53	2.76	2.35
PLEDGE STATUS						
Pledged	4.11	3.93	2.41	1.86	2.41	2.23
Did not pledge	4.60	4.13	4.16	2.94	3.11	2.57
REGION						
East	4.03	3.94	2.81	1.50	2.69	1.90
North Central	4.47	4.05	3.00	2.74	2.90	2.52
South	4.42	3.91	4.79	2.44	2.40	2.44
Southwest	4.20	4.36	3.54	2.95	2.72	2.60
West	4.43	4.00	3.10	1.40	2.49	2.42
INSTITUTION TYPE						
PWI Public	4.34	4.08	3.23	2.01	2.66	2.33
PWI Private	4.32	n/a	2.96	n/a	2.68	n/a
HBCU Public	4.22	3.91	3.41	2.43	2.83	2.36
HBCU Private	4.35	4.00	4.30	3.36	2.50	2.59

Note: PWI = predominantly White institution; HBCU = historically Black college or university.

amount. For policy endorsement, students in the South were less support-ive than in 1992, while students in the East made the greatest gain in endorsement.

Similar gains were made across all three scales by institutional type, although the patterns of responses remained the same. Students attending public HBCUs continued to have the least awareness of the policy, and in absence of private PWIs, public PWIs had the highest level of hazing tol-erance. No private White institutions participated in the original study. Finally, students attending private HBCUs endorsed the policy less than they did in 1992, while other students made only moderate gains.

The intent of the study was to determine Black Greek undergraduates' perceptions of the no-pledge membership intake process in 1999, and compare this sample versus the students completing the same instrument in 1992 to assess the effectiveness of the membership intake program implemented in 1990. Overall, the 1999 undergraduates had a more favorable attitude toward membership intake, even though in most instances their support was only moderately greater than that of their predecessors.

However, the undergraduate culture continues to maintain a core assumption about the benefits of pledging, which explains low to moderate gains in accepting the membership intake program. In the seven years since surveying the initial population, only 5 percent fewer believed that they have the ability to screen out aspirants through this new process. This perception alone would seem to fuel undergraduate feelings that justify the perpetuation of pledging.

Therefore, while moderate gains have been made in changing student attitudes about membership intake (based on the continuous supply of news reports), the basic underlying assumptions about pledging as a part of the Black Greek experience remain consistent. As indicated in a study by Kimbrough and Sutton, students expect to participate, and admittedly do participate in a pledge experience for full acceptance into the organizations.[82]

While only those students who admitted they pledged differed significantly from those who did not in all of the scales and represent an identifiable area of concern, there continue to be some recognizable patterns based on selected variables that might serve as indicators for subgroups needing specific attention. These patterns can provide assistance for student affairs administrators in determining where to focus educational efforts. Referring to Table 3, the relationships based on these variables are better explained. Fraternity members' attitudes have translated into 81.2 percent of hazing cases reported and compiled for this study. With students in the South less tolerant of hazing, they may be more likely to report hazing cases, which might explain their high numbers in the summary of media-reported cases. Conversely, the higher tolerance regions should be examined as areas where there is a greater likelihood of hazing.

In several of the subgroups, students were very knowledgeable of the membership intake program, moderately endorsed the policy, but continued to tolerate hazing. While in all three scales the 1999 students scored more favorably than those participating in 1992, this increase has not translated into a decrease in hazing incidents. Most important, over half of this sample participated in a pledge program, even though they were initiated for the most part six to nine years after the formal end of pledging.

The fact that the majority of the sample participated in a pledge process indicated that the students consciously ignored the over-a-decade-old policy. The gains as reported in Table 7 have not translated into any noticeable reduction of hazing incidents, nor have they prevented further deaths.

However, the lowering tolerance for hazing may be translating into more incident reports being filed by students. This would suggest that further and more widespread education, particularly for aspirants, could help either reduce the total number of incidents, or continue to hold those who violate the rules accountable. The fact based on this data is that most gains are moderate, and when considering that the hazing tolerance scale contains ten items, students were willing to participate in over half of the tasks associated with pledging that appear on this scale.

The plethora of hazing cases toward the end of the decade punctuated the fact that many students and alumni fully support underground pledging, which includes brutal hazing. In February 1999 at Lincoln University in Pennsylvania, a twenty-one-year-old student was beaten while attempting to join Alpha Phi Alpha Fraternity. He suffered internal injuries that required at least two operations (including a colostomy) and numerous weeks of recovery.[83] Seven Alpha Phi Alpha members were suspended from school, but police investigations determined that two Delaware men, both twenty-eight years of age, used paddles on the aspirants, and both were charged under the state's antihazing law. As the Chester County district attorney explained, "These two defendants were out of college. You can't dismiss it as some I-didn't-know-better college prank."[84]

As membership intake enters its second decade, it appears that the national, historically Black Greek–lettered organizations may have begun to retreat from the earlier mandate of membership intake. Modifications in the programs over the past few years appear to signify that there is recognition that the current undergraduate culture is much stronger than legislative efforts by graduate members. The task, then, will be to find a common ground of acceptance for some kind of program that both graduate and undergraduate members can endorse and follow, before these organizations face monumental lawsuits that will jeopardize their existence.

4
Was Eight Enough?

WHEN EIGHT BLACK FRATERNITIES AND SORORITIES DECIDED IN 1930 TO form an alliance that would consider the mutual interests of the constituent members, the feeling probably was that these groups defined the Black fraternal experience. There is no evidence that these persons knew of any other collegiate Greek-lettered organizations at that time, and they probably did not foresee any other developments. And even though Sigma Pi Phi was twenty-six years old at that time, there isn't much to suggest that the conveners of the meeting that formed the National Pan-Hellenic Council were very aware of its existence, if at all.

So these organizations, known as "The Great Eight," "The Big Eight," and "The Elite Eight" were the complete definition of Black fraternalism in America for decades. Even after the founding of Iota Phi Theta in 1963 at Morgan State University, there was a strong sentiment that existed in these organizations that no other group would rise to the ranks of a national fraternity or sorority to be inducted into the NPHC. But as the 1990s dawned, it was clear that Iota Phi Theta was for real—and growing. Meeting resistance from a very conservative National Pan-Hellenic Council, Iota Phi Theta sought and was granted membership in the National Interfraternity Conference (NIC), which is today known as the North American Interfraternity Conference. Iota Phi Theta met the NIC's established set of standards, and they gained admission in 1984. The NIC also accepted Kappa Alpha Psi as a member, as they were the first group to hold membership in the two umbrella organizations.

But the issue of Iota Phi Theta did not go away as some had hoped. At the NPHC national convention in 1995, held in San Diego, California, considerable discussion was held on the floor about the proposed expansion policy for the organization. While members of Iota Phi Theta were invited to participate in the conference, delegates were asked to leave business sessions deemed open only to affiliate members. Much of the sentiment expressed in the meeting was a fear that any expansion would cause a flood of new members into the organization. One member even commented that she did not want to have the president of NPHC with a Spanish first and last name. It was clear that the general body was opposed to any expansion efforts.

At that conference, Daisy Wood was elected national president of the NPHC for the third time. She made a commitment to the Iota members that they would gain membership during her term in office. She reiterated this commitment at the closing banquet of the Association of Fraternity Advisors (AFA) conference that December. It was obvious that a showdown was developing between the general membership and the leadership of the organization.[1] And there was even dissention within the leadership of NPHC. One officer questioned expansion because of a potential to open up membership to other minority groups, namely White women and Asians.[2]

Early in 1996 the national presidents of the eight NPHC member organizations, along with the executive board of the NPHC, reviewed the expansion guidelines developed in 1993. The guidelines limited the number of applicants dramatically, especially with limitations in terms of the number of years in existence, and national organization structure. The guidelines were mailed to all active councils in July of that year for review. After accepting applications, only one organization met the requirements—Iota Phi Theta. So the organization applied for membership, and a special committee approved the application. In November 1996, the National Pan-Hellenic Council officially announced that Iota Phi Theta Fraternity was the newest member of the group.

The organization was fully inducted into NPHC membership during the 1997 undergraduate leadership summit, held in Indianapolis, Indiana, thirteen years after Iota Phi Theta had gained admission into the predominantly White NIC. And the monikers for the NPHC member organizations changed to "The Noble Nine," and the most popular, bearing a book by the same name, "The Divine Nine." But resistance is still apparent in the organizations. Especially from the senior members in the organizations, there is an air of snobbishness that continues to look down at Iota Phi Theta. Some can be heard mocking the titles the organization uses for officers (i.e., the president is known as a "Polaris"), and many Greek functions, even in 2000, continue to omit the fraternity. While attending a Delta Sigma Theta graduate chapter event in the Atlanta area during the spring of 2000, the chapter president had members of each Greek organization stand when she called the name. She omitted Iota Phi Theta.

The history of Black fraternal organizations is riddled with inaccuracies. As noted in chapter 1, only within the last decade has Sigma Pi Phi been recognized as the first Greek-lettered organization. Members of Kappa Alpha Psi, through their history book, have been aware of the Alpha Kappa Nu Greek society at Indiana University in 1903, but the group was unknown to the rest of the Greek community. Members of Alpha Phi Alpha Fraternity read in their history book about the rumored Pi Gamma Omicron Fraternity at Ohio State University, and the group's existence is still in question. Until this text was written, there has been no mention of the

Gamma Phi Fraternity that existed for several decades at Wilberforce University. This is a peculiar fact because noted historian Charles Harris Wesley authored history books on Sigma Pi Phi and Alpha Phi Alpha as well as served as president of Central State College, located across the street from Wilberforce. But this book serves as the first proof that the organization existed.

A closer inspection of history reveals that numerous Black fraternal organizations have existed or are in existence. Many of the groups prior to the 1960s would be classified as local organizations. On some campuses, before Greek organizations were allowed, these local groups fulfilled some of the needs for affiliation. In the 1960s and 1970s the organizations represented the times—expressions of Black power and parodies of the Greeks. The 1980s and 1990s saw groups develop that reflected student desires for individualism and creativity, along with expressions of consciousness that rejected Greek life in favor of African fraternities and sororities. This chapter will review the development of fraternities and sororities outside the NPHC, with special emphasis on groups that represent the future of Black fraternalism in America.

THE MATURATION YEARS: 1910–60

The first two decades of the twentieth century laid the foundation for Black fraternalism in the United States. Between 1906 and 1922 the eight organizations that form the old guard for the National Pan-Hellenic Council were founded on four college campuses. In the cases of Butler University, Indiana University, and Cornell University, the organizations filled a void for Black students who were denied opportunities for involvement on those campuses at that time. Essentially, these organizations formed a support system not only for the members but also for all Black students. At Howard University, the cradle of Black Greek civilization, Greek-lettered organizations filled a void for students who were unfulfilled by the activities offered at that time.

As the NPHC organizations prepared to grow and mature beginning in the 1920s, the fraternal idea had caught on in several instances. At Howard University in the mid-1910s, much of student life was in a simplistic form. The 1914 *Howardina* yearbook indicated that the students at Howard amused themselves through senior superlatives. The yearbook indicated which students were selected as the most dignified, the most scientific, the most elegant, the most henpecked, the class baby, the ugliest, the vainest, the old maid, and the greatest "heart breaker."

At that time the Tau Sigma club for men, and the Alpha Phi literary society existed. The Alpha Phi literary society was described as "the oldest of the student orgs. at Howard. It was organized in 1872, and for nearly ten years was the only medium for student expression, aside from the regular routine of college work."[3] But with the establishment of the Beta Chapter of Alpha Phi Alpha in 1907, and Alpha Chapters of Alpha Kappa Alpha (1908), Omega Psi Phi (1911), Delta Sigma Theta (1913), and Phi Beta Sigma (1914), the Greek ideals were firmly planted.

The established fraternities though were for undergraduate students. So Howard saw an emergence of graduate level organizations shortly after the national groups were formed at Howard. In 1913, medical, dental, and pharmaceutical students at Howard formed the Chi Delta Mu Fraternity. In 1916 law students added the Tau Delta Sigma Fraternity. Women graduate students joined the ranks of creating fraternal organizations soon after. Women law students formed Epsilon Sigma Iota Sorority in May 1921, and the medical sorority, Rho Psi Phi, was founded in January 1922. The influx of Greek-lettered organizations created a push for student governance on the campus, and at the beginning of 1920 school year "the administration of Howard University turned over to its students a constitution which permitted them to elect from their own members a group of students to compose what should be known as a Student Council."[4]

After the formation of Gamma Phi Fraternity at Wilberforce in 1905, Alpha Phi Alpha founded the Xi Chapter in 1912. By 1920 there were five Greek-lettered organizations on the campus, including Gamma Phi. In 1920 students formed Gamma Kappa Phi Sorority, and in 1921 three students formed the Royal Crescent Club, a social organization that appeared to function like a fraternity. These groups were excluded when, in 1924, Kappa Alpha Psi initiated the formation of an Inter-Fraternal Council on the campus. So the evidence indicated that there were clear distinctions between the NPHC groups that had multiple chapters by the mid 1920s in some cases, versus the more local groups. By 1930, Phi Beta Sigma was on the campus at Wilberforce, and the existence of the Royal Crescent Club became limited. After 1935 the organization disappeared from the campus.

One interesting sorority at Wilberforce was Sigma Pi, which functioned almost as an honor society. The 1928 *Forcean* yearbook described the group as a compilation of "Junior and Senior members of each of the sororities on the campus. It was organized in 1922 and has for its purpose, the bringing about and maintaining of better relationships between members of their groups."[5] This group probably could be seen as a prelude to the Inter-Fraternal Council at Wilberforce.

Moving into the 1930s, the national Black Greek organizations continued to grow and mature. By 1930, Alpha Kappa Alpha had 34 undergraduate chapters, while Alpha Phi Alpha had 49 and Kappa Alpha Psi about 36. Most of these chapters were in the Midwest, and many at predominantly White institutions that were accredited. Over the next two to three decades, many of the new chapters were formed at historically Black colleges in the South and Southwest. At several of those institutions there were student organizations that predated the Greek-lettered groups, but as predominantly White fraternities replaced literary societies on many college campuses during the late 1800s, the same happened at HBCUs in the 1930s and 1940s.

The oldest women's group at Tennessee A&I State College by 1940 was the Delta Tau Iota group. Indeed, social organizations patterned themselves after Greeks in many cases, evident by the usage of Greek letters. A decade later, Greeks exploded on the campus: Sigma Gamma Rho (first), Phi Beta Sigma, Omega Psi Phi, and Kappa Alpha Psi in 1931, Alpha Kappa Alpha in 1932, Zeta Phi Beta in 1933, Alpha Phi Alpha in 1934, and Delta Sigma Theta in 1936. In an oddity, appearing in the 1939 *Ayeni* yearbook was a picture of a women's student organization, the Swastika Club. While the swastika has an ominous notion in contemporary Western culture, it is associated with prosperity and good fortune in many ancient cultures. In early Christian and Byzantine art it was known as the gammadion cross, or crux gammata, because it is formed by four Greek letter gammas that are joined at the base.[6] The Swastika Club at Tennessee State described as its aims (1) to create a desire for better literature, (2) to promote high scholarship, and (3) clear and straight thinking.[7]

This pattern of mass colonization by Greek organizations appeared at numerous HBCUs during this period once the universities reached accredited status. At Alabama State, three groups were formed between 1936 and 1937. Alabama A&M added five organizations between 1948 and 1950. Greek organizations began at Jackson State in the late 1940s as well. The 1948 *Jacksonian* stated

> Of unusual interest to the students of Jackson College was the recent approval of Greek-letter Organizations on the campus. Although Phi Beta Sigma was the first to establish any undergraduate chapter at Jackson College, other sororities and fraternities will soon be represented among the popular student organizations.[8]

By 1950, Jackson State students organized a Pan-Hellenic Council to meet the needs of the newly formed chapters.

Fraternities and sororities were added at Tuskegee beginning in 1948. Prior to that time, social organizations dominated student life. The 1941 *Tuskeana* yearbook indicated

> When we speak of social organizations, we have reference to those organizations which play the role of undergraduate chapters of social fraternities and sororities on our campus. These organizations from their beginning have been the leading coordinating force among the students at Tuskegee Institute. Each year they increase greatly the scope of their purposes and the

magnitude of their influence. In addition to sponsoring the most attractive and colorful dances of the year, these organizations have become rivals in their benevolence to the underprivileged, both local and national.[9]

Not only did the social organizations at Tuskegee attempt to fill the role of Greek-lettered organizations, they often used Greek letters as well. There existed the Delta Sigma and the Alpha Pi Gamma women's organizations in the early 1940s. The men were a little more direct in sharing their intentions, as they formed a social organization called the Pre Frat Club. The student newspaper, the *Campus Digest,* documented the addition of Greek chapters. The university established seven chapters in April 1948. The paper indicated, "prior to the establishment of these organizations, there had been much controversy which had prevented their beginnings."[10] But the students were optimistic about the establishment of the chapters.

By 1950, Greek-lettered organizations were establishing roots across the country. Many historically Black institutions were sufficiently accredited so that the organizations could establish chapters in accordance with their guidelines. And in many instances Greek chapters replaced various social organizations developed to fulfill that role, but lacked the full interest of students due to the local nature of the organizations. On campuses where the expansion of national groups was slow to develop, different types of local groups developed.

At Coppin State, male students established a chapter of Beta Sigma Tau. The yearbook caption indicated, "Beta Sigma Tau, the first national intercultural and social fraternity, was founded in Chicago, Illinois on May 24, 1948."[11] In addition, Pi Beta Sigma Sorority was founded on the campus to be "an intercultural sorority that would lack the barriers of race, creed, and national origin."[12] Established as the sister organization to Beta Sigma Tau, the group planned to have members from Coppin State, Morgan State, Goucher College, Loyola, and Notre Dame. It would not be until the late 1960s before Greeks were introduced to the campus, establishing a Pan-Hellenic Council in 1968.

Much of the period between 1910 and 1960 was an opportunity for NPHC groups to establish chapters nationally. Much of the growth occurred in the southeastern United States at historically Black colleges. In between the founding of these eight organizations and their expansion to many campuses, social organizations inadequately fulfilled fraternalism roles. In many cases these groups patterned themselves after fraternities and sororities, indicating the desire students had for this type of affiliation. The experimentation with local social organizations unknowingly served as a prelude to the later innovations of students in expressing fraternalism on college campuses.

BLACK POWER, BLAXPLOITATION ERA: 1960–80

The 1960s were an exciting time in history. The movement toward civil rights occupied the actions of students on campuses as well as their peers, family, and friends in the local communities. Many college students became history makers themselves as they integrated large, southern universities. Greek-lettered organizations emerged soon after on these campuses, almost repeating the history of the groups founded on predominantly White campuses.

But the 1960s were also a time when Black students, increasing in numbers due to better access to higher education, sought new ways to express and experience brotherhood and sisterhood. As the eight National Pan-Hellenic organizations expanded, they eclipsed local social groups, much like the introduction of White fraternities in the 1850s to college campuses extinguished interest in literary societies (along with colleges developing extensive libraries, replacing a primary function of these groups). During this period of time, two distinct philosophies emerged as represented in the organizations created at the time.

One philosophy could be described as a Black Power approach to fraternalism. In February 1960, four students from A&T in Greensboro, North Carolina, initiated a sit-in when they were refused service at a variety counter. From that point in time the civil rights movement began in earnest. Groups such as the Student Nonviolent Coordinating Committee (SNCC) and the Southern Christian Leadership Conference (SCLC) joined in on the freedom rides throughout the South. The decade would see more than two hundred thousand march on Washington, the passing of the Civil Rights Act of 1964, and the assassinations of John F. Kennedy and Martin Luther King Jr.

In 1966, when Stokely Carmichael became the chair of SNCC, he insisted that Negroes had to think in terms of Black power to combat White power. This became the new focus for the decade. John Hope Franklin writes

> Slowly, then more rapidly, the optimism gave way to pessimism and even cynicism. . . the feeling, bolstered by bitter experience, that justices and equality were not to be extended to blacks under any circumstances. This created the gloomy atmosphere out of which the Black Revolution emerged.[13]

The Black Power conference of 1967 as well as the formation of the Black Panthers signaled the arrival of a new age, one that was reflected on college campuses.

Intertwined in the Black power age of fraternalism was the Blaxploitation era. Blaxploitation films evolved in the 1970s targeted toward Black audiences. They used the popularity of Black actors, often portrayed as superheroes. Black America's stars were Richard Roundtree, Jim Brown,

Pam Grier, and Antonio Fargas. Movies such as *Shaft* (1971), *Black Caesar* (1973), *Cleopatra Jones* (1973), and *Three the Hard Way* (1974) provided the impetus for fashion, music, and the catchphrases of the day (e.g., "power to the people").[14]

The culture of Blaxploitation was in opposition to mainstream groups such as CORE and the NAACP, organizations concerned that the films would have long-term negative effects on Black youth. Author Nelson George attests to the impact the films had on culture, from the turtleneck sweaters and leather jackets worn by Shaft to the relentless use of the word "nigger" in the films. He indicates

> Never in the history of American cinema had there been so many aggressive, I-don't-give-a-damn black folks on screen. That is so crucial. Blaxploitation movies reserved little space for the singing of Negro spirituals, turning the other cheek, or chaste kisses. In fact, characters who possessed these qualities were often the brunt of much-appreciated derision. In blaxploitation black people shoot back with big guns, strut to bold jams, and have sweaty, bed-rocking sex.[15]

This ethos was definitely at play in the founding of numerous fraternities and sororities during this period that had these values as well as in openly parodying mainstream Greek-lettered organizations.

Table 8 lists numerous organizations founded during the Black power, Blaxploitation age. Those organizations that exemplify the characteristics of Blaxploitation are fairly obvious in their names. Groups such as Nun Phi Nun, Hound Phi Hound, and Vash Na Ha were short-lived groups formed to parody NPHC organizations. Other organizations saw themselves more as reflections of the Black Power ideology espoused by Stokely Carmichael and saw their purpose on campus as challenging the status quo of the more conservative Greeks.

Two groups deserve special consideration during this era. The first is the Iota Phi Theta Fraternity, founded on the campus of Morgan State College on 19 September 1963. The founding of the fraternity was significant for many reasons, but one would be that it occurred one month after the March on Washington, during the month when four Black girls were killed as the result of a Birmingham church bombing and two months before the assassination of John F. Kennedy. Under this backdrop, twelve nontraditional students formed the fraternity. Lawrence Ross Jr. in the book *The Divine Nine* writes

> Each of these students was three to five years older than his peers; some had families with children; others had spent time in the service. Almost all of the founders had full-time jobs in addition to their studies. Another common denominator among the founders was that many had known each other for most of their lives. This, combined with the maturity of the founders, provided their different outlook on the meaning of fraternity.[16]

A Fly Block Fraternity—A Chapter

Groove Phi Groove Fraternity—Lion Chapter

Groove Phi Groove and A Fly Block Fraternity, 1970 (Courtesy Lincoln University Archives)

TABLE 8

Sample of Fraternities and Sororities of the Black Power, Blaxploitation Era:
1960–1980

Group name	Founding date	Location
Groove Phi Groove Social Fellowship (men)	1962	Morgan State
Zeta Delta Phi Sorority	1962	CUNY Bronx
Iota Phi Theta Fraternity	1963	Morgan State
Phi Eta Psi (Iota Mu Pi) Fraternity	1965	Mott C. C.
Nu Lambda Bama Sorority	1966	Howard
Tau Gamma Upsilon Fraternity	1968	Morgan State
Swing Phi Swing Social Fellowship (women)	1969	Winston-Salem State
Gamma Sigma Sigma Fraternity	circa 1971	Morgan State
Nun Phi Nun Sorority	circa 1972	Morgan State
Man Phi Blood	circa 1973	Mississippi Valley State
Woman Phi Blood	circa 1973	Mississippi Valley State
Ria Bibi Yaikinsha women's social group	circa 1973	Alabama A&M
Nasiha Roho Adinasi men's social group	circa 1973	Alabama A&M
Yo Psi Phi Fraternity	1975	Morgan State
Iota Phi Lambda Sorority	circa 1976	Norfolk State
Omicron Xi Epsilon Sorority	circa 1976	Norfolk State
Vash Na Ha brotherhood	circa 1977	Norfolk State
Malik Sigma Psi Fraternity	1977	C. W. Post College
Sigma Phi Rho Fraternity	1978	Wagner College
Phi Eta Psi Fraternity	circa 1978	Alabama State
Nu Phi Kappa Fraternity	circa 1978	Alabama State
Phi Delta Psi Fraternity	circa 1979	University of Detroit
Groups with Unknown Dates/Locations	Notes	
Wine (or Whiskey) Psi Phi Fraternity	present at Howard in 1974	
Delta Psi Chi Fraternity		
Beta Phi Upsilon		
Alpha Gamma Omega		
Epsilon Zeta Epsilon (EZE) Fraternity	Michigan area	
Groove Phi Soul	present at Shaw University in 1977	
Nu Gamma Muchuba	present at Shaw University in 1977	

It is evident that the fraternity faced some challenges in its early years on campus, many of them in relation to the more established fraternal organizations. Ironically, this struggle would last the better part of thirty years as the organization fought to gain membership in the National Pan-Hellenic Council. Iota Phi Theta did not appear in the Morgan State yearbook, *Promethean*, until 1965, and the first substantive description of the fraternity appeared in the 1971 book.

Alpha chapter, the first of Iota Phi Theta, was founded September 19, 1963 by 12 men who felt they were too old and mature to go through a ridiculous pledge season. It was originally called "I Felta Thigh" fraternity. "I Felta Thigh" entered Pan Hell in 1965. The name was then changed to Iota Phi Theta. In 1966 Iota withdrew from Pan Hell and became a major influence in forming the Council of Independent Organizations.[17]

This council included Alpha Phi Omega, Gamma Sigma Sigma, Groove Phi Groove, Tau Alpha Upsilon, and the Pershing Angels and Rifles. By 1970, twelve groups held membership in the Council of Independent Organizations. As noted earlier, it would not be until 1996 that Iota Phi Theta would join the old guard Greek-lettered organizations in the National Pan-Hellenic Council.

The second fraternity of note in this period is one not very well known by most. Fifteen students at the C. W. Post College of Long Island University founded Malik Sigma Psi fraternity on 13 May 1977. The fraternity was conceived under a new concept that represented the new consciousness of students of color. In fact, the founders were men of African and Latino decent. The fraternity ushered in African fraternalism, a concept that challenged their campus immediately. When originally organized, the fraternity had an all-Swahili name. The rules of C. W. Post College indicated that in order to be recognized as a fraternity, at least two Greek letters had to be used in the name.

While potentially seen as an area of conflict, the founders decided to strategically name the fraternity, a move that embodies the concept of African fraternalism. They used the Swahili and Arabic word *malik* first, a word meaning king or ruler. Malik represents the concepts of the fraternity—manhood, achievement, leadership, integrity, and knowledge. Furthermore, it is a part of Malcolm X's Swahili name (El Hajj Malik El Shabazz), and the fraternity points to him as their Black shining prince for his contributions to Black America. They next chose the Greek letters Sigma, which means progression, and Psi, an ancient symbol meaning man. The fraternity members explain the meaning of the fraternity by reading from right to left, as is done in Arabic. So the meaning of Malik Sigma Psi is man's progression to become king or ruler.[18]

These actions epitomize Malik Sigma Psi. Elquemedo Alleyne, a member who wrote the unpublished information booklet for the fraternity, explained the reasons for a new approach to fraternalism. "The founders of Malik Sigma Psi chose to reject the popular conception of 'Black Greekism' because of its inferiority complex that miseducates our people against recognizing Africa as the true beginning of civilization. Malik Sigma Psi chooses instead to emphasize our Africanness and prefers therefore to be called 'African Fraternalists.'"[19] The fraternity teaches that fraternalism is an African invention, and through the Greeks studying Egyptian culture, they developed Western civilization, which led to the formation of social organizations in American higher education that evolved into fraternities and sororities. With Black fraternities and sororities developing in the early 1900s, they adopted the label of Black Greeks.

Malik Sigma Psi then used two Greek letters to appease the administration at the college. But in their quest to develop African fraternalism, they explained the usage of these letters as well. The fraternity rejects the notion that fraternalism can only be defined through Greek letters. The predominantly White fraternities Farmhouse and Triangle are other examples of creating fraternities without Greek letters. Members of Malik challenge Greek letters from an Afrocentric perspective.

> It must be revealed that the "Greek alphabet" is in actuality a derivation of the African Coptic alphabet which was used as part of the secret languages of the Egyptian Priests of the Mystery System. Thirdly, we admit that if it were not for the thievery of the Greeks in their plagiaristic writing and their destruction of the Black civilization, the truth would not have been revealed today that there is no such thing as a "Greek Alphabet" but a stolen African alphabet.[20]

Despite the differences noted by Malik Sigma Psi, the organization operates much like any Black fraternity. The colors of the fraternity are black and orange. The members wear jackets and jerseys with the symbols MΣΨ on them, although many mistake the Malik to be the Greek "Mu." The fraternity also employs a hand sign and uses a call of "Malik" to acknowledge each other. The fraternity also participates in the art form of stepping as do other Black fraternities. As of the late 1990s, the fraternity was primarily a northeastern fraternity, with chapters currently or at one time located at SUNY Buffalo, Hofstra, Stonybrook, Westbury, and Adelphi. The fraternity has had a chapter as far south as Virginia at Norfolk State University. Roughly two thousand men have been initiated into Malik Sigma Psi Fraternity.

The fraternity has also developed a system for recruiting and pledging new members that resembled NPHC pledging prior to 1990, but with some modifications. The process begins with an open house on the campus. This program is open to not only interested men, but also women and campus administrators. The members present fraternity and chapter history, an explanation of the terminology used, and a discussion on the concept of African fraternalism. After this open house, a more specific meeting is conducted for interested men only. Generally only a few men are selected to participate in the eight-week pledge program. The elaborate program consists of three to four stages, with pledges starting off in all-black uniforms and *kufis* (African hats), and then adding orange during certain phases.

During pledging, the aspirants learn greetings they present to members that are constructed as mini-history lessons, discussions of the nature of African people, and the stolen legacy. Pledges are also required to make a shield that is to be a representation of that student. In the literature, the fraternity indicates "entry into the kingdom of Malik teaches unity and solidarity and is patterned after African rites of passage on that continent. . . . Pledging is an important part of initiation into our brotherhood. We feel NO need to beat, break down or dehumanize our potential members especially when we, as people of color in this country, undergo a daily pledge process."[21] The fraternity notes that it is a nonhazing organization but engages in physical and mental building. During this process the aspirants are given Swahili line names, similar to the tradition of NPHC groups. Many members generally continue to go by that name after initiation. All of the line names begin with the word Malik, and they may refer to each other by that name.

As indicated, several founders of Malik Sigma Psi were of Latin descent. Latin students have joined the fraternity with regularity since its existence. But this has caused conflict in some cases with Latin fraternities, many of which were founded beginning in the late 1970s. Latin fraternities in some cases have chastised Latinos who joined Malik rather than one of their groups, much like Black fraternities and sororities criticized their Black peers who joined predominantly White groups, most often labeling those students as "sellouts." Malik Sigma Psi has remained steadfast though in its acceptance of Latin men, and even Freddie Perez of the Young Lords Movement is an honorary member.

The period between 1960 and 1980 was one of rapid growth in fraternalism for Black students. With greater access to higher education for many students, particularly nontraditional students, new fraternities such as Iota Phi Theta met their needs while reflecting the mood of the mid-1960s. Many organizations created in the 1970s were campus versions of Blaxploitation films, creating fun-loving and highly stereotypical organizations that were short-lived. And this period also initiated the African fraternalism movement through Malik Sigma Psi. The dominant presence of the NPHC organizations has prohibited these groups from growing in many cases, keeping most of them small in number, or shortening the life span of the organization to a few years and on only one campus. Yet their existence is important to note in fully exploring Black fraternalism in the United States.

INDIVIDUALIST/MULTICULTURALISM ERA: 1980–PRESENT

By 1980, over fifty Black fraternal organizations had been in existence. Although the eight NPHC members at that time were a dominating presence, it became clear that many students sought to express brotherhood and sisterhood in alternative forms. With some of the successes of the civil rights movement, Black students increased in numbers on college campuses through the new pipeline to previously segregated White universities in the South. The spirit of the eighties was that of a "me" generation, and nationally there were increases in the terms created that referred to self. This sentiment impacted college life, and consequently, fraternalism.

Table 9 is a listing of groups formed during this era, most appropriately defined as an individualist/multiculturalism era. The standard theme provided by these groups was that they sought to create their own fraternities and sororities. These students wanted to be founders, and leave their mark on student life on their campuses with hopes that their ideas would spawn into nationally recognized organizations. Other students, seeking to bring together students of different races and backgrounds, sought to build fraternal groups that openly embraced multiculturalism.

The final major theme of this new fraternalism was an open expression of Christianity. At least five organizations developed that incorporated "Christian" in the title, with others, including Delta Psi Epsilon Sorority, indicating that they were founded on Christian ideals and principles. It is apparent in these organizations that while they desired the brotherhood and sisterhood afforded by traditional Greek groups, they were not willing to participate in a culture that had become increasingly hedonistic. So these organizations offered a new option for students.

With the development of World Wide Web technology in the 1990s, it has become easy for these new groups to become noticed and to provide their own propaganda about their groups. The main issue faced by the groups was why they felt a need to begin new groups when others existed. Alpha Beta Sigma Sorority indicates, "The founders of Alpha Beta Sigma are all entrepreneurs. These Ladies did their research, and didn't come across a sorority which they felt would cater to all their ideas. As strong African women we know that if you want something done, and you want it done a certain way, then you go out and do it yourself. And so this is what we did."[22] The Pi Psi Fraternity, founded at Michigan State indicated, "We like to use the saying 'a fraternity should fit your personality like a glove.' What a better fit than to establish an organization of your own."[23] And some had very specific niches they sought, like Delta Phi Upsilon Fraternity that indicates its purpose as "cultivating and encouraging high scholastic and ethical standards, improving the social stature of gay people, promoting unity among black gay men and supporting a progressive interest in the education of such men."[24]

An example of a fraternity developed during this period of time is Gamma Alpha Chi. The organization was started at Louisiana State University on November 5, 1990. The founder was Troy W. Howard, described as a student who had an interest in NPHC fraternities and went to interest meetings. However, he did not believe the fraternities on that campus functioned as they were meant, so he turned to a residence hall organization he was a member of, and it formed into the fraternity after university approval. Thirteen men constituted the initial chapter.[25]

TABLE 9

*Sample Fraternities and Sororities of the Individualist/Multiculturalism Era:
1980–Present*

Group name	Founding date	Location
Mu Sigma Upsilon Multicultural Sorority	1981	Rutgers
Beta Pi Phi Fraternity	1985	Western Illinois
Delta Phi Upsilon Fraternity	1985	Florida State
Phi Omicron Psi Fraternity	1986	VCU
Elogeme Adolphi Christian Sorority	1987	Bradley
Omega Phi Chi Multicultural Sorority	1988	Rutgers
Alpha Nu Omega Christian Fraternity	1988	Morgan State
Alpha Nu Omega Christian Sorority	1988	Morgan State
Gamma Phi Delta Christian Fraternity	1988	U. of Texas
Alpha Lambda Omega Christian Sorority	1990	U. of Texas
Gamma Alpha Chi Fraternity	1990	Louisiana State
Phi Alpha Psi Sorority	1991	VCU
Phi Psi Nu Fraternity	1992	U. of Nebraska
Delta Psi Epsilon Sorority	1992	Oakwood College
Pi Psi Fraternity	1993	Michigan State
Alpha Gamma Psi Sorority	1993	U. of Michigan
Gamma Omega Delta Nu Sigma Fraternity	1993	SUNY New Paltz & Binghamton U.
Phi Rho Eta	1994	Southern Illinois
Tau Kappa Omicron Multicultural Sorority	1995	U. of Michigan
Sigma Alpha Phi Fraternity	1996	Bowie State
Theta Psi Sorority	1996	Michigan State
Gamma Phi Eta Fraternity	1996	Georgia Southern
Xi Gamma Phi Sorority	1997	Georgia Southern
Alpha Beta Sigma Sorority	1998	SUNY Buffalo
Alpha Tau Omega Phi Fraternity	unknown	U. of Pennsylvania
Eta Phi Beta Sorority	unknown	St. Augustine's
Alpha Omega Alpha Christian Sorority	unknown	SE Missouri State

From LSU the fraternity expanded and developed chapters at several schools in the southwest: Southern, Grambling, Louisiana Tech, the University of New Orleans, and the University of Southwestern Louisiana. By the end of the 1990s approximately two hundred men had been initiated into the organization. Members indicate that the organization does not consider itself a historically Black fraternity, as some of the founders were White, but all of the manifestations suggest otherwise. The colors of the fraternity are black and white. The members use hand signs and a call of "G-Chi" or "1–9–9–0." The fraternity also participates in stepping as well.

The motto of the fraternity is "Educate ourselves to serve others, and educate others to better the world." Its national philanthropy is sickle cell anemia, chosen due to a member's affliction with the illness.[26]

The fraternity conducts a pledge process similar to the kind NPHC groups used prior to 1990. Potential members attend an interest meeting, and then are interviewed by members. The members then engage in a period of observation, a time where the aspirants are viewed during their day-to-day routines. Once selected, the pledges participate in a process described by members as private, but in reality mirrors underground pledging of NPHC groups. There are no outward manifestations of pledging for aspirants, but the pledges are assigned numbers that will appear on their paraphernalia once they are initiated. Pledging for Gamma Alpha Chi is dependent on the aspirants, and generally lasts from two weeks to two months.

Gamma Alpha Chi is a group that would like to grow and develop into a major national organization that could gain membership in the National Pan-Hellenic Council. But like many of the groups that developed during this period, the perception is that the organization is only a fad or destined to be short-lived. Members say that other Greeks might look at their letters and ask, "What the hell is that?" They joke that it is a shame for Greeks not to know Greek letters. Other fraternities simply call them a "fake frat" and completely dismiss the organization. Rumors even exist that indicate that the founder was denied membership in another group, a reason given for the founding of many of the groups during this era. But some, including campus administrators, think groups such as Gamma Alpha Chi can help to keep NPHC groups honest about what their purposes are on campus and in the community.[27]

The next twenty years will be crucial in determining which of these groups develop a strong enough foundation to persist. Some groups, such as Tau Kappa Omicron Multicultural Sorority founded at the University of Michigan, only existed for one year. The challenges are great, as these organizations are undoubtedly affected by the negative incidents of the high-profile NPHC groups. With many of these organizations trying to maintain pledging customs that NPHC organizations used prior to 1990, universities are likely to mandate that any expansion to campuses where they are not currently located requires them to follow NPHC policies, especially with regard to pledging and new member intake.

AFROCENTRIC ERA: 1985–PRESENT

The final era, running concurrently with the individualist/multiculturalism era, focuses on Afrocentrism. The late 1980s and early 1990s were a time on college campuses when Black students began to embrace their history and culture. This was a period when Malcolm X posters were in residence hall rooms, popular T-shirts bore the slogan "By Any Means

Necessary," and students wore medallions in the shape of Africa around their necks. The Spike Lee movie *Do the Right Thing* gave birth to the hip-hop anthem for Black college students, "Fight the Power," by the group Public Enemy. More students grew dreadlocks and wore *kufis*. Students took this spirit to college administrators and began to actively demand more Black faculty and staff, the adding of multiculturalism to the curriculum, and the creation of Black studies programs and departments.

Students also began to actively read to learn more about their culture and history. Molefi Asante, father of Afrocentrism, provided numerous texts to define this new concept for a conscious student body. Na'im Akbar of Florida State University emerged as a popular speaker and author, promoting an involved Black student body. Students also began reading classics, including those written by Carter G. Woodson and E. Franklin Frazier. And these students many times openly criticized the fraternities and sororities, most often challenging the notion of them being called Black Greeks, using the rationale offered by Malik Sigma Psi Fraternity.

Table 10 lists the organizations formed during this era. They are more likely to describe themselves as African fraternities and sororities, rather than African-American Greek-lettered, as none of them use Greek letters in their names. They are few in number and are probably seen as eccentric by many college students. Again, the overwhelming visibility and popularity of the "Divine Nine" groups has stifled the growth of this aspect of Black fraternalism. But an examination of these groups reveals a very unique culture that rounds out a century of Black fraternalism in America.

TABLE 10
Sample of Fraternities and Sororities in the Afrocentric Era: 1985–

Group name	Founding date	Location
Kemet (African fraternity)	1988	Atlanta University Center
Auset (African sorority)	circa 1990	Spelman
Ndugu (African fraternity)	circa 1995	Clark Atlanta
Nzinga (African sorority)	circa 1995	Clark Atlanta
Malika Kambe Umfazi	1995	SUNY Buffalo
Hetheru	unknown	Tuskegee
Order of Akande (coed)	unknown	Albany, NY
Auscar	unknown	NY city
Kush	unknown	NY state
Exodus	unknown	NY state

Note: Nzinga is the Congo spelling of the sorority. It also is written as Njinga, which is the Bantu spelling of the sorority.

One of the organizations that epitomizes the Afrocentric era is Kemet of the Atlanta University Center.[28] The organization began forming around 1987, as many students attending Clark were reading the book *Stolen Legacy* by George G. M. James. They were also inspired by a conference held on the campus of Morehouse College in 1986 on Africa and Kemet. In January 1988, ten men founded the fraternity. Many of the men were history majors. Baruti Kemet, a Georgia State University alumnus initiated in 1996, says that there are "no dummies in Kemet." The members have also been referred to as "readers" and "treehuggers."[29]

The ten founders of the fraternity are called "The Ten Lights of Ra," and a member of the fraternity might be called "Another Light of Ra." The members see themselves as vessels of knowledge to others. This is substantiated by the fact that the organization has produced newspapers in the Atlanta University Center. But there aren't many outward manifestations of the fraternity. The do have a hand sign, but there is not a great amount of paraphernalia. Members may wear a ring composed of four colors in a certain order, and occasionally a hat may be worn that signifies membership in the organization.

The members are referred to as the Asen of Kemet, and they are organized into "nomes" instead of chapters. Members of the organization live in several states, including California, New York, Indiana, and Tennessee. By 1996 roughly two hundred men had been initiated into the organization, and there is a national structure to the fraternity with specific guidelines. The organization functions primarily by consensus decisions, with no formal leadership. There are selected elders from the community that function as guides or advisers, but they are not known by those outside of the organization.

I was invited to attend the Resurrection March held 29 April 1996 at Clark Atlanta University. The march was a modern-day rites of passage ceremony for the initiates, and in theory, similar to a Black Greek probate show. Students learn about membership opportunities by attending an interest meeting, called an "ashe." Signs are posted that announce the meeting, but the members don't actively recruit students. Those selected participate in the pledge program, which does not have a prescribed length of time for completion, but is, according to the members, guided by the ancestors.

The Resurrection March began as the aspirants marched through the campus carrying a log while chanting "Kemet is coming! Kemet is coming!" Everything the organization does contains a great amount of symbolism. The log represented the African story of Osa and Seth. On the front of the log, eyes were painted to represent the eyes of Heru, and represented the battle of Heru and Set. The log was placed on the ground and the aspirants prepared for the ceremony to begin.

One member of Kemet led the ceremony. He initially asked an elder in the crowd for permission to begin the ceremony. Once permission was granted, the brother leading the ceremony gave the welcome. He instructed the crowd

What is KMT?

Founded in January of 1988, KMT (pronounced Kem-et) ASEN, is an Afrikan brotherhood based on the principles, customs and traditions put forth by our ancestors. The name "KMT" means "Land of the Blacks," and is the original name of Egypt, as established by its Afrikan inhabitants.

KMT ASEN is an organization of Afrikan men bound together by four fundamental principles; (1) Afrika is at the center, (2) Afrikan Women, our mothers and sister, are keepers of the center, (3) Family is the basis of Afrikan life and, (4) One must better ones self to better serve the needs of ones people. We, the men of KMT, have as our ultimate goal, the liberation of the Afrikan world, at home and in the diaspora. Responsibility to the community, a knowledge and understanding of our history and intense study of the world and its environment are key points in this process.

The ASEN is a family unified by common experiences, a clan with the same last name, holding the rituals of our ancestors dear. No man may stand alone against the storm of white supremacy and its winds of racism, rains of sexism and hail of oppression. When one completes the "Crossing," the brother is welcomed into the house of KMT; shelter from the storm. No longer alone, each brother unites with the ASEN to travel Eastwards, implementing plans and building relationships big and small to string the yoke of oppression, white supremacy, and realize the Light of a redemptive Afrikan world.

Our common experiences are hidden beneath layers of contradictory and contentious behaviors that are recognized pathologies of the way we live in the west. The "Crossing" is designed to bring the initiate into the ASEN with a new perspective of himself. Beginning with the ancient dictate, "Know Thyself," physical, mental and spiritual development are fostered in an intensive environment conducive to such growth.

The organization is made up of men who, at one time or another, have sojourned through the Atlanta University Center (AUC). Some of our members are an integral part of the AUC community, as productive and contributive students to its life. Others of our members have gone on to various institutions and are either pursuing higher degrees, or are engaged in careers impacting our community.

The ASEN stands humbly, for man is the medicine, and before the voice stirs from within the village, we have answered.

Kemet information meeting flyer, 1996

to participate in the ceremony, initially by repeating the word "Medassi," a word of thanks. While the leader of the ceremony appeared to have been the leader of the pledge process, the organization does not use any formal leadership. Even the pledge process was led through group consensus.[30]

The second speaker was identified as one of the founders of the organization, or one of the ten lights of Ra. The crowd was led in a libation ceremony, where they were asked to call out the names of ancestors. For each, a libation was poured, and the crowd was asked to respond, "Ashay," which means, so be it. The crowd was then told that the initiates pledged (and the term pledged was used) for ten weeks and thirty-four days. Since there were ten founders, ten is a significant number. The leader indicated that during this time they turned their backs to the west, which they equated with death, and faced east, toward the temples. The rationale for this statement was that in ancient Kemet, the cities were to the east while the tombs were to the west.

After this explanation, each candidate introduced himself. They would give their birth names, along with their genealogy. So the candidate would say that he was the son of this man and this woman, who was the son or daughter of this man and woman, and so forth. After each candidate spoke, a member of the fraternity gave a blessing, and then each candidate's face was physically cleaned with soap and water, and then dried with a towel. The narrator informed the audience that this was a symbolic cleansing of their Western death, or providing them with an understanding of a view of the world other than that of the West.

Additional blessings were given. Then a mixture representing blood, milk, and water was poured over the log. This represented the fluids of their mothers and signified a new birth. Ironically, during this time it began to rain. Rain is a symbol of cleansing in some African cultures. Within minutes the ceremony was being held in a thunderstorm with heavy downpour. The candidates were asked three times if they feared the resurrection. Each time they said "No." Once affirming their intentions to "cross over into the light," or be initiated, they held an African idol above their heads, one by one, and gave the African name they received during the pledge process. This could be interpreted as similar to the line names of Black fraternities and sororities, but with much more symbolism and meaning for each student.

Once each candidate announced his new name, amid the cheers of the crowd, members of the African sorority Auset came and presented the men with gifts. They reaffirmed the candidates as African men as well as their role in supporting them. Kemet has four fundamental principles, one of which states that women, their mothers and sisters, are keepers of the center. One of the conflicts Kemet feels it has with NPHC fraternities is due to their perception that the other fraternities disrespect women openly.

Kemet does not wish to be treated as the traditional Greek-lettered fraternities, mainly because they believe an African fraternity is completely different. The pledge process of Kemet contained what they called "physical and mental challenges," probably activities that campus administrators might challenge as being hazing. But Kemet justified its process through an annotated bibliography about African culture that they would recommend for campus administrators to read.

Once defined exclusively by eight nationally recognized organizations, the realm of Black fraternalism easily includes over seventy-five organizations that have been or are currently in existence. It appears that very regularly, students attempt to begin national organizations that represent their chance to influence history. In the process, these fledgling organizations often end up using the letters, signs, or symbols of existing organizations, causing temporary conflict. While many of these groups have been and will always be considered local organizations, their place in the history of Black fraternalism is important as they have provided a sense of the times in which the students lived, and offered ways to make meaning of their college experience.

5

That Thing You Do

SINCE THE INCEPTION OF COLLEGES IN AMERICA, STUDENT CULTURES ON college campuses have evolved. For the majority of college campuses, literary societies were replaced by fraternities that brought a sense of rebellion to campuses. In the mid-1800s after the explosion of fraternities and sororities, Black college students saw these organizations as a way to become part of the mainstream college culture. However, these Black groups also provided support for students, especially on the predominantly White campuses. They mirrored their White counterparts by using Greek letters, by forming chapters, and by incorporating secret handshakes and rituals.

But the historical legacy of African-Americans indicates that as a people, Blacks have taken American customs and added their own flair. Jazz music became the classical music of Black America, using European instruments. Black Americans transformed Christian church services into rhythmical, emotional gatherings to provide a culturally based meaning to worship. Basketball went from a game of set shots and long jumpers to a game played above the rim, characterized by earth-shattering dunks.

The same happened as Blacks formed Greek-lettered organizations. The creativity of the members, along with the innate qualities of their African ancestry, transformed collegiate Greek life into an expressive, exciting culture on college campuses. Since the early 1900s, Black fraternal organizations have added plots, step shows, hand signs, and calls to college life. But to this point in time, these cultural artifacts are not very well understood, with little documentation surrounding their genesis. Much of the history of these organizations, their customs, and traditions has been passed down through oral histories, tales, and legends. Practically no substantial studies have attempted to illuminate these fascinating aspects of Black fraternalism.

Yet, through such inquiry, the development of these aspects of Black fraternal life can be explained and chronicled. Many of these artifacts now help define Black Greek–lettered organizations, but most members have little substantive knowledge as to the development of these customs, or the meanings they have in relation to many African customs and traditions. This chapter seeks to define these concepts and chronicle their development during the first one hundred years of Black collegiate Greek life.

PLEDGING AND RELATED ACTIVITIES

As chronicled in an earlier chapter, pledging in many ways was the defining experience in Black collegiate Greek life. The pledge process lasted as long a semester in some instances, and was whittled down to two weeks before ending in 1990. During that time the pledges were the center of attention for Black students, and their activities were highly watched. The activities of the pledges defined themselves as aspiring Greeks, but more important than that, their activities provided the foundation for much of the culture of Black Greek life.

The initial innovation in the culture was the naming of groups working toward membership in the organizations. In 1919 the Kappa Alpha Psi Fraternity defined its aspirants as Scrollers and inaugurated the Scrollers Club. Students at Tennessee State University wrote, "The Scrollers Club which is an integral part of Kappa Alpha Psi Fraternity, was founded on the campus of Ohio State University, May 19, 1919 for the purpose of unifying the men who aspire to the achievements that Kappa Alpha Psi offers."[1] William Crump further explained that pledge clubs existed from the organization's beginning, but with an increase in pledges after the war, the pledge clubs were needed for "thorough, effective, and more or less standardized orientation."[2] The name Scroller was chosen because of the scroll on the fraternity's badge.

This need for standardization expanded to other organizations. In 1921, Alpha Phi Alpha instituted the Sphinx Club first at Howard University. The purpose of the organization was spelled out in the 1945 *Bison* yearbook at Howard:

> The Sphinx Club of Beta Chapter of Alpha Phi Alpha is a brief stopping place where the members of the fraternity in theory attempt to study a man's character, to get acquainted with him, and to let him get acquainted with them in order that both the fraternity and the sphinxman may decide intelligently whether or not either wishes to continue the friendship and cement it into brotherhood.[3]

While pledge clubs developed during the 1920s, their purposes varied among the organizations. Likewise, each organization developed a name for its pledge club. In 1930, Zeta Phi Beta at Howard indicated, "Those young ladies who wish to become Zeta members and have expressed that desire are 'Archonians,' pledge members."[4] Some organizations indicated that pledge clubs were made up of freshmen students. Delta Sigma Theta indicated, "The Pyramid Club is composed of freshmen women who have expressed their desire to become affiliated with Alpha Chapter and have exhibited desirable qualities in their activities on the campus."[5]

During the development of the pledge clubs, each organization defined what the club was for and the purpose of the organization. At Wilberforce in 1923, Delta Sigma Theta, like the chapter at Howard, had a Pyramid Club composed of freshmen women. They indicated that the "club has for its aims the highest in scholarship, ideals and womanhood. The symbol of the club is the triangle: the base for fidelity, one side for enthusiasm, the other for womanhood."[6]

Later years saw more development of the clubs. The aims as described included values that the new members were to learn. Members of the Sphinx Club at Howard in the mid-1940s were responsible for sponsoring a project as well as learning about the aims of the fraternity. Scrollers of Kappa Alpha Psi during this time had to learn parliamentary procedure along with fraternity ideals. In the late 1950s, Lampados, or pledges of Omega Psi Phi, were to prove themselves worthy of membership, including maintaining their scholastic average and performing service. Pledges in the Crescent Club at Jackson State were "expected to practice good manners anywhere and at all times."[7]

The concept of pledging evolved over the years. As indicated, the activities associated with the term varied in length, being shortened during the 1980s and officially ending in 1990, only to be reborn as underground pledging. But the term and associated terms have varied as well. The first term used for those attempting to gain membership was "pledges," used in relation to the Ivy Leaf Club at Wilberforce in 1923. A year later in the Howard yearbook, the word "pledgee" was used to describe a dance held by the Scrollers of Kappa Alpha Psi. The term pledgee was later used at Tennessee State in the early 1930s.

Throughout the 1940s, 1950s, and 1960s the terms pledgee and pledge were used interchangeably. During that time the terms "pledging" and "probation" were also interchangeable. The term probation emerged in the 1950s. It symbolized the status the pledges had with the rest of the campus. In essence, they were on probation from interacting with persons other than members of their pledge club, members of the organization, and faculty or staff. At Jackson State in 1964 the phrase "pledgees on probation" signified the state the pledges were in during that time. The term probation was prominent until about the 1970s, when the term pledging became preferred.

An important element of pledging that evolved was the single file line image of initiates moving across campus. This image is important in African-American history in several regards. Slaves were marched to ships in chains when they were transported to America. And when Harriet Tubman led slaves to freedom on the Underground Railroad, they were instructed to walk in single file line, literally stepping into the footprint of the person in front of them in order to prevent detection. As pledging developed in Black fraternities and sororities, this phenomenon was visible. A picture of the members of the Alpha chapter of Alpha Phi Alpha in 1907 shows the chapter members standing in a line according to height. This is the earliest image of the concept that would develop for the next sixty years.

Zeta line with numbers (Courtesy Jackson State University Archives)

It would not be until the early 1950s before the organizations solidified the line concept. Aspirants while pledging were referred to as the pledge club, using the specific term that the organization created (i.e., Archonian Club, Aurora Club, etc.). In 1951 at Howard, the word "line" was used to describe the pledge club. This term accurately described how the group looked at they marched across campus. The word line in relation to the pledge class appeared at Tuskegee in 1954, Central State in 1956, and at Alabama State in 1961 and Tennessee State in 1965. By the 1970s persons pledging were almost unilaterally referred to as "the line," and pledges went from being "on probation" to being "on line."

As indicated, the symbolism of the line has strong African roots. The image of a Black Greek pledge line was similar to candidates participating in an African rites-of-passage ceremony. Candidates could be seen standing close together, back to front, and in some instances with arms connected or locked. As pledge programs evolved, this same symbolism existed. Lines would be punished if they were separated or if someone "broke the line" physically. Again, pledging served as a history reenactment of sorts. Slaves clung to each other to prevent separation, just as pledges attempted to during their process.

As mentioned, lines were always tight, mirroring in some regards the traveling slaves on the slave ships. During the 1950s when the terms pledging and probation were used interchangeably, the terms "ship" and "ship-pie" emerged as another means to describe a pledge class. At Jackson State in 1959, each pledge club was referred to as a ship, such as the Zeta Ship, or the Sigma Ship. As of the writing of this book, the term ship is presently not used in Mississippi. However, it is still prevalent in a few midwestern states, including Illinois, Iowa, Kansas, and parts of Indiana.[8] The symbolism includes calling the first person in the line the captain, and the last person the anchor, although these designations may vary depending upon the circumstances. Conway indicated

> On a visit to Goree Isle in Senegal, I painfully observed the "door of no return." Through that single passage, across a plank, manacled in unbroken lines, millions upon millions of Africans left that place on ships bound for the Americas. Lithographs of slave ships clearly show Africans tightly packed for that journey. Interestingly, in the Midwestern United States pledgees have been sometimes called "shippies."[9]

As the line symbolism and concept solidified, additional aspects of the culture of pledging emerged. As early as 1956 at Central State, the pledge club or line received an additional name that would identify their place in history. The Kappa Alpha Psi line there was called "The Tragic 19" in a yearbook photo.[10] There was no immediate proliferation of line names on the campus. Five years later at Howard, the Delta Sigma Theta line was clearly deemed the "Eveready 42," inaugurating the use of collective line names. The next year Howard University would be introduced to "The Fine 29" of Alpha Phi Alpha, "The Grand 16" of Kappa Alpha Psi, and "The Slick 21" of Omega Psi Phi. By 1969 the use of collective line names appeared at Jackson State.

Once a numerical adjective was added to the pledge club, the next logical designation was for each individual to assume the number that represented their place in the line. By the 1960s, pledges could be seen with objects bearing their specific number. College yearbook photos in the 1960s showed members wearing paraphernalia that bore not only the term and year that they pledged, but their number in the line. As the collective line was named, soon each individual member received a nickname, called a "line name." Individual line names were not really evident until about 1970. Greek chapters did not appear in the *Delvian* yearbook of Mississippi Valley State until 1970. In the 1973 yearbook, each member of the Omega Psi Phi chapter had an individual picture with his nickname, or line name, underneath.

Several other features developed along with pledging that helped to define the process as well as the Black Greek experience. As early as the 1940s, pledges could be seen carrying objects of significance to that organization or group. Lampados of Omega Psi Phi began carrying lamps. Ivies of Alpha Kappa Alpha might carry an ivy plant. Pyramids of Delta Sigma Theta might carry a plastic duck. While some of these activities may have appeared to be whimsical, there are African traditions that closely mirror these practices. Ishmail Conway indicated,

> In Senegal and Gambia, some initiates carry lanterns, plants, and doll-like figures as treasures. During the initiation periods, ethnic groups (the Mandkinka, the Serrer, the Jollar and the Fulani), have young male initiate groups carry lamps. This fanal lantern symbolizes their impending enlightenment as adults.... Women carry dolls of reed and bone; not as playthings, but because the material represents "life symbols of human structural development."[11]

There were however, some anomalies in the traditional objects carried by the pledges. In the early 1950s the Delta Sigma Theta pledges at Howard carried panda bears rather than ducks. Auroras of Sigma Gamma Rho at Jackson State in the 1950s could be seen carrying a baby doll and a bottle. But during this time one uniform feature developed through all organizations. Over time, many pledge clubs could be seen carrying paddles decorated in the organization's colors and bearing the symbols. Based on the analysis of pledging, the paddle was not only a visible symbol of pledging but a behind-the-scenes instrument of punishment.

The pledge process created language that defined the various roles members and aspirants played. One of the key features was that brotherhood and sisterhood were acted out while persons were pledging. As with predominantly White fraternities and sororities, Black Greeks employed the terms "big sister," "little sister," "big brother," and "little brother." As early as 1931 the distinction between the classes of members was evident. In the Howard yearbook that year, the page dedicated to the Ivy Leaf Club declared, "Ten of us freshmen are building new hope on the first step of the ladder of a nation-wide sisterhood. We are the little sisters 'of the Alpha Kappa Alpha Sorority.'"[12] The page also referenced the members as big sisters.

The rites-of-passage programs for African tribes also communicate various roles that the initiates would play in society. Rites-of-passage ceremonies were normally tied to some biological process. For women it would revolve around their first menstruation, and for men, circumcision.[13] For example, the Xhosa tribe of South Africa, of which Nelson Mandela is a member, uses the ritualized circumcision for "youths to heal, reflect on their lives and learn about the role of men in Xhosa society. They are allowed no clothes, only a blanket."[14] Much like pledging, there are some physical challenges associated with circumcision.

> Days after being circumcised, Mornay Myira is recovering in an initiation hut built on sweeping grasslands.... Myira is streaked with white clay, sym-

bolizing purity. A poultice of leaves covers his wound. "The first four days after I was circumcised were hell," says Myira, a college student. "I had to change the dressing every few hours. It was constant pain. I couldn't sleep. Plus we're not given water so I was extremely dehydrated."[15]

In addition, the initiates swallowed the severed foreskin, fearing that an evil spirit could cook it up if thrown away and cause the initiate to die.

As indicated in the discussion of pledging, prior to the advent of the practice in fraternities and sororities, college freshmen were uniformly hazed on college campuses. Oftentimes they were subject to weird dress and being called names. For instance, in the early 1920s, freshmen at Lincoln University were called dogs and were subjected to harsh punishments. While the uniform dress that developed as a part of the pledge process for Black Greeks was generally in good taste, the use of derogatory names was a significant part of probation and pledging. As early as 1925 at Wilberforce, Sigma Gamma Rho and Delta Sigma Theta called their aspirants "barbarians." The Delta Sigma Theta description was more informative, as on the page listing the chapter's social calendar, they discussed the nine barbarians, indicating a pledge club of nine women.

The practice did not take hold until the 1950s. As early as 1950 at Central State, the term "barb" was used as a shortened version of barbarian. The term "worm" was also used for sorority pledges. At Tennessee State in 1955, the term "dog" was applied to the pledges of Phi Beta Sigma, Alpha Phi Alpha, and Omega Psi Phi. The Alpha Kappa Alpha pledges were called "worms" while the Delta Sigma Theta pledges were called "barbarians" as they were at Wilberforce. Students at Howard also used barbarian, but for a while the members of Alpha Kappa Alpha called the new pledges "plugs" in the late 1950s. By 1961 at Howard, Alpha Phi Alpha pledges were called "Apes."

As late as 1962 at Wilberforce, the dog symbolism persisted. Captions in the yearbook indicated "ΚΑΨ dogs are coming" and the "Dogs of ΑΦΑ."[16] But around this time, and as early as 1950, an interesting phenomenon developed. Members of Omega Psi Phi unofficially adopted the dog symbolism and carried it to the next level. Probates of the fraternity could be seen on college campuses wearing dog collars and leashes, drinking from bowls, and barking. Over the next four decades the canine reference would become pervasive, as members of Omega Psi Phi would become known as the "Que Dogs," barking to acknowledge each other, just as other groups developed calls during the late 1970s and early 1980s.[17]

Once the distinction was established between members and pledges, the big sisters or big brothers reinforced the subservient nature of the pledges by requiring them to "greet," or make a loud, verbal acknowledgment of the members. In 1954 at Tennessee State, a yearbook caption under a picture of a Zeta Phi Beta line read, "Please, Most Noble Greek, May We Be

Barb's of DST Off to the Desert

Dog Lucius Ware

Apes of A Phi A

Death March

Kappa Louis Jackson
with
Robert Roule
and
Loomis Peebles

Use of derogatory pledge terms, 1953 (Courtesy Central State University Archives)

Seated?"[18] At Howard in 1955, women pledges could be seen bowing with a caption reading, "Hello Milady."[19] This probably represented a greeting as well. At Jackson State, a picture of Scrollers was described in the caption as "Today, along our way to the land of Kappa Alpha Psi, we greet our superiors."[20] The practice of greeting would grow so that by the 1980s, pledges could be heard giving long and elaborate greetings to big sisters and brothers and sometimes to other Greeks or to sweethearts.

A final concept that emerged during pledging was the "crossing of the burning sands." Numerous theories exist as to what the phrase means. Conway indicated,

> Then, there is the final march across the "burning sands." There are also gifts and celebration by the community when the pledgees complete the period. Today this is known as "going over." Imagine the heightened expectations brought on by the ending [of] the journey through the southern Sahara. Picture returning to the West African fishing city of Cayar after fishing in the Atlantic; after mooring the vessels on the hot sands of the beach, you celebrate the safe return.[21]

In essence, crossing the burning sands, also known as "crossing," or "crossing the sands" signified the end of the pledge process. It was the symbolic process of moving from the status as a non-Greek student into the ranks of a brotherhood or sisterhood.

It appears the term was first used around 1945. At Howard, the phrase "cross the burning sands" appeared in an article about the Lampados of Omega Psi Phi. At Tuskegee in 1950, a news article discussed the Lampados Club of Omega Psi Phi.

> Like the whole of "Greekdom," the Club requires and encourages the highest standards of morality and teaches the duty of service to mankind. It fosters the participation of its members in social action and philanthropic programs, and teaches the principals of democracy and the duties inherent in good citizenship. The ambition of the Lampados is to cross the burning sands into dear ol' Omega Land, where the hand of brotherhood awaits them.[22]

The phrase also appeared in the 1950 yearbook of Alabama A&M, *The Heritage*. Students there wrote "the first weary but determined men who crossed the burning sand to the fruitful plains of fraternal brotherhood" as an introduction to the new members.[23] Jackson State students, in describing a Phi Beta Sigma line, indicated, "These four are striving to cross the burning sands. If they can just make it, how their faces will change."[24] These descriptions highlight the fact that pledging was a strenuous process, one that the pledges look forward to ending by "crossing the sands."

GENERAL OUTWARD EXPRESSIONS OF GREEK LIFE

The Black Greek culture has developed both visually and audibly. Over the existence of the organizations on college campuses, undergraduates used a great deal of creativity in developing organizations and a culture that would provide a unique imprint on student life in higher education. In fact, Greek life as a whole on college campuses has added to the culture of student life. While their White counterparts built houses that bore Greek letters, sophisticated processes for recruiting new members via an annual event known as rush, and social events that for years revolved around kegs, Black students boastfully bore their letters in many unique ways, used their hands to form signs that indicated membership, and even created audible sounds to acknowledge each other from a distance.

One of the similarities between the two types of campus fraternal organizations was the wearing of letters. Due to economic circumstances of the students, very few early photos exist of members wearing some kind of garment with letters. A simple pin with the letters was probably the extent of paraphernalia up through the 1940s. The first type of paraphernalia used for Black Greeks was a simple sweater with Greek letters. A photo from Tennessee State in 1948 pictured a member of Delta Sigma Theta wearing a sweater while holding a paddle. Throughout the next twenty years, sweaters would develop into the primary form of paraphernalia worn by collegiates. By the late 1950s and into the early 1960s, sweaters were very visible on campuses. Most pictures of the representatives of the campus Pan-Hellenic Council showed them wearing their individual organization's letters on heavy, wool sweaters.

By the late 1960s, when line names and numbers evolved, the sweaters became artifacts of these innovations. Members sometimes would list the year they were initiated on the sleeve of a sweater. Some would indicate their line number on a sleeve, or sometimes on the front of the sweater. Before line names developed, students would sometimes have their given name on the sweater as well. In one instance, chapter officers had their office written down the sleeve. In many cases the writing on the sweaters was in script, designed and sewn on the sweaters. These sweaters seemed to add an air of importance to the members as the bold designs made them easily identifiable from a distance.

During the fashion trend dominated by sweaters, on a few campuses, a different trend emerged but was short-lived. On several campuses students wore fraternity and sorority blazers. The blazers had an emblem, such as a shield or a crest, embroidered over the pocket. Tennessee State was one of the campuses where students expressed Greekdom via this route. In 1961 the yearbook pictured members of Alpha Phi Alpha wearing their blazers that included the chapter designation sewn under the fraternity shield. The next year's yearbook pictured members of Zeta Phi Beta wearing blazers as well, accented by pearl necklaces. Both the sweaters and the blazers were part of a larger student culture during the 1940s through the 1960s. Students dressed more formally more often, and were often pictured in shirts and ties, skirts and dresses. The Greek paraphernalia were generally items that could be worn along with the standard dress of college students during those times.

Beginning in the mid-1960s, some of the formality of student dress began to erode and students began to use more casual means to express Greek life as well. Actually, there were hints before this time. In 1951, a student wore an ΑΦΑ cap at Howard University. But the next major initiative was the use of T-shirts. Some of the first T-shirts with Greek letters appeared in a 1965 yearbook worn by members of Delta Sigma Theta. With the next ten years, T-shirts would proliferate on campuses and become a major form of expression of Greek life. By the mid-1970s most Greek members were pictured wearing their T-shirts, versus ten years prior when sweaters dominated. Into the 1980s and 90s, T-shirts became a dominant form of expression. Any national convention of a Greek organization is characterized by large vendor areas, most of if not all of them selling the latest T-shirt with the catchiest themes. T-shirts evolved from simplistic shirts bearing only the Greek letters to vehicles to express sentiments of members, such as popular shirts that challenged the idea of membership intake with the slogan "Paper burns, sands are forever."

Along with the T-shirts came the development of fraternity and sorority jackets. Some of the earliest jackets were seen on the campus of Wilberforce University in 1957. The members of Kappa Alpha Psi wore very elaborate windbreakers for that period of time, professionally done and multicolored. This was more of an anomaly. It would not be until the mid-1970s that jackets became more prominent. The early jackets usually would contain a screen of the fraternity or sorority crest as well as the Greek letters. But for the most part, jackets started off as being fairly plain, just as the sweaters and T-shirts.

By the mid-1980s, jackets became more than paraphernalia, and in many instances, walking artwork. Collegians began to use the jackets as showcases to provide detailed information about their experience as a member of their sorority or fraternity. Not only did the jackets have Greek letters, one normally would see the name of the chapter where the member was initiated, and sometimes an indication as to the school where the chapter resided. With the sweaters of twenty years before, the year of initiation was indicated on the jacket, but by the 1980s the specific term was also indicated, whether is was fall (indicated by an F, the letters FA, or the word FALL), winter (usually indicated by WTR or W), or spring (usually indicated by SPR). In some cases summer initiates indicated that as well on the jacket.

On the back of the jackets the prominent figure was the number of the person in line. Even the postpledging, membership intake years beginning in 1990 did not end this practice. Above the number generally appeared the line name of the person, solidifying the tradition of giving line names or nicknames begun during the late 1970s. Other innovations appeared on jackets. Often the real name of the student may have appeared on the front of the jacket, and sometimes the names of all the persons initiated together if not too many. During the 1990s many students added specific designs to the jackets that signified mascots or organization-specific symbols. Finally, the bottom of jackets in some cases revealed slogans and sayings that became popular within the organizations, such as "Yo Baby Yo" or "Another Fine Delta." Even toward the end of the first century of Black fraternalism, jackets are the most prominent and distinctive paraphernalia worn by collegians, although the realm includes hats, sweaters, T-shirts, ties, shorts, boxers, socks, shoes and shoelaces, and even recently, thongs. Black Greeks in particular have developed an extreme liberalism as to where the letters are placed and in ways to wear them.

Sayings that sometimes appeared on jackets, such as the phrases "Yo Yo," "Skee Wee," and "GOMAB," are examples of calls. Calls are audible sounds made by members as a means to signify or acknowledge membership in a particular organization, or to acknowledge or "call" a member who may be in range where they could hear the call and respond. Instead of yelling the person's name, the fraternity brother or sorority sister would use the call to get the person's attention. These actions are also steeped in African as well as African-American traditions. Alternately named whoops, hollers, cries, and artwhoolies, they were a form a yodeling employed in the Congo and Angola among tribes (whooping), or sung by slaves (cries and artwhoolies). Call was also the name of the practice of Black vendors who peddled and advertised their products.[25]

Being verbal customs, it is difficult to determine when or why they appeared. Discussions with older members of the organization yield varying responses as to when calls were first used. In a dissertation, Marcella McCoy explored some of the customs of Black Greek–lettered organizations. The topic of calls was raised through interviews with persons initiated throughout a period from 1941 to 1994. Some of the subjects indicated they heard calls as early as the late 1960s, but there was a great deal of inconsistency. One of the ways used to determine the origins was to look for these phrases written in student publications. At Alabama State in 1981, the phrase "OO OOP" was viewed on a T-shirt of Delta Sigma Theta members on the campus. Three years later at Alabama A&M, the phrase "SKEE WEE" appeared. It is probable that these calls were mid-1970s inventions, but a much more detailed analysis of this aspect of Black fraternalism is needed and warranted.

Yet, during the 1980s and into the twenty-first century, calls have become ubiquitous outward expressions of Greek life. Any gathering of Greeks is likely to create an environment where calls are produced widely. With the advent of step shows, events that created a venue for many Greeks to congregate, calls became a critical part of the environment of the show, and they were used by members who participated in the shows. Today's college campuses are grounds where calls are normally heard on a daily basis if there are numerous and active Black Greek members.

The compliment to the call is the hand sign, or hailing signal. Again, the oral history of Black Greek customs has never pinpointed the exact origin of this custom. Theories include an introduction of gang hand signs as more former gang members entered colleges and universities. In interviews for her dissertation, the members who spoke with McCoy clearly had no definite idea when hand signs became prominent. One member, initiated into his fraternity in 1980, indicated that they used hand signs. But those initiated in the late 1960s were unaware of when the practice began.

A review of pictures from college campuses of Greeks were absent of any types of hand gestures until the 1970s. General chapter pictures as well as candid shots showed no evidence of hand signs, gestures developed to identify membership within particular fraternities or sororities. Around 1970 at Morgan State, the precursor of a hand sign seemed to appear. In a picture of Kappa Alpha Psi members, a member is shown holding up his three middle fingers. This early hand sign also appeared on the campuses of Alabama A&M in 1976. The hand sign for the fraternity as used today, making a circle using the thumb and index finger while extending the last three fingers (very similar to the "okay" sign used by many Americans), appeared at Tennessee State by 1976, and Norfolk State in 1977. From that point on the hand sign proliferated on college campuses.

Omega Psi Phi also appears to have had a precursor hand sign. At Morgan State in 1978 this precursor was in the form of members holding both arms straight up in the air. A similar hand sign was seen a few years later at Alabama State. But the current version of the hand sign, which when done with both arms looks like the Greek letter psi (Ψ), was present by 1980. A T-shirt of an Omega member at Morgan during this time clearly displayed the present hand sign for the fraternity.

Hand signs for the rest of the organizations appear to be a 1980s invention. Oral history for Alpha Phi Alpha members indicates the present hand sign, known through popular culture as the Hawaiian "hang loose" sign, was developed around 1975 at Florida State. The present sign was found in a photo from 1981 at Tennessee State. But through an analysis of yearbooks from almost twenty HBCUs, no other hand signs were prominently present until 1984. Particularly of note was the complete absence of any sorority hand signs. A photo from California State University at Long

Early Kappa Alpha Psi handsign, 1975 (Courtesy Lincoln University Archives)

Beach in the early 1980s showed a member of Alpha Kappa Alpha holding their sorority hand sign, characterized by holding out the pinky finger. Even though a seventies invention, within a decade hand signs became ubiquitous. Since that time practically all undergraduates pose for pictures while using their respective hand signs.

The language of members of Black fraternities and sororities can be viewed as a culture in and of itself. Members created a lexicon that uniquely describes their organizations and related activities. As with many practices and traditions that evolved over time, their beginnings are not clearly understood. However, it is fairly evident that many of these practices are almost as old as the organizations themselves.

One of the most basic sets of phrases are those used to describe members of the same fraternity or sorority. With all fraternities, Black or White, the common term used to describe members is "brother." Black fraternities continue to use this term when referring to members of their particular organization. This term also developed a broader usage, particularly during the 1960s as Black men began referring to each other as "brother," and likewise to women as "sister" as a symbolic gesture recognizing that they all were going through the same struggle. The words in essence became slang, and a group of Black men could be referred to as "the brothers," and the women could be called "the sisters." Various spellings evolved as well for the terms, including "bruthas" and "sistas."

But with the fraternity experience, the word "frat" evolved to describe men in the same organization. One of the earliest usages of the word was at Wilberforce University. In the 1920 yearbook the chapters often listed fraternity brothers who were faculty members. They were called either "Fratres In Facultate," or "Frates In Facultate."[26] The actual word frat was later used in 1928 at Howard University. The word "frater" was also used at this time, and must be considered the word from which frat derived. The Latin word *frater* in essence means brother and thus has been applied to the Black fraternal experience.

An explanation of fraternity life using the word frat appeared later in a 1939 Tennessee State yearbook. John Wilson, at that time a member of the Lampados Club of Omega Psi Phi on the campus, wrote, "A man loves each separate member of his club or 'frat,' as an individual; he is loyal to his club or 'frat' as a social unit, and to each member of it because [of] his membership in it."[27] Since this time, the word frat has become a unique aspect of the Black Greek culture. Not only do members refer to each other using the term, but also nonmembers often ask about another's fraternity brother using the term (i.e., "Where is your frat, Brent?"). In addition, the term has been used to describe numerous members of the fraternity, or the fraternity as a whole. The whole organization is sometimes called "the frat."

While men have used the words "brother" and "frat" to describe members, they have primarily used the word brother when referring to each other or using it as a title (e.g., Brother King). Sororities have also used two terms, but slightly differently. As with predominantly White sororities, the word "sister" is used to describe members of the same sorority. As indicated earlier, this term has taken on a broader meaning since the Black Power movement, and all Black women are referred to as sister or sisters depending upon the setting.

Black sororities, almost from their inception, used the word "soror" to indicate women who share membership in the same organization. The word soror also is used as a title to introduce or greet a member of the same organization (e.g., "Hello, Soror Nobles"). This word is a shortened version of the word sorority, with Latin roots indicating sisters or sisterhood. As with the usage of "fratres" and "frates" at Wilberforce in 1920, the word "sorores" was used before the listing of members in the faculty. In the 1924 *Bison* yearbook of Howard University, the shortened word "soror" first appears in the Delta Sigma Theta section. In essence, the word originated roughly within the first decade of Black sororities on college campuses. The term evolved as did frat and now is the primary way the members of a sorority are identified. The plural form of the word, "sorors," is also prominently used as a part of the Black Greek experience.

An interesting quandary is the usage of the terms in Pan-Hellenic situations. At conferences of the National Pan-Hellenic Council, the umbrella body for the nine largest Black Greek–lettered organizations, an effort is made to show unity among the members of the various organizations. To that end, all of the fraternity men are referred to as "frater." Of course, this is a neutral term, as in a general sense none of the fraternities use this term as a title or greeting. However, all of the women are referred to as "soror." It is clear that there is some uneasiness in that the term soror evolved to be sorority specific. In the 1990s the title "Greek" has been used instead of frater or soror as a more neutral title or greeting.

Before the advent of line names, other types of nicknames were used to describe Black fraternities and sororities. Just as with White organizations, names have been shortened to quickly identify groups. As Beta Theta Pi members are known as Betas, and Delta Delta Delta members are known as Tri-Delts, members of Iota Phi Theta are known as Iotas and members of Zeta Phi Beta are known as Zetas. This practice is rather old. As early as 1935 at Wilberforce, the yearbook headings used nicknames (the Alphas, the Kappas) instead of the entire name of the organization.

Two more specific nicknames evolved as well. Members of the Omega Psi Phi Fraternity are also known as the Ques, and the organization, Que Psi Phi. It isn't clear at this point when the term originated. One of the earliest usages of the term appeared in the 1951 Howard yearbook. The pictures of the various pledge lines were captioned, and the Omega line was termed the "Que Pro line."[28] On the Omega Psi Phi page of the 1957 *Tuskeana* yearbook of Tuskegee University, the words of a song entitled "Ring Those Bells" also used the term:

> Oh, ring those bells, on 'Skegee's campus
> Let them peal out loud and strong.
> Shine down Que's, now all together,
> Que's have brought the best men home.[29]

At Tuskegee, the chapter was not organized until 1948, so the phrase became in use within ten years on that campus. The term began appearing on other campuses after this time: Alabama State, 1966; Tennessee State, 1967; Mississippi Valley State, 1970; Jackson State, 1972. Alternately, the phrase "Que Psi Phi" appeared around the same time: Alabama A&M, 1970, and Mississippi Valley State, 1973.

The other prominent nickname is Nupe, a reference to a member of Kappa Alpha Psi Fraternity. The fraternity is unique in that it has two names, Kappa Alpha Psi and Phi Nu Pi. In fact, Kappa Alpha Psi was founded as Kappa Alpha Nu at Indiana University in 1911, but changed several years later. In any event, the meanings of the terms are obviously ritualistic, known only by members of the fraternity. The term Nupe, however, appears to be derived from the name Phi Nu Pi.

The earliest usage of Phi Nu Pi in print appears in the 1920 Howard yearbook on the Kappa Alpha Psi page. But it would be years later before the word Nupe would become the unofficial nickname of fraternity members.

In fact, through this study, the word did not appear until 1977 at Mississippi Valley State. It was also seen at Tennessee State in 1980. This term's usage appears to coincide with the development of line names for organizations and is more of an unofficial nickname than the more standardized usage of the word Que.

As each organization experimented with different terms to uniquely describe their groups, in addition to the formal name of the organization, there were several ways that the collective Black fraternal community on college campuses described themselves as an umbrella organization. While efforts to form a united Pan-Hellenic Council commenced in the mid-1920s, culminating with the formation of the National Pan-Hellenic Council in 1930, college chapters used a variety of names to describe the umbrella organization on their campuses.

From the onset there was no consensus about what name would be used to describe the Black Greek–lettered organizations. While the National Pan-Hellenic Council was officially formed in 1930 in Washington, DC, the students at Howard University in 1931 called their umbrella organization the Inter-Fraternity Council. And within the next few decades there were several iterations of the name for the umbrella body on that campus, along with different versions of its organization. In 1945 the *Bison* yearbook indicated

> The Panhellenic Council organized January 1945 under the leadership of Ernest Oppman, a non-Greek, whose primary purpose was to unite the Greek letter fraternities and sororities into one cooperative body dedicated to benefiting the campus as a whole. The whole aim of the Council is to promote the Greek-letter ideals of scholarship and character, and to develop these ideals through concerted effort, friendly rivalry, and a full-orbed recognition of the over-all, fundamental purposes to which each of the organizations is individually committed.[30]

Within four years the name of the organization had been changed to the Greek Council. The 1951 yearbook indicated, "The Greek Council was formed in the spring of 1949. Its purpose is to foster better relationships among the nine Greek letter organizations and to promote civic and cultural activities on the campus."[31]

This pattern was prevalent at many campuses. At Tuskegee, the Inter-fraternity Council existed as early as 1950, and by 1966 it was called the Pan Hellenic Council. In 1957 at Tennessee State, the umbrella organization was called the Inter-Fraternity Council, and by 1964 it was termed the Pan Hellenic Council. Wilberforce was one of the few campuses to use the term Pan-Hellenic Council as early as 1947, and at Jackson State, the Pan-Hellenic Council was formed in 1950.

While the use of the term Pan-Hellenic Council, or simply Pan, became in vogue on Black college campuses by the 1960s, the formation of umbrella organizations on predominantly White campuses experiencing rapid growth added new terms to the Black Greek lexicon. As Black Greek–lettered organizations established chapters on predominantly White campuses, their umbrella councils sought names to differ from the Interfraternity Councils (IFCs) that represented the predominantly White fraternities, and the Panhellenic Councils (known simply as Panhellenic) that represented the predominantly White sororities.

The resulting names reflected the heritage of the members, and included Black Greek Council, Black Greek Committee, Pan Greek Council, Black Greek Association, and even Multicultural Greek Council (a term used especially in places where Latin fraternities and sororities, as well as other culturally based groups, fit best in this type of council versus an IFC or Panhellenic). While efforts were made in the 1990s for local councils to affiliate with the National Pan-Hellenic Council, even into the twenty-first century some of these terms are still used to describe Black fraternal councils.

In addition to the terms used in the Black fraternal experience, there are also several artifacts that serve as organizational monikers. These various objects have provided a sense of identity for Black fraternities and sororities. While some are similar to those used by predominantly White fraternities and sororities, these monikers are also an example of the creativity that is an essential element of Black fraternal life.

Fraternities and sororities all use pins that are generally worn in formal situations, and are usually formed by the letters of the organization. In the Black Greek experience, pins were involved from the inception, and even before the inception. Before students at Cornell officially formed Alpha Phi Alpha Fraternity in December 1906, one month prior to the vote to form the fraternity a committee was appointed to design the pin of the organization.[32] Not only were pins created for members, but also for persons who were pledging the various organizations.

In addition to the pins, during the late 1960s, as pledging evolved, pledges wore lavalieres that represented their various organizations. The lavalieres, also called blocks, were generally wooden objects normally cut into a specific shape and worn by the pledges at all times during the process. The wooden object may have been cut in the shape of a pyramid, an ivy, a scroll, or a crescent, and corresponded to the appropriate organization. In some cases it would be painted or decorated and include the number of the person in line. The lavaliere was generally strung using a leather strap or small rope and in most cases worn beneath the clothing. But, depending upon the campus, lavs may be worn for all to see.

In some cases the lavaliere (known simply as a lav in some parts of the country) was an object to be protected at all times by the pledge. Losing the lavaliere, either through carelessness or a physical challenge of a member, technically meant the person was no longer pledging the organization. Therefore the lavaliere was an important development in the culture of pledging.

The first lavalieres were seen at Howard in 1964. Lavs were also seen at Central State and Coppin State in 1968, Tennessee State in 1969, and Wilberforce in 1972. One of the most interesting lavalieres was found at Wilberforce in 1973. The Alpha Phi Alpha chapter had an interest group, students who declared interest in the organization but were not currently pledging. The group was known as the AMOT (Alpha Men of Tomorrow) Club. In a picture for the yearbook, the AMOTs wore lavalieres in the shape of a fist, similar to the Afro picks of that time, with the word AMOT written on the wrist of the fist.

From a cultural viewpoint the lavaliere has similarities to some African customs. The Ndele of Southern Africa wear charms from time to time. The charm is called a *dambo*. The word *dambo* means dance. The purpose of the *dambo* is to keep the wearer in touch with ancestors. It is also meant to be private, not to be seen by everyone.[33] The lavalieres worn by pledges from the late 1960s until 1990 symbolically linked pledges to those who had pledged the organization before them, just as the Ndele who use the *dambo* in a similar manner.

A few larger symbols of Black fraternalism have been used by organizations over the years. One of the earliest was the banner. In the mid-1920s, Black fraternal organizations designed and developed simple banners that bore the Greek-lettered name of the organization. This practice expanded in the next decade as the pledge classes in the 1930s were pictured with banners that held the name of the club. At Wilberforce in the mid-1930s, each pledge class was pictured in the 1936 *Forcean* yearbook with a banner bearing its name (e.g., Archonian, Scrollers, or Pyramid).

Around the same time, members created penlights to represent the organizations. A penlight is a wooden structure cut in the shape of either the letters of the organization or some representative symbol. It usually contains light bulbs, as the penlight is constructed so it may be plugged in and illuminated. Penlights historically have been used for formal chapter programs and events as visual representations of the organization.

The first penlights appeared in the 1920s. At Wiley College in Texas, the 1925 yearbook, the *Wild Cat,* pictured the Phi Beta Sigma chapter with a penlight in front of a chapter house. The penlight was a wooden structure with the Greek letters $\Phi B\Sigma$, the Phi on top of the Beta and Sigma. Six light bulbs were attached to the center of the Phi, with three additional light

Alpha penlight and paddles, 1977 (Courtesy Wilberforce University Archives)

bulbs on each side of the letter as well for a total of twelve. A cord stretched from the primary structure to a small wooden Greek letter Beta that had six light bulbs affixed to it. The Beta indicated that the Wiley chapter was the second for Phi Beta Sigma, or its Beta chapter.

The largest of the symbols of Black fraternalism on college campuses is known as the plot. A plot is a structure that symbolically represents the organization, and appears in various forms. The most prevalent is a structure built with bricks and concrete to form some form of object that represents the organization. For instance, an Alpha Kappa Alpha plot might be in the shape of a large ivy, or an Omega Psi Phi plot might be constructed in the form of a large Greek letter Omega. A great number of plots are formed either in the shape of the letters or some symbol linked to that organization.

But other forms of plots currently exist. Some are represented through an area on campus where the trees and sidewalks are painted in the colors of the organization, with the letters of the organization. These areas may be repainted annually, usually around homecoming festivities. Several trees at Alcorn State University in Mississippi take on this appearance.[34] Another form of plot consists of a professionally done granite plaque that lists the name of the organization, the national and local founding dates, and the date it was erected. At the writing of this book, this type of plot existed at Tuskegee University as well as at Howard University for Alpha Kappa Alpha. A third form consists of benches and garbage cans painted in the organization's colors with the letters.

There is no clear explanation as to why or when plots became artifacts of Black fraternities and sororities. These structures are unique in that they overwhelmingly appear only on historically Black college campuses. Very few predominantly White institutions have Black Greek plots. This may be due to the fact that these chapters only appeared on the campuses for the most part in the late 1960s and into the 1970s.

From available evidence, the earliest plot-type structure is the Omega sundial erected at Howard University in 1929. The monument was constructed after the death of Col. Charles Young, the second honorary member of the fraternity, who died in 1922 in Liberia.[35] But this initial monument bears little resemblance to most plots on college campuses today, and probably could more appropriately be labeled as a precursor to a plot. In function it is a plot, as Omegas at Howard gather every Friday at noon around the monument.

A more modern form of plot appeared in 1954 at Alabama State University. This Kappa Alpha Psi plot lay flush in the ground in the shape of a diamond, a major symbol for the fraternity. Yet with this early form of plot, it would be another twenty years before plots became a regular fixture on Black college campuses. Students in the mid-1970s began constructing plots at Alabama A&M, Howard, and Albany State. At this point in time, however, there is no clear evidence as to when plots became uniform parts of the Black Greek culture.

There is, though, a clearer cultural rationale for the establishment of plots. The Moletji tribes of southern Africa create shrines dedicated to their ancestors. These shrines are made of clay and a part of the courtyard floor. They are used as a place where members of a family make regular, spiritual contact with their ancestors and are sometimes joined there by their neighboring kinsmen and friends.[36] In contemporary times the plot is a Black Greek version of a Moletji shrine. For campuses with plots, especially historically Black colleges, the plot plays a central role in the culture of Black fraternities and sororities as a meeting location. This is very evident during homecoming activities as alumni meet at the plot to get reacquainted or meet current chapter members. This spirit of gathering many times evolved into impromptu step shows at the plot as well.

BRANDS

One of the most controversial outward expressions of Greekdom is the brand. From a cultural viewpoint the brand is very much an African concept. An article in the *San Francisco Examiner* entitled "Brothers in Scars" described the folklore as a reason for the proliferation of branding.

> One story of the genesis of ritual scarification comes from Nigeria, where the king of the Yoruba people was said to have sent two slaves to his deceased mother's homeland to learn her name, as he had never known her in life. He believed that knowing her name would give him power to conquer neighboring lands. As it turned out, only one slave returned with the name. As punishment, he gave the other slave 122 lashes with a sharp razor. The king's wives found the scars that formed on the slave's body to be beautiful, and so the king scarred himself with the razor and advised all leaders to do the same as a sign of nobility.[37]

However, branding also has negative connotations. In a dissertation about branding, Sandra Posey indicated that most associate the word with animal husbandry. She writes, "Others associate it with neo-tribalists, a loosely connected marginalized group of individuals that attempts to adopt the alleged ideals of tribal societies and uses scarification as a rite of psychological transformation or public statement."[38] But branding was also associated with slavery as the means to denote ownership, and thus the strong negative stigma the practice has for many persons today.

Posey's study focused on the Omega Psi Phi Fraternity. This organization is associated with the practice of branding far more than any other fraternity or sorority. Despite the ubiquitous nature of branding with Omegas, members have no concrete understanding as to why or how the practice began. Posey indicated,

> During the interview process, a number of members indicated having knowledge of branding's origins, but explained that this was a topic that could only be shared among insiders. Others did not ascribe this level of confidentiality to the information. Perhaps because the national governing body does not officially recognize branding in its organization, there seems to be a lack of consensus surrounding what can and cannot be revealed. Some went to the extent of not wanting to talk about brands at all, let alone reveal anything about branding's history.[39]

And the varying stories told support the lack of consensus. One member indicated that he believed the founders all had brands. Another shared that Col. Charles Young, who was the second honorary member of the fraternity, originated the practice. In fact, several members linked branding to wartime America. One indicated that branding helped identify bodies of members who were killed, while another said that bodies were branded after the men were deceased. Others linked the practice to African tribal rites, while others claimed it was an extension of slavery. One member explained thusly,

> There has [*sic*] been accounts of certain slaves that would show off whip marks to say, you know, "I was a slave." I was a slave and I went through something. And that point of view came about when you had the field slaves and the house slaves. And the field slaves would show the marks of working in the cotton fields, the marks of working in the briar patch and say "Look what I went through. You didn't go through anything. I mean you were in the Big House. You didn't go through anything."[40]

Posey indicated that the member who provided the previous quote was attributed to a man initiated after 1990, and that the brand was a means of gaining respect. The man further indicated, "It's all about how hard did you pledge, you know, how long did it take you to be made, you know, what did you go through? And for an individual now not to have a brand, it's like you didn't go through anything. . . . But that's just my opinion."[41]

Much of the theorizing about the history of brands as recorded by Posey was offered by young members, men between the ages of twenty-seven and thirty-six. Yet, the more mature members of the organization provided an almost completely different account of why the practice began. One member, fifty-four, succinctly stated,

> History will not record who was first [Black fraternity to brand] but no, it's not an extension of tribal rite in Africa. Somebody got drunk one night and said, "Hey, let's put a brand on us." "I'm gonna get a tattoo." "Yeah." That's how those things start. Then after a while they develop a life of their own so I mean some guys . . . might want to intellectualize this is some grand design, carrying on my African ancestors. I ain't going for all of that bullshit.[42]

The national vice president of the fraternity at the time of the study, Adam McKee, indicated amusement at calling it a tradition when no fraternity history "speaks to or even alleges to branding as a procedure for the fraternity."[43] A third member, age sixty-eight, was confident that no branding took place between 1950 (when he was initiated) and 1970. He declared that members who brand "think that's the only way you can be a real Q which is asinine. . . . I just don't believe that you need to disfigure your body."[44]

It is clear that the history of branding is fuzzy at best. The artifacts of Black fraternal life do not clearly indicate when or where branding began. The earliest reference to the process was recorded in the Afro-American newspaper in Washington, DC. A 1935 article made mention of a fraternity that was notorious for branding its new members.[45] In a study of Black fraternal public rituals, Marcella McCoy interviewed several persons who had brands or claimed knowledge of its origins. One man indicated that when he was initiated into Omega Psi Phi in 1950, brands were given on the chest above the heart, so that they were visible only when the shirt was removed. This may explain limited knowledge of the practice, as well as limited branding, between 1935 and the 1950s.[46]

The practice appears to have gained some momentum during the 1950s but was still fairly isolated in its usage. By the late 1950s women were getting brands as well. In McCoy's research, her focus group's discussion of brands was affected by a 1958 initiate of Zeta Phi Beta Sorority who admitted she possessed a brand. McCoy wrote, "The other female in that interview group who pledged a different sorority at the same campus was shocked to learn that women were being branded and even more surprised to learn that her acquaintance 'subjected' herself to allowing someone to brand her."[47] The woman's explanation validated the thoughts of the senior members of Omega Psi Phi Fraternity about why branding began. She indicated that she was branded immediately after initiation because the older members told them "All true Zetas get branded! I guess I just thought it was a part of the program. I thought everybody got it. I didn't know."[48]

As with hand signs and calls, it appears that brands became increasingly popular during the late 1970s and exploded in the 1980s. Again, the pop culture phenomenon, Spike Lee's *School Daze,* exposed the existence of brands. One scene pictured one of the Gamma Rays, the sweethearts or little sisters of the fictional Gamma Phi Gamma Fraternity, licking the brand of a fraternity member in a sexual manner. By the late 1990s, newspapers noticed branding, and the practice was exposed to a wider audience. And these articles continued to provide confusion as to its origins. The justifying and intellectualizing of the practice of branding by undergraduates not only provides a sense of various realities, but symptoms of multiple cultures that exist within the organizations.

An article in the *San Francisco Examiner* in 1997 claimed that Black fraternities "began performing brandings in the early 1900s. Legend has it that these fraternities used the brands to distinguish brothers from imposters trying to spy on secret meetings."[49] In an interview with the *Detroit News*, Eric Silverman, a professor of anthropology at DePauw University, theorized that branding was "a way of taking the symbol of horrible oppression and turning it into something positive . . . It's the African-American male seizing command of his body and conveying the message to white America—'I'm taking command of my body. It's for me

Kappa brand, 1965 (Courtesy Wilberforce University Archives)

to do what I please, not for you. I'm inflicting pain on my body in a positive way.'"[50]

Women have emerged in the 1990s as active participants in branding. In an article for the Indiana University campus paper, a member of Zeta Phi Beta indicated she was branded her initiation night "as a permanent symbol of a very precious time period in my life."[51] She indicated that a hanger formed in the shape of a Z, after being heated on a stove for an entire night, was used to create the brand. A student at Old Dominion University, in an interview with the *Washington Post,* described her brand in the following manner.

> I always wanted to get a brand. In my case, other than the fact that I think some of them look nice, for me it's a certain rush that you get. . . . It kind of excited me in a sense. . . . A lot of people were like, "Are you crazy?" But once it healed, a lot of people told me it looked nice. I think the frats think it's sexy, especially where I got it [her right outer thigh]. It's not like it's on my arm and it's a big keloid. It's kind of ladylike in a sense.[52]

The story done by the *Post* caught the attention of a granddaughter of one of the founders of Delta Sigma Theta, herself a member of the sorority, as was the student interviewed. The article and picture touched off great debate within the organization regarding the appropriateness of branding

for sorority members. But the fact remained that the practice gained popularity with women by the end of the twentieth century.

STEPPING DEFINED

Not only did the Spike Lee movie *School Daze* provide commentary on
Black America—from the clashes between the college educated and the local
townies to the problems of color consciousness represented by the jigaboos and
the wannabees—the film provided a glimpse into Black fraternity and sorority
life. Lee's character in the movie, Half Pint, is the focal point for the mythical
fraternity Gamma Phi Gamma as he pledges along with other students, who
are collectively known as the Gammites. But in addition to the atrocities associated with pledging, the 1988 movie also provided a glimpse of an exciting
form of expression known within the Black Greek community as stepping.

As with most Black fraternal traditions and activities, there is a significant amount of variance in the understanding of what stepping is, where it
came from, and when it began as a part of the Black Greek experience. This
variation of understanding is evident in the news articles that have been written about stepping. For the most part, stepping and step shows were not even
written about until the late 1980s, after the movie *School Daze.* One of the
earliest articles ironically appeared in the *Wall Street Journal* in 1989. The
article described the practice as a "step dance" as well as stepping.

> Stepping draws from several music traditions—African drumming, minstrel
> shows, rap, church gospel—and has evolved into a uniquely American dance
> form. Its synchronized and syncopated moves date back to the 1940s, when
> lines of fraternity pledges marched in lockstep around campus in a rite of
> initiation. It had a boot-camp mentality to it, meant to strip pledges of their
> individuality and promote group unity.[53]

The article further explains that the "first true step dance" was a product
of the 1960s. The shows had a spiritual quality to them, according to the
author, and used call-and-response techniques similar to Negro spirituals as
well as elements of the civil rights movement. It evolved then in the 1980s
to become a more physical activity, including the use of both subtle and vulgar sexual references. By the time the article was written, it was noted that
the culture of stepping had broadened into television via the NBC comedy
A Different World as well as in an advertisement by McDonalds.[54]

In a story on stepping in the *Washington Post* in 1990, the reporter provided an intriguing description of stepping:

> Stepping is tap dancing without tap shoes, James Brown without the music of
> the JB's, Cab Calloway sans piano, a marching band without John Philip Sousa.

It is jazz, funk, rhythm and blues, and rap without instruments. Stepping is lean and mean. The music comes from the synchronized interplay of hands and feet, from chants and hollers. It is a way to make music using the body as instrument.[55]

Maurice Henderson, an expert interviewed for the *Wall Street Journal* article, also provided commentary about stepping in the article. He indicated that stepping began in the mid-1940s for men, but that women didn't step until the 1950s. Henderson indicated that stepping began "as a celebration, but it is subconsciously rooted in the African tradition of celebrating culture and heritage."[56] He further chronicled stepping through the 1980s, and indicated that it seeped into the culture of rap music as rappers began to incorporate stepping into their choreography.

Other experts lended differing accounts about stepping during the 1990s. Articles in the *Dallas Morning News* and the *Flint Journal* concurred that stepping began in the 1940s and 1950s, but that organized shows began in the 1970s.[57] In an article in the *Atlanta Journal-Constitution*, Frank Mercado-Valdes, creator of the STOMP national championship, indicated, "It was ultimately refined by the end of World War I. . . . Many people believed that the first steps were performed by former GIs who combined drilling with traditional West African dance."[58] And in the *Charlotte Observer*, Elizabeth Fine, author of the first book on stepping, *Soulstepping: African American Step Shows,* indicated that the practice may have begun as early as 1925, as Kappa Alpha Psi and Omega Psi Phi pledges were described as dancing to invisible music during Hell Week.[59]

The speculations about the roots of stepping invariably include discussions of African origins. Henderson's comments in the *Washington Post* included the theory that stepping "is based on African dance, especially West Africa."[60] Mercado-Valdes of STOMP added, "Its origins are associated with West African dancing."[61] But one of the prevalent theories is that it evolved from South Africa and the gumboot dance. In an article for the *Corpus Christi Caller-Times*, the following explanation was offered:

The gumboot dance—named for a rubber-like boot—was performed as a pastime for people working in South African gold and diamond mines during the late 1800's . . . the gumboot dance may have been incorporated with modern stepping in the 1970's as South African dancers were recruited to American dance companies such as the Alvin Ailey American Dance Theater and the Dance Theater of Harlem.[62]

Very few serious studies have examined the roots of stepping at this present time. But overall they support the notions that stepping does have African roots, whether they have been perpetuated today purposefully or through some type of cultural instinct. In a study of dance in the African-American tradition, Jacqui Malone in the book *Steppin' on the Blues* spends a chapter on the history and development of stepping. Malone provides an excellent description of stepping as it appears today.

> What we call stepping today grew out of song and dance rituals performed by Greek-letter chapters as a way of expressing loyalty toward their organizations. Over a period of approximately fifty years, this constantly changing dance form has evolved and absorbed many cultural influences, including military drilling, black social dances, African American children's games, cheerleading, vocal choreography, martial arts, the precision marching of historically black college bands, South African "gumboot" dancing, music videos, acrobatics, and American tap dancing. Like many other vernacular forms, stepping has the ability to assimilate almost anything in its evolutionary path and still retain its distinctive character.[63]

Malone further indicates that even though stepping uses western and central African dance styles, to say that it came from Africa is somewhat misleading. She points out that, "It would be more accurate to view stepping as a uniquely African American dance genre that was created in the United States."[64]

Through her research, Malone found some direct links to African customs and dance rituals. Some step routines include the crossing of hands above and below the thighs, most often by clapping. This is an aspect of play among girls in the Kongo. The term *nsunsa* indicates games and play that are done using hands and feet in the Kongo. In addition, the body used as a drum is fundamental in the Kongo and a part of their activities.[65]

Another aspect of stepping is the use of canes. Some organizations, particularly Kappa Alpha Psi Fraternity, have become proficient using canes as a part of routines in which they are spun and even tossed while keeping a beat or series of interconnected beats. This too is a part of many African cultures and may be witnessed in Zaire, Sudan, South Africa, Zambia, and Mozambique. Malone indicated, "Among such nomadic groups as the Mbuti, who have no drums, sticks and other implements are carried for musical purposes and used in conjunction with rhythmic stamping, hand clapping, complex body movements, and vocal techniques."[66] Conway further posited that with the Mandkinka, the initiates carried ritual sticks and wore masks during ritual dances as a means to invoke the spirits to bring fertility to the participants.[67]

Stepping owes a great deal to African culture, but as Malone asserts, it has become a uniquely American form as it has incorporated numerous elements of American and African-American music and dance. As described earlier, slavery added a culture to America that is perpetuated not only in music but also in step shows. Within the culture of the Black church, spirituals continue to be an important historical art form. They are known by several varieties, including the call and response, the syncopated and segmented melodies, and the slow and sustained long phrases. Of these, the call and response is probably the most prevalent form appearing in stepping today.

Beyond slavery, numerous art forms and cultural aspects of African-American life have impacted stepping as speculated earlier. A 1991 article in the *Drama Review* provided additional insights into stepping. The author, who described herself as a White folklorist, offered a definition of stepping that supports the notion of the eclectic nature of stepping.

> Stepping, or blocking, is a dynamic and popular performance tradition among African-American fraternities and sororities. . . . This complex performance event and ritual involves various combinations of dancing, singing, chanting, and speaking, and draws on African-American folk traditions and communication patterns as well as material from popular culture, such as advertising jingles, television theme songs, and top-40 hits.[68]

Fine's study focused on step shows at Virginia Tech in Blacksburg, Virginia, from 1984 through 1989. Her definition also introduced the term blocking, which, as she defines, refers to the block or yard where the fraternity and sorority members socialized as well as stepped. Additional evidence suggests the term was used in the state of Virginia at several schools, including Norfolk State University and Old Dominion University.

Fine's study analyzed the more contemporary aspects of stepping as they relate to African-American folk traditions and customs. She indicates that the shows include "call-response, rapping, the dozens, signifying, marking, spirituals, handclap games, and military jodies."[69] She also indicates that organizations develop "trade steps" (also known as signature steps) that add to the organization's identity. Examples include the "Serious Matter" step of Alpha Kappa Alpha and the "Grand-daddy" step of Alpha Phi Alpha. In referring to stepping as folklore, Fine explains that the routines are transmitted orally primarily, although in recent years videotape has become an effective tool. The practice of road tripping, or of visiting other chapters, was also indicated as a means of exchanging steps as well as attendance at fraternity or sorority conventions.

Fine as well as Malone discussed the verbal jousting that is a significant part of step shows and stepping. Fine explains,

> Stepping is a form of ritual communications that employs at least three distinct types of acts: cracking or cutting, freaking, and saluting. In the crack or cut, one group makes fun of another group, either verbally, nonverbally, or both. "Freaking" refers to a member who breaks the norm of synchronization and unity, in an attempt to get greater audience response. . . . Saluting is a ritualized greeting in which a fraternity or sorority greets another Greek organization by imitating the steps, style, or symbols of that organization.[70]

She further explains that cracking is a modern form of the dozens and signifying, a method of indirect criticism through innuendo. It also represents
nonverbal parodies, also referred to as marking. Fine summarizes the use
of these techniques as a part of a social drama that is a part of Black Greek
life. Fine asserts, "To establish and maintain a unique Greek identity, each
fraternity and sorority must define itself with symbols and styles that distinguish it from any other group. . . . Stepping performances have become
a key venue for displaying and asserting group identity, as well as for nego-
tiating the status of each group within the social order."[71]

Malone also discusses the importance of "oral commentary and verbal
play" within the context of stepping. According to Malone, the language
used in stepping is not only functional but must be entertaining in order to
have an impact in the entire scheme of the show. In fact, she asserts that
while the actual movement and precision of stepping is key, the creative and
witty speech patterns as well as verbal play are critical elements in stepping.
This verbal aspect of stepping is also a reflection of African culture living
in African-Americans. In fact, the entire satirizing of different organizations
is a part of the West African country of Benin, where during a monthly dance
known as *avogan*, men and women from different parts of the city take turns
satirizing one another. Just as with step shows, the people in Benin who can
talk about their rivals the best gain the most prestige.[72]

Malone uses numerous terms to describe the verbal wordplay within the
context of stepping: woofing, playing the dozens, marking, sounding, signifying, jiving, cracking, rapping, and joning. But she notes that students
did not use these terms to describe the role of verbal insults within steps
shows, but rather used the single term "cracking," just as with Fine's analysis, and defined it as a way to "put down" a person or group, or to show disrespect for them, either in jest or seriously. Malone further explains,

> Usually fraternities crack on other frats, and sororities limit their cracks to
> rival female groups. In this practice we see a close link to the songs of allu-
> sion/dances of derision of African music and dance styles. By diminishing
> the status of their opponents through witty verbal surprises, sorority and fra-
> ternity members draw cheers from the audience. . . . Delivered with just the
> right amount of rhythmical punch, a successful crack can bring the house
> down.[73]

Both Fine and Malone use the phrase "the dozens" in reference to an
aspect of the verbal wordplay involved in step shows. The dozens can be
described as verbal duels used to trade insults. During the 1980s and 1990s,
modern forms of the dozens emerged through "your mamma" jokes that
became popular in Black high schools and even college campuses.[74] These
types of jokes were also known as "snaps" and the activity known as snap-

ping. Some sitcoms in the 1990s attempted to capitalize off of this African-American custom and added snaps as a part of some shows. In a dissertation, Marcella McCoy offers further definitions and gives the cultural origin of the practice.

> Sometimes the insults are exchanged as verse in songs accompanied by foot stomping and hand clapping. The focus was on genealogy and the point of it was total humiliation. Yet the loser was the one who, because his emotions took control or because his insults were too weak, took refuge in physical abuse. The winner was the one with the cruelest wit who managed to keep cool. The term "the dozens" itself refers to slave auctioneers selling "items" they felt were flawed in some way by the dozens. Every slave knew that he was included among a dozen only if something was physically wrong with him (age, illness, deformity, etc.). Thus, to be part of a dozen was humiliating.[75]

The snaps, especially "your mamma" jokes, are accurately described by this definition.

The Evolution of Stepping

Through all of the explanations about when stepping began and concerning the cultural influences on stepping, there is still no clear explanation as to when stepping began and how it evolved. The persons interviewed through newspapers relied on their personal memories and oral histories as to when the practice began. While the study of the history of pledging indicates that probates routinely began marching around campus as early as the late 1930s, and became ritualized during the 1940s and 1950s, stepping is more accurately described as a 1960s invention that has evolved into a complex form of expression in less than forty years.

There initially appears to be an activity that serves as the transition from the simple marching of the pledges or probates to the evolution of step shows. In 1953 at Central State, the term "death march" is used. The death march was a final activity of pledging, most invariably associated with fraternities, where probates spent literally hours marching as a final test of their worthiness. In many cases probates had to hold an object or objects, like a cinder block, and they may have had to recite poems or history while moving slowly, sometimes one step at a time every few minutes. The term death march also appeared at Jackson State in 1962 as the yearbook pictured Phi Beta Sigma Crescents holding some kind of torch along with their shield. Death marches evolved from the 1950s to the late 1980s and in actuality were nothing more than public displays of hazing.

While the term death march appeared in 1953 at Central State, another term appeared that has meaning in today's language of stepping. In 1958 at Central State, the yearbook used the caption "Alpha Walk." Pictured was a group of pledges engaged in a slow-moving progression across the campus. It probably was a version of the death march seen five years earlier (a practice most often attributed to Omega Psi Phi). However, the Alpha Walk evolved into a form of signature step employed by members of Alpha Phi Alpha Fraternity. By 1965 at Central State, the picture of what was captioned to be the Alpha Walk was much more lively, performed this time not by pledges but by brothers of the fraternity.

Based on the use of the death march and the Alpha Walk, it is reasonable to assert that pledging activities gave rise to public performances in the 1960s. On some campuses, on the last day of probation, each line was required to perform publicly.[76] In 1961 at Tuskegee, the lines of Greek organizations began public performances. A caption in the yearbook read, "The Twist was never like this."[77] Pictured was a group of Alpha Kappa Alpha Ivies, each dressed in dark skirts with fur jackets and wearing berets. Each was holding a paddle decorated with the letters AKA. They are pictured with their left leg stretched back while looking over their left shoulders. It is evident that these women were performing some type of choreographed movement or dance step.

This type of performance was also seen at Alabama A&M during this time. Students on that campus had a special week known as "Greek Week." In a yearbook article, the students indicated, "The third week of April is set aside as 'Greek Week.' All open probation and initiation activities are held at this time."[78] Corresponding photos showed various activities associated with probation, but some of the more interesting ones pictured probates dressed up in costumes. Omega Psi Phi Lampados wore turbans and held fake swords while Alpha Phi Alpha Sphinxmen were dressed as Egyptians.

The performances of the probates began to take on more sophistication in the mid-1960s. In 1965 at Alabama A&M the probates were seen performing inside some facility, apparently a gym, that provided a formal venue for activities. Yearbook captions around the time called these performances "Greek Talent." At Howard in 1965, students used the term "Greek Weekend" to describe programs where pledges presented skits and songs. Students at Alabama State coined the phrase "Greek Night" as a similar activity. In fact, Greek Night was a major activity for the Greeks, as indicated in the yearbook, "Activities of the social fraternities and sororities are coordinated through the Pan Hellenic Council. . . . Major activities for this year have been Greek Night, Rush Week, Probation and a Formal Convocation."[79]

After the initial movement to formalize performances through Greek Talent, Greek Night, and Greek Weekend, the word "show" was used to more accurately describe the activities of the probates, or pledges. It must be emphasized that at this point, these performances were almost exclusively done by those aspiring for membership. At Tennessee State in 1966, the term "Greek Show" was used, while at Central State in 1967 students used the term "probate show." A definition of the Greek Show was offered in 1968 on a page of the *Tennesseean* yearbook,

> A looked forward to event of social Greek letterdom initiation week is the annual Greek Show. This year's probates showed a world of talent in on-stage renditions in the styles of present-day rock artists.[80]

The corresponding photos show the probates singing and dancing, much like the styles of groups such as the Temptations or the Four Tops. One caption read, "Jere Johnson (temporarily crutched) solos while his Alpha Phi Alpha brothers back him up with harmony and dance."[81] Although the caption indicated that they were Alpha brothers, it meant as pledge brothers and not as initiated members of the fraternity, although the show was done just prior to initiation. Another indicated, "Alpha Kappa Alpha neophytes harmonize" while moving in unison. In all the pictures the probates are dressed alike in either costumes or in nice outfits such as tuxedos.

While the shows of the 1960s solidly reflected popular culture and showcased the talent of new members who sang and danced similar to the groups of that era, stepping evolved to include a more active and physical aspect of the performance. As indicated, in 1965 at Central State members of Alpha Phi Alpha performed an "Alpha Walk" that was an active movement that resembled what today is called stepping. Other activities solidified the emergence of a new aspect of Greek talent that became to be known as stepping.

One of the movements associated with stepping is called a "hop." In essence, a person hops using alternative legs to push off. Hopping today is most associated with Omega Psi Phi, probably because it is with this organization that the term is first seen. At Howard in 1969, Omegas are seen hopping on campus, but the term used was "bop." A yearbook caption explained, "Brothers demonstrate 'Omega Bop' for spectators on Fridays."[82] Malone further explained that this was part of Howard tradition established in the 1930s as members of organizations met on campus to sing and dance, and Omegas performed around the Omega Sundial.[83] The 1970 *Bison* caption clearly supported this notion—"Omega Bop is performed around dial on Fridays."[84]

At Tennessee State the word "hop" was used in 1969, also in reference to Omega Psi Phi. The yearbook captured a picture of what was called the "Que Hop," clearly an activity that would today be called stepping. In fact, the caption in the yearbook suggests that the activity had been around long enough to be associated specifically with the organization, reading, "Ques demonstrate their well-known Que hop."[85] The following year at Tennessee State, members of Phi Beta Sigma are shown stepping as well, under the caption, "Sigmas puts [*sic*] everything into their 'New Hop.'"[86]

Stepping continued this evolution in the 1970s, although there was clearly no consensus as to what the activity itself would be called, or what the large shows would be called. The actual words "stepping" and "step" are 1970s inventions. The term stepping appears in the 1970 Tennessee State yearbook. But the word does not catch on until the late 1970s and 1980s. The word stepping appears at Norfolk State in 1979, the word "step" in 1980 at Wilberforce, and the more relaxed "steppin'" in 1981 at Howard.

The Greek Show would evolve into an event performed only by members. This was the situation on the campus of Tennessee State in the early 1970s. Beginning in 1966 the phrase "Greek Show" indicated a performance by probates. But in 1971 the phrase "Presentation Day" emerged. Students defined Presentation Day as follows:

> Traditionally, Presentation Day is a day of performance by the Greek probates. It is usually the second Sunday in November. The Greek Social organizations present their lines to the public for the first time on this day, generally this performance is done in front of the Student Union.[87]

An interview conducted by McCoy revealed that on some campuses probates participated in two performances. In 1969, the line performed twice during the nine-week pledge program, once in the middle and once at the end.[88]

By the 1980s, students on this campus qualified the Greek Shows by calling them "Probate Greek Shows." Greek Shows were then the performances done by initiated members.

As indicated in the study by Fine, the term "blocking" also referred to stepping in Virginia. At Norfolk State University, the "Block Show" became an important part of activities during homecoming. In the 1979 yearbook, the show was explained:

> Block show competition has become a recent addition to the Homecoming activities. Various sororities and fraternities, along with the social groups, are given an opportunity to entertain the Spartan family as well as compete for a trophy recognizing them as the number one sorority or fraternity on campus.[89]

As indicated, Norfolk State shows included social groups such as Groove Phi Groove. The conversion of Greek shows from probate activities to competitions featuring initiated members is a product of the late 1970s. Malone noted that the first competitive Greek show at Howard took place during the 1976 homecoming week.[90] In addition, some schools, such as Morgan State, called the performances "Greek Sing" in 1980, although that term existed as early as 1969 at Coppin State in relation to the performances of probates. Coppin State students clarified that term by 1972 by calling it "Probate Sing" in order to emphasize the role probates played in the performance.

As mentioned by Fine, popular culture also has influenced stepping, and stepping in turn has influenced it. Beyond the appearance in the movie *School Daze,* stepping was prominent in the television comedy *A Different World*

Probate show activities, 1983 (Courtesy Central State University Archives)

through a fictional fraternity. The terms Greek Show and stepping became clear in the 1980s. Greek Shows evolved into major spectacles that filled large arenas. Events such as the Bayou Classic (a football game) sponsored Greek Shows that could draw thirty thousand spectators. Stepping had evolved from displays of singing and choreographed dancing to synchronized, syncopated, and soulfully synthesized hand and foot movements performed energetically.

More recent TV shows, including *Moesha* and *The Parkers* on UPN, have also explored Greek life and stepping. But the whole stepping style was given widespread exposure through the development of music videos. One of the earliest was a video by rapper Chubb Rock that featured members of the Omega Psi Phi Fraternity. Background dancers employed what they termed a stepping style, and in some cases, as with MC Hammer, many of the moves appeared to be influenced by stepping, if not stepping itself. While the probates of the 1960s sang the tunes of the day, the Greeks of the 1980s and 1990s stepped to the tunes. In fact, sometimes stepping of fraternities and sororities kept tunes alive. The song "Atomic Dog" by George Clinton of P-Funk fame has become the unofficial theme song for members of Omega Psi Phi. One nationally televised performance of the song by Clinton even featured Omega steppers.

Beginning in the late 1980s, stepping essentially became part of popular culture. Steppers began appearing in numerous television commercials. Independent producers developed annual step competitions to be broadcast on syndicated networks, such as the STOMP program. Even the 1996 Olympic Games, held in Atlanta, featured a segment during the opening ceremony that included a team of steppers. More and more segments of the broader American public, not just Black Americans, have been exposed to stepping.

But one of the developments in the 1990s was that more and more people outside of Black fraternities and sororities were also stepping. On Black college campuses, there had been more of a tradition of either non-Greek step shows, which might include auxiliary groups such as sweethearts or the Alpha Phi Omega Fraternity. There may have also been step shows where freshman residence halls competed against one another. But unique groups also began to participate in the process. On predominantly White campuses there have been instances where Black Greeks taught their White counterparts how to step. In many instances this was seen as a way to build bridges in a diverse Greek community.

But stepping has become a part of high schools and churches. Some high schools have functioning step teams that perform for various events or even compete against other schools. In a Corpus Christi newspaper, the Miller High School step team was described as formed by a teacher who did not have any direct experience stepping. But the group, formed in 1999, was started "to encourage students and keep them involved in school activities."[91] The school team won a competition that included fifteen other teams, with a possible prize being to step as a part of the Macy's Thanksgiving Day parade.

The same is true for churches. This has become an activity in the 1990s that involves youth, who provide a spiritual message being backed by the contemporary gospel music of the day. Indeed, the music of artists such as Kirk Franklin, whose hit "Stomp" used R&B and funk samples, have facilitated the stepping of church groups. Church step groups now can be seen performing before major gospel concerts.[92]

6

The Future of Black Greek Life

THROUGHOUT THE PREVIOUS FIVE CHAPTERS I'VE ATTEMPTED TO PROVIDE information that should serve as a foundation for a thorough understanding of Black fraternalism in America. Since the history of Black Greek–lettered organizations has been incomplete in the past, one objective was to provide a more complete history, one that includes the introduction of a previously unknown Black fraternal organization, Gamma Phi Fraternity, which should rightfully be considered the first collegiate, Black fraternal organization. After providing this historical foundation, I sought to explain how pledging evolved, since so many persons maintain various myths about the development of this process and its role in Black Greek organizations.

After the decision was made in 1990 to end pledging, Black Greek–lettered organizations experienced new pains as pledging evolved into an underground form. I attempted to explain how a martyred pledge process has produced numerous injuries and even one death, although undergraduates, confirmed through a research study, yearn for a sanctioned pledge process. I attempted to expand the realm of thought when one thinks of Black fraternal organizations, and sought to expose the reader to over seventy organizations that are fraternal in nature. I especially sought to enlighten readers about African fraternalists and African fraternities, as these two movements in Black fraternalism represent a new consciousness within Black college life.

Finally, I wanted to give some meaning to the rituals and traditions of Black fraternities and sororities. Black Greek–lettered organizations have developed a rich student-based culture. While current members habitually yell their calls and "throw up" their hand signs, virtually none of them know why they do these things, or even when the practices began. These chapters hopefully gave readers a solid understanding of these traditions, although there is still additional research that must be done in order to more closely pinpoint some of the practices, including why Black Greeks started building plots.

But this is history. These events, traditions, and practices are occurring or have occurred. And Black fraternal organizations continue to exist, although perilously, into the twenty-first century. The question becomes, after almost one hundred years of existence on college campuses, what is in store for these organizations over the next hundred years? Have all of the issues of the first century of existence been resolved, and if not, how can they be resolved? Are there issues or challenges that are just beginning to emerge that will play an integral role in the success of these organizations in the future? And are there unseen issues that might emerge in the next century that Black fraternal organizations must address in order to survive?

This chapter will attempt to address the challenges of Black fraternal organizations in the next century. Some of the issues presented are those that remain unresolved today. The two major persistent issues include resolving the issue of pledging and membership intake, and the future of undergraduate chapters. In terms of challenges not fully addressed, the first is one that is latent within the Black community, and an unspoken taboo within Black fraternal organizations—the issue of gay and lesbian members. Finally, I will attempt to gauge the impact of a fraternal development that, while not directly related to Black Greek–lettered organizations, has been influenced by their existence. This development is the establishment and rapid growth of Latin fraternities and sororities. These four issues are major challenges for Black fraternalism in the next century.[1]

To Pledge or Not to Pledge

The 1990 decision to formally end pledging has affected Black Greek life, particularly the nine NPHC organizations, in a manner that could have been predicted but was ignored by national officers. In essence, the national organizations sought to change culture through legislation. The rationale at the time was that by ending pledging, Black Greek organizations could avoid potential lawsuits caused by hazing. In reality, the legislation *did* change the culture. The culture of pledging, developed over a period of approximately seventy years, moved from a sanctioned, aboveground process to a semisecretive, underground process that cannot be closely supervised by fraternity/sorority officers and advisers or university administrators.[1]

This mutated process, known as membership intake, has been a complete failure. Much of the failure is due to the refusal of national officials to closely listen to the undergraduate members who have, since the 1992 study by John Williams, consistently sought a process to formally select and educate new members. They have endorsed through their underground culture a rites-of-passage process in order to be a fully respected member in the organization.

It is important, before discussing the alternatives to the present membership intake process, to fully understand the culture of membership intake and the undergraduate impressions of the process. As a part of my 1999 survey that followed up on the work of Williams, I allowed undergraduates to discuss their feelings about membership intake through an open-ended question. Through these responses, several clear themes emerged that provided an insight into undergraduate thought at the end of the twentieth century.

The first theme was that the new system weakens and does not promote fraternal bonds. Today's undergraduates seek close relationships through their fraternal organizations, and even though none of them have experienced a true pledge process, their belief is that by pledging, one develops deep bonds of brotherhood and sisterhood. The sharing of common experiences, through trials and tribulations, are viewed as the only means by which bonding can occur.

This desire for close and meaningful relationships is symptomatic of today's college students. Levine and Cureton indicated that today's students come from blended families, and look in many places to form close relationships. They noted,

> For these students, there were frequently no roots, no sense of place, and no strong relationships. They yearned deeply for all of these things but feared they would never have them. The bottom line is that students are coming to college overwhelmed and more damaged than those of previous years.[2]

This need of today's students seems to explain the determination of undergraduates to conduct and endure an unsanctioned pledge process in order to gain a sense of belonging. From another developmental point of view, some can look at the willingness to participate in this process as a way for students to gain a sense of competence.[3]

Undergraduates participating in the study echoed the importance of forming bonds. One responded,

> "Although I strongly disagree with any physical, mental, or emotional abuse involved in hazing, I believe that the current membership intake process needs to be revised in order to create a stronger bond between new initiates and in order to make members feel as if they have worked hard for their letters."

> • Senior female, '98, didn't pledge, East (year in school, gender, year initiated, and school location)

Another, commenting on the challenges of pledging and how they lead to bonding wrote,

> "Under the no-pledge policy it doesn't allow for the bonding (strong bond) of brotherhood & sisterhood because people are not put in positions to sacrifice for one another to create a bond that can't be broken."

> • Junior female, spring '98, pledged, North Central

There is an undeniable feeling among present undergraduates that pledging is a necessary ingredient for strong bonds with fraternities and sororities.

The second major theme through the responses was that undergraduates felt the new process would make new members less knowledgeable about the history and traditions of the organizations. One student responded,

> "I went through the no-pledge member intake process and was very disappointed. I felt that I didn't learn any sorority traditions. . . . There is nothing that I learned that I couldn't have read out of the history book. I felt cheated after my process was over."

• Senior female, '98, didn't pledge, West

The pledge process historically was a time not only for pledges to prove their worth to the organization but to learn the history of the organization. Through the duration of the pledge process, anywhere from six to sixteen weeks, pledges were required to learn both national and chapter history.

However, there never has been an effective means to measure how much pledges learned while pledging. In fact, most of the learning done was under great duress, as pledges answered questions regarding history in an effort to avoid punishment by big brothers or sisters. This rote memorization was short-term, and many members did not recall basic history once they were off line. Basic history was watered down to simple facts, such as the date of founding, and the names of all the founders. Yet, pledging is still viewed as the best means by which to teach new members the history of the various organizations.

The third major theme was the honest admission that membership intake did not end pledging, but rather, forced it underground. In the study, over half of the population, although all were initiated after 1990 when pledging was banned, insisted that they had participated in a pledge program. The following statements confirmed this fact:

> "The no-pledge policy hasn't really changed the amount of hazing that occurs; it only changes the penalties for being caught."

• Senior female, '98, pledged, South

> "My impression is that most Black Greek fraternities & sororities (nationwide) still pledge despite the no-pledge policy."

• Senior female, '99, didn't pledge, West

> "The greatest effect of the no-pledge policy was to force people 'underground.' Now pledging is kept quiet (in most cases), but it still occurs."

• Senior female, '97, didn't pledge, North Central

Most officers within the organizations have struggled to understand why today's undergraduates have chosen to perpetuate pledging. The single most offered reason for the persistence of pledging is the need to gain respect from peers.[4] The completion of pledging is seen by undergraduates as the necessary step in order to be considered full and complete members of the Greek community. A student succinctly summed up the reason why pledging still exists:

> "Everyone knows the non-pledging policy is not really in action! Every organization at every school pledges in some form or another. Some are just better at covering stuff up. If there is a non-pledging organization on your campus—everyone knows it and they don't get spoken to or even ignored or ridiculed at events. *Skaters* is what they're known as! Sometimes those that don't pledge at first will just to gain that respect from their fellow Greeks."

> • Senior female, spring '95, pledged, West

Several minor themes emerged from the study as well. Some students felt that the new process did not allow for the weeding out of aspirants. Pledging has been viewed historically not just as a vehicle to educate new members, but to siphon off those who attempted to join for the "wrong reasons," mainly, to wear the letters or participate in the social activities. This sentiment is expressed by the following comment:

> "The problem with intake is that you cannot truly weed out the slackers or people who truly are not devoted to your organization."

> • Senior female, spring '98, didn't pledge, East

However, there is no evidence that indicates pledging accomplished either goal—educate new members or weed out insincere aspirants.

Pledging was seen as an opportunity to then test the resolve of potential new members. One student indicated,

> "Coaches don't allow their players to just sign onto a team. They have to earn it. I do not believe in beating a pledge physically. I think challenging them mentally conditions and prepares them for membership in an organization that often asks them to give 110% all the time."

> • Senior male, spring '96, pledged, West

As this student explains, the culture of Black Greek life supports the core value of pledging as a means to prepare persons for lifelong membership.

Yet, there has never been any empirical evidence that indicates members remain active or that they "give 110% all the time" to their organizations. On the contrary, since the 1960s there has been a recognition that members do not maintain active status throughout their life. In a 1962 letter written by Alpha Phi Alpha founder Henry Arthur Callis, he indicated that the fraternity boasted of "25,000 Alpha's in the United States. Yet our active membership rarely exceeds 6,000 of which 2,000 or so are undergraduates."[5] The idea of lifelong membership is one that must be revisited by Black fraternal organizations.

The other minor issue revealed through the study was that membership intake was seen as causing a division between members initiated prior to 1990 and those initiated after that date. Theoretically, when the new member intake program was instituted, all vestiges of pledging should have ended. These would have included the numbering of new members, assigning of individual and collective line names, etc. However, to prohibit these traditions would have instantaneously created two classes of members, essentially highlighting the fact that those who had been initiated under membership intake were different from those initiated prior to 1990.

The traditions continued, more so due to the fact that newer members were participating in illegally sanctioned pledge programs. However, there was still the sense that the new program singled out new members. The following comments support this notion.

> "Older members often 'challenge' newer members on history that supposedly is not taught anymore. I have seen many tears and feelings of discomfort because of this."

> • Senior female, '96, pledged, West

> "The no-pledge process brings nothing but division among fraternity and sorority members both young and old. The old members say 'these young bro's or sorors don't know what the organization is all about . . . well then stop being lazy and teach us . . . we are asking for help. . . .'"

> • Senior male, '94, pledged, West

These students indicate that during the membership intake era, there are still older members who challenge or test newer members because they were initiated after 1990. They feel that they must "pledge" in order to be respected not only by their peers but by older members, often called "old heads," who may harass or disrespect them.

All of these themes, along with the empirical data presented in chapter 3, indicate that membership intake is the primary issue threatening the existence of Black fraternal organizations, particularly those affiliated with the

National Pan-Hellenic Council (NPHC). Even after twelve years of the new process, the vestiges of pledging remain active in an underground form on college campuses. The efforts to address the situation have primarily been through moratoriums, periods where initiating new members is prohibited, while national officials attempt to develop a new means to eradicate underground pledging.

The reason that membership intake failed was because it was a legislative action and not a cultural change. Pledging has to be accurately classified as a culture that in many regards has taken on a life of its own. Edward Hall, in the text *Beyond Culture*, describes the relationship of people with their extensions—their language, tools, institutions, etc. The problem with these extensions, according to Hall, is that they may develop a life of their own and can take over. This was the essence of the fear associated with Y2K, as our dependence on computers potentially created a way for our extensions (the computers) to completely halt normal functions.[6]

The same is the case with pledging. Pledging began evolving in the 1920s for Black Greeks. Over time these probationary periods developed into complex rituals that included pledges dressing alike, marching together in single file lines, and greeting or saluting members. Further evolution saw the pledges receiving numbers associated with their place in the line, an individual nickname (or line name), and a collective line name that gave the group of pledges a unique identity.

By the time we reached the 1980s, pledging had a life of its own. The culture, in this case pledging, was learned by each new line, and the importance of this ritual became subconscious and habitual for members. The policy change of 1990 only forced the extension to operate at a different level, but not end it. Interestingly, Hall described leaders in the West as victims of linear and compartmentalized thinking, incapable of evaluating situations comprehensively or weighing priorities for the common good.[7] The decision of 1990 epitomizes this fact, as the organizations tried to change one aspect of the culture, pledging, without changing any of the interrelated aspects—line names, line numbers, probate shows, etc.

There have been several ideas presented in order to address the issue of pledging and hazing in fraternities and sororities, especially for Black Greek–lettered organizations. In Hank Nuwer's *Wrongs of Passage,* the final chapter presents eighty-four strategies to combat hazing. The strategies are presented as suggestions in general, for universities, for fraternities, and for parents. They include adopting a zero-tolerance policy for hazing on campuses, publishing a fraternal rap-sheet, in essence, a record of violations by each organization, and try hazing cases in the courts rather than on campus. Nuwer also advocated for more research and the collection of hard data.[8]

As a part of his doctoral research, Williams offered several comments directly related to Black Greek membership intake. His suggestions included more training for undergraduate officers, with national organizations subsidizing costs, more communication between the organizations and universities, and funding for additional research. Williams also has promoted the investigation of creating a process that serves as a rite of passage that undergraduates have indicated they value, so much so that they will continue to carry out a process that may potentially destroy their organizations.[9]

With regard to membership intake, I offer several recommendations that should be seriously considered if Black Greek–lettered organizations are earnest about addressing the problems of hazing and pledging. Membership intake is the most serious issue facing these organizations, yet is the one that has been studied and discussed the least. The following three recommendations are at least a start in gaining a sense of control over the problems associated with membership intake. A second set of recommendations fall under the next major issue, chapter advising, but it should be noted here that both are needed in order to successfully address the problems of membership intake.

1. Intensify serious educational opportunities.

While the research presented in this book indicates that students are more knowledgeable of the rules regarding intake, their actions that perpetuate underground pledging indicates that a different type of education must occur within these organizations. Students are cognizant of the rules but have not been convinced to change the culture of their chapters despite the potential consequences. The students, in essence, despite having more knowledge of the rules, have chosen to directly defy them based on their own value systems.

The argument must be made that the organizations have done poor jobs in educating undergraduate members. Most state, regional, or national conferences of the major Black fraternal organizations contain a great deal of pomp and circumstance, politicking, and imaging events such as public programs. The same is true with the regional and national NPHC conferences, which are poorly attended. Very rarely do the organizations devise and offer educational sessions that will truly address the problems of the day, such as membership intake, and undertake a concerted effort to attempt to solve the problems.

One reason is that there are no clear answers to the issue of membership intake. The national organizations adopted the policy as a means to ensure long-term survival. Undergraduates have semisecretly continued the former process, which neutralizes the point of membership intake because the organizations continued to be sued and are vulnerable to a major lawsuit with the next death. Because membership intake is such an emotional issue, many times national and regional meetings are not the best forums to engage in the meaningful dialogue, processing, and brainstorming needed to work through all the related issues.

Therefore, new and creative educational efforts must be implemented by the various organizations. Ideally, through the National Pan-Hellenic Council, the umbrella body for the nine largest fraternal organizations, a working institute should be implemented in order to bring together national leaders, undergraduates, and student affairs professionals to honestly and openly dialogue about membership intake. Much of the issue is emotional, and time must be devoted to process the feelings. But thoughtful discussions and debates could lead to the creation of programs for educating new members.

But educational efforts should be much more comprehensive than discussions about membership intake. The educational program offerings at the various conventions are weak at best. National organizations, including the National Pan-Hellenic Council, must begin to invest in the undergraduate membership in order to better prepare them to operate their chapters and councils. Most often, there are few truly worthwhile programs available for undergraduate members.

Much of this is due to conferences planned by persons who do not work with undergraduates on a regular basis, who are not trained in student affairs, and who do not have any conception of the principles of student development. All national fraternal organizations have members who work in student affairs on college campuses, and these organizations must do a better job in utilizing members who have been trained to plan programs for undergraduates. These persons must be contracted to plan educational sessions at conferences.

This lack of responsiveness to undergraduate needs and the underutilization of members trained in student development theory led to the creation of the Black Greek Leadership Conference. Initiated in 1986, the conference is planned and implemented by student affairs administrators who are members of Black Greek–lettered organizations. The conference is devoid of politics, pomp and circumstance, and participants can attend numerous educational sessions, along with relevant keynote speakers, and social events. While less than thirty undergraduates generally attend a regional NPHC conference, up to five hundred students will attend a Black Greek Leadership Conference. This model should be replicated by each national organization, as well as the NPHC, so that students have several opportunities to attend leadership conferences.[10]

But a change in philosophy must occur for national organizations. Historically Black fraternal organizations, although espousing a lifelong commitment by members, have failed to put resources into their undergraduate members. This is in opposition to predominantly White fraternities and sororities that routinely sponsor undergraduate leadership academies in order to train their collegiate members. Some of these organizations sponsor weeklong institutes for up to two hundred undergraduate members that teach the principles of leadership, chapter management, etc. In most cases the undergraduates are responsible only for covering travel expenses.

Black fraternal organizations have been slow to adopt this concept, even though this type of approach would make sense in terms of training future leaders of the organizations. The first substantive such effort in Black fraternal organizations was made by Alpha Phi Alpha Fraternity in 1998. Dr. Ralph Johnson, a longtime student affairs administrator, pitched the idea for an undergraduate leadership academy, a weeklong program for college brothers to gain an intensive understanding of the fraternity and the associated issues.[11]

Collegians participated in sessions on student development theory, ethical development, service learning, and the meaning of the ritual. Their only cost was travel to Baltimore, site of the academy, chosen because the corporate headquarters is there and participants could visit the office to meet with officials. After four classes, ranging in size from seven to twenty-three participants, the program is viewed as a modest success. While it was hoped that more college brothers would have been able to participate, numerous alumni of the program have gone on to hold regional offices within the fraternity.

This program has to be just the start for all Black fraternal organizations. Dr. Johnson gave a presentation about the academy at a national student affairs conference in hopes of stimulating other organizations to begin similar programs, but at this time none have responded. Ideally, the National Pan-Hellenic Council would design and implement a similar program for undergraduates. Once again, the North American Interfraternity Conference (NIC) has sponsored the Undergraduate Interfraternity Institute (UIFI) for numerous years. While some Black Greeks have participated in this program and gained a great deal of understanding on universal Greek issues, a similar program focused on their issues could be beneficial to addressing not only hazing and membership intake, but unity within Black Greek–lettered organizations.

2. Impose *severe,* nationally driven sanctions for hazing.

Over the years there has been a great deal of inconsistency in terms of the penalties associated with hazing cases. Much of this is due to the difficulties associated with investigating and hearing hazing-related cases for college fraternities and sororities. In many instances university administrators as well as national officials often have great difficulty in clearly and accurately determining what happened in a hazing case.

Subsequently, a wide range of sanctions has been given to chapters and individuals due to hazing-related cases. In the past several decades the longest suspension of a chapter was the Alpha Rho Chapter of Alpha Phi Alpha Fraternity, located at Morehouse College. The chapter was closed in 1989 after the death of Joel Harris due to a hazing session. It would be a full decade before the fraternity reopened the chapter. This decision was the fraternity's, as the institution, pressured by alumni who wanted their sons to have the opportunity to join the Alpha Rho Chapter, was open to reactivating the chapter years earlier.

The "standard" sanction for a hazing case involving an injury appears to be between two and four years of closure. The 1999 hazing case at Norfolk State University involving Delta Sigma Theta Sorority resulted in a four-year suspension of the chapter, as the potential member was hospitalized in critical condition.[12] The philosophy behind four-year sanctions is that within this period of time, all students who were members of the chapter should have graduated, and therefore, the organization would have an opportunity to start a completely new chapter. Yet, with the average graduation time today for college students being six years from entrance to completion, plus the culture of Black fraternal organizations that includes chapter alumni visiting the present members, thus continuing to maintain influence on the activities, the effect of a four-year suspension is minimized greatly.

Therefore, the sanctions used must be sufficient enough to deter hazing. One of the first ways to do this is to completely turn over hazing cases to the court systems. As indicated, author Hank Nuwer suggests this course of action to prevent hazing. Nuwer writes,

> Educators make lousy law-enforcement officers and judges. Serious offenses that violate state law should not be tried by university judicial groups in place of state courts. . . . When illegal acts have been committed, law-enforcement authorities must take over and try the cases in state courts.[13]

Students would have to begin to seriously consider their actions if they have knowledge that hazing crimes will be handled by local police and courts, as many university students view campus police or public safety as inconsequential entities. Moving all hazing cases to the courts through local police would highlight the seriousness of these crimes for students.

In addition to using the courts, national organizations and universities should also make decisions based on the outcomes of the cases with regard to the future of the chapter. A new standard should be a minimum suspension of ten years for any hazing offense that is tried and proven to be a criminal charge. Since most hazing cases that come to light and are reported are those that result in injuries, the severity of penalties handed down by campus officials must be comparable. A ten-year closure of a chapter as a minimum sanction for a criminal hazing act would make a strong statement that hazing will not be tolerated. Presently, neither national organizations nor universities promote possible sanctions for criminal hazing that result in a minimum of a ten-year sanction for a chapter. This kind of penalty would at least get the attention of students in the organizations.

The next step is to promote sanctions of permanent charter revocation. There should be some actions that immediately cause the chapter to be closed forever, with the name of the chapter given to a newly formed chapter at a later date, or maintained historically as a permanent reminder that egregious hazing crimes will not be tolerated. If a chapter is convicted of a criminal hazing and closed for ten years, and then, once reactivated, is convicted again for a second criminal hazing, it should be permanently closed and the charter revoked. If a chapter culture of hazing cannot be changed after a ten-year closure, that chapter should be closed forever and the charter revoked. This type of action will most likely need to be executed by the university, as the political forces within an organization would probably push not to permanently close a chapter.

The other crime, which should garner an immediate charter revocation, is a hazing death. Since 1989 there have been three Black Greek hazing deaths. As mentioned, the Alpha Phi Alpha case caused the chapter to be closed for ten years. Southeast Missouri State University permanently closed the Kappa Alpha Psi Fraternity chapter there after the 1994 death of Michael Davis. It is noted that the Kappa Chapter at SEMO was closed for one year in 1988 for a hazing case where a pledge was beaten with a cane, a criminal hazing activity. Most recently, a student died at Tennessee State University in 2001 while pledging Omega Psi Phi. Although it is unlikely that undergraduates intentionally murder students through hazing activities, the death of a student through this kind of activity must not be tolerated by universities or national organizations. More than establishing a "zero tolerance" policy, specific sanctions must be communicated to fraternity and sorority members. By clearly stating that hazing deaths will cause chapters to permanently lose their charters, the message will be sent about the seriousness of hazing, a message that has not been sent in previous years.

The final element for sanctions must be the imposition of strong personal sanctions for those involved in major hazing cases. Members of Kappa Alpha Psi Fraternity at Southeast Missouri were expelled after the hazing death in 1994. More recently, nine members of Delta Sigma Theta were expelled in 1999 after hazing left a student in intensive care. Students involved in criminal hazing cases should face the most severe of sanctions that a university can offer, that being expulsion. If universities are to truly take a stand on hazing, they must intensify the level of sanctioning for hazing crimes.

Simultaneously, the courts should treat hazing cases as crimes that bear higher penalties. After hazing cases involving his fraternity at Kansas State University and the University of Maryland-Eastern Shore, syndicated columnist William Raspberry suggested that fraternity hazings should be treated as assaults.

> Somehow the message doesn't seem to get out that this sort of behavior is not to be tolerated—and not merely because it brings embarrassment to a justly proud fraternity. Maybe it's necessary for law enforcement officials to stop treating physical hazings as boys-will-be-boys misdemeanors and prosecute them as the assaults they are. Perhaps a little jail time might get the attention of some frat members who don't seem to hear more measured warnings.[14]

With today's students being oriented around issues of self, it appears that there must be actions targeted to their personal welfare in order to change the culture that supports hazing. In effect, the consequences must be raised to a level that makes it completely irrational for students to engage in hazing.

While hazing cases that have provided large settlements were targeted toward national organizations, several settlements included financial costs to individual students and their families. A future case that results in a substantial garnishment of future wages of students for hazing crimes would go a long way in changing the culture that promotes hazing. One litmus test for the ability to sue collegiate members will be the success of the Omega Psi Phi Fraternity, which in 2000 sued members of the University of Louisville chapter after the fraternity lost a settlement of nearly one million dollars for a 1997 hazing case. If the fraternity is able to win a decisive judgment against its own members, it will set a precedent for holding students financially accountable for violating fraternity or sorority policies if they continue unsanctioned and illegal hazing activities.

3. Create a well-defined, highly structured, and educational pledge program

The final recommendation is probably the most controversial and yet the most important in really addressing the culture of pledging. Based on the study by Williams in 1992 and my follow-up study in 1999, it is clear that undergraduate members still want some type of pledge program. While their contemporaries in predominantly White fraternities and sororities have reduced the length of time for pledge programs during the 1990s, they have maintained the practice of pledging. Notable within predominantly White fraternities, Zeta Beta Tau and Tau Kappa Epsilon moved to end pledging in 1989, but TKE abandoned the move and ZBT has had hazing abuses in the late 1990s. And while Lambda Chi Alpha instituted an associate member program in 1972 to technically replace pledging, the activities of the associate members are indistinguishable from those of pledges in many instances, including being hazed.

Indeed, pledging has been an issue with the entire Greek community. Since the moves made by Lambda Chi Alpha, Zeta Beta Tau, and Tau Kappa Epsilon, many Greek-lettered organizations have moved to reduce liability by shortening pledge programs. During the 1990s many organizations adopted four- to six-week pledge programs in an effort to curb hazing abuses. Additionally, several universities implemented mandatory pledge program limits, even by publicizing the dates by which all fraternity or sorority pledges would be initiated.

Yet the decision in 1990 by the largest Black fraternal organizations was to abandon pledging altogether. However, a well-structured pledge program should serve as a compromise between undergraduates who continue the practice under a veil of secrecy that threatens the life of the organizations, and national leaders who believe that the no-pledge program is prolonging if not completely saving the existence of the organizations.[15] The question becomes, how does this pledge program look?

I envision a pledge program that resembles in many cases a highly challenging university course that contains many experiential components. At the heart of the program would be a thorough history lesson of African and African-American history. Many current undergraduates still wish to know more about themselves and their history, and through pledging these needs could be met. The next component would be to teach the history of the organization that the aspirants were joining along with the history of other fraternal organizations, especially Black Greek–lettered organizations. Most of the history taught through intake programs is a cursory overview that provides only basic names, facts, and dates. Thorough history sessions could spur conversation and debate as aspirants seek not only to understand the founding of their organizations but the climate on their campuses for students of color, or for women, two groups challenged by higher education in the early 1900s.

A third component would be to provide aspirants with an understanding of the culture and traditions of Black Greek–lettered organizations. The aspirants would learn the African origins of the customs employed by Black Greeks and the history of these practices. These sessions would include passing on the oral traditions of the organizations. Some of this would be done through step practices, as a part of many step shows is the use of chants that employ traditional slogans and saying of the organizations. The step practices also would be a fun way to learn one of the most visible aspects of Black Greek life that must be considered a "perk" of membership.

The fourth component would be a complete exploration into leadership development and chapter management. Many experiential programs exist that provide leadership training for college students. These modules could be designed, modified, or created for members of a pledge class. Through these sessions, members would learn how to lead, their strengths as leaders, and how to work as a team. It is to be expected that chapter members would also fully participate in the team-building exercises, as undergraduates indicated through the research that bonding was an important aspect of pledging. By including chapter members, the bonding will occur across the chapter, not just by members of the "line" as they have historically worked together to fight off the challenges of big brothers or sisters.

Leadership development could include sessions on effective writing, speaking, and debate. As we continue in the Information Age, the need for more effective communication is paramount. My personal experiences with Greek members over the last ten years indicates that many write poorly, speak poorly, and cannot form decent arguments to support their ideas. Opportunities to write position papers, give speeches, and engage in debates would add critical thinking exercises that are needed for today's leaders. From my own pledging experience, I remember engaging in all of these activities while on line, and continuing active debates with members once I was initiated. These activities would provide opportunities to synthesize materials from the classroom in an out-of-class environment.

New members would also learn how to effectively operate the chapter. They would get experience planning programs from top to bottom, which would include how to schedule rooms using university facilities, how to arrange audio/visual equipment, contacting speakers, and so on. New members would also meet with university officials in an effort to form healthy relationships instead of perpetuating the "us versus them" mentality that many students, particularly Greeks, tend to maintain.

Finally, the pledge program would include opportunities for community service. However, there should be structured opportunities for reflection so that the service takes on more of a service-learning approach. Service-learning is a concept that is gaining popularity within higher education, as many courses seek to integrate the tenets of the practice within the curriculum. Structured volunteer experiences followed by facilitated discussions led by university staff or graduate members could add a significant dimension to the pledge experience, providing much more meaning than standard volunteer activities.

A program such as this would foreseeably take four to six weeks to implement. Throughout the week, one to two hours could be spent going though history sessions. Some of the history sessions could be offered in lecture format by members (both undergraduate and graduate) as well as university faculty, staff, or community members. A by-product of the pledge program should be to expose outside persons to the organization by helping to train its future members. Weekends would be used for step practices, experiential leadership development, team-building activities, and service-learning projects. In some instances, four-hour time blocks would be needed to complete service projects or to complete team-building programs (such as ropes courses).

Table 11 presents a model for a structure pledge experience. It by no means would be guaranteed to eliminate hazing. With a history of over six hundred years relative to higher education, hazing is a culture firmly rooted in campus life. However, the implementation of a pledge program could

TABLE 11

Sample Pledge Program

WEEK	Monday	Tuesday	Wednesday	Thursday	Friday	Saturday	Sunday
1	African history and culture	African history and culture	African history and culture	African history and culture	African history and culture	Team building Step practice	
2	African American history Critical essays	African American history Critical essays	African American history Critical essays	African American history Critical essays	African American history Critical essays	Team building Step practice	Discussion of essays
3	African American history Public speaking	African American history Public speaking	African American history Public speaking	African American history Public speaking	African American history Public speaking	Service learning Step practice	Oratorical contest
4	Fraternal history Debate	Fraternal history Debate	Black Greek history Debate	Black Greek history Debate	Black Greek history Debate	Service learning Step practice	Debate
5	Organization history Chapter management	Organization history Chapter management	Organization history Chapter management	Organization history Chapter management	Organization history Chapter management	Service learning Step practice	Chapter management
6	Organization history Plan/Produce campus event	Organization history Plan/Produce campus event	Organization history Plan/Produce campus event	Organization history Plan/Produce campus event	Organization history Final Exam	Initiation	

Notes: Step practices could be held several times a week based on schedule; each weekday would require one to two hours of work by aspirants, plus time for individual reading, preparation, and assignment.

possibly lessen the need for undergraduates to rebel and perpetuate underground pledging. In any event, the rebirth of pledging, which can still be called membership intake, is an experiment worth implementing in an effort to curb hazing.

Under Advisement

The second major issue affecting Black Greek–lettered organizations in the next century is redefining the role of advisers. The connection between undergraduate and graduate members evolved during the early years for Black Greek–lettered organizations. As early as 1911, Alpha Phi Alpha established a graduate chapter in Louisville, Kentucky, which ushered in an era of involvement by former undergraduates as well as men who gained membership through the graduate chapters.

Since formation of the initial graduate chapters, the major Black Greek–lettered organizations have worked to establish graduate chapters in numerous cities throughout the world. Most organizations today have at least three hundred graduate chapters. These chapters operate as do the undergraduate ones, which includes conducting nationally mandated programs as well as membership intake activities. For those who do not join the organizations through the undergraduate ranks, these functional graduate chapters provide them with a fraternity or sorority experience geared toward the older member.

As a part of the evolution of graduate chapters, they developed the role of advising the undergraduate chapters and members. While none of the house histories of the NPHC member organizations specifically address the advising relationship of graduate and undergraduate members, it is fair to speculate that as the organizations grew and developed, and as collegiates graduated and sought to help their respective chapters, they also served in an advisory capacity. The informal advice given to undergraduate chapters eventually evolved into formalized advising structures where local graduate chapters became sponsors of collegiate chapters.

As a part of the supervisory function assumed by graduate chapters, one member was deemed the chapter adviser. This sole person was to be the primary link between the undergraduate chapter, the graduate (sponsoring) chapter, and the national organization. The adviser would be expected to attend chapter meetings and functions and work with university officials as well as monitor all pledging activities. Many undergraduate functions required the signature of the adviser, either for university recognition or for paperwork associated with pledging. All in all the chapter adviser was responsible for a great deal of the successes, and failures, of an undergraduate chapter.

Yet, with the abuses associated with pledging as documented in chapters 2 and 3, the effectiveness of the adviser must be questioned and the role of the adviser redefined in this next century. Very few, if any, of the reports about Black Greek hazing indicated that the adviser was present when the abuses occurred. Conventional wisdom indicates that many of the hazing sessions (called "sets" in many instances) happened late at night at an off-campus location, probably after the adviser had gone to bed for the evening. It also appears that advisers have been missing as many Black Greek chapters post low chapter grades each term, often ranking at the bottom for all Greeks on predominantly White campuses. Other underadvised chapters conduct no campus programs or engage in community service.

If Black Greek–lettered organizations are to thrive on college campuses in the next century, a new paradigm must be employed with regard to advising. This new method for advising will require more of graduate chapters that sponsor collegiates, as well as national organizations. In addition, the umbrella organization for Black Greek–lettered organizations, the National Pan-Hellenic Council, must also play a more meaningful role in the advising and development of college chapters for all organizations.

The first action should be the creation of an advisory board. For years, one person has advised undergraduate chapters. In many cases the chapter adviser was a person in name and on paper only. This individual did not always attend chapter meetings or events and usually participated in pledging only by signing the required paperwork. In effect, undergraduate chapters functioned on their own, for better or for worse. This fact is even more pronounced for chapters that exist on campuses that may be one to two hours away from the nearest graduate chapter.

Black Greek–lettered organizations should develop advisory boards, in essence, small teams or committees in which one person has the overall responsibility as the lead chapter adviser and works closely with the chapter president to advise chapters. Others on the board would assist with all chapter functions, but also have specific areas in which they would provide guidance and expertise. For example, one adviser should work with chapter finances and serve as a mentor/personal adviser to the chapter treasurer. Another adviser would focus on programming and work with the chapter officer responsible for developing a plan for chapter activities, both on and off campus. This could include community service opportunities.

A final adviser should be responsible for membership activities. This would be a tremendous responsibility since membership intake is the area for greatest liability. The adviser would work with the chapter officer responsible for intake and would make sure that the process is implemented as outlined by the national organization. The adviser would also ensure that the chapter continues to provide ongoing membership education, which would include organization-sponsored activities as well as relevant conventions and institutes. The membership adviser should also work to monitor academic progress of undergraduates, providing support for those who struggle academically.

This model for an advisory board would require the commitment of four persons. One would continue to take the lead and serve as chair of the advisory board. The other three members would have specific areas to ensure chapter success. However, the board would provide flexibility for busy graduates so that all undergraduate events could be attended and membership intake more closely supervised. A stronger graduate presence could serve as a deterrent to hazing and other negative undergraduate chapter activities.

The suggestion to add more advisers must be accompanied by a word of caution. In some cases today, graduate chapters and advisers practically control collegiate activities. The vast majority of these cases involve sororities. Having worked in student affairs with Greek organizations, I have often held conversations with sorority women who lamented over advisers who told them what step shows they could participate in as well as who they must invite to join the organization. Quite frankly, many sorority advisers have been overzealous in their roles and have created animosity with their collegiate sorors. And even though some graduate advisers have been overbearing in recent years, they have not been able to prevent hazing abuses. The ultimate goal of an advisory board is to better assist undergraduates to operate their chapters within the rules of the organization, but provide enough room for their own successes and failures.

The next phases of advising should be led by the national organizations. After endorsing and mandating chapter advisory boards, national officials should assess which chapters actually need to create and maintain advisory boards. As indicated, some chapters exist in remote college towns where the nearest graduate chapter is over one hour away. National organizations should critically assess the viability of chapters that cannot establish such boards and strongly consider closing those chapters.

One of the features of the Black fraternal system, especially through the nine largest organizations, is that their popularity caused Black students on every campus to want chapters. As second generation Black college students started becoming more numerous in the 1980s, they had been exposed to graduate members as children. These members included their parents and relatives as well as teachers, coaches, and church members. Many formed opinions as to which organization they wanted to join, beliefs that they brought with them to college. The result was that, even on campuses with a small Black student population, students wanted particular organizations on that campus. On campuses with as few as three hundred Black students, it is conceivable that four or more Black Greek chapters exist.

Therefore, the NPHC organizations each have (with the exception of Iota Phi Theta), well over two hundred undergraduate chapters, and in some cases, more than three hundred. The number of chapters is significant when compared to predominantly White organizations, many of which have less than two hundred chapters. While Black students integrated White schools en masse during the 1970s, undergraduate chapters grew likewise in subsequent years. This uncontrolled growth of chapters, without improvements in individual chapter advising and national support, has created a crisis in advising. It is important that national organizations first assess all chapters, both undergraduate and graduate, as that is not a routine process. But for undergraduates, serious consideration should be given to closing chapters that cannot develop committed advisory boards. This is especially true where the nearest graduate chapter is several hours away.

The second phase for national organizations is to begin routine chapter assessments, both for graduate and undergraduate chapters. Each organization should develop a national staff position of director of evaluation and assessment, who would lead in this initiative. This director would be responsible for annually disseminating assessment instruments to chapters, compiling data that the national leadership can use in addressing the strengths, weaknesses, and needs of the respective chapters. The director would also begin tracking chapter performance through the required reports.

Using this data, organizations could develop a standard for progressive discipline for chapters based on the annual reports, thus recommending chapters to be closed due to lack of performance. The director would also be responsible for maintaining a record of hazing cases as a means to evaluate the effectiveness of membership intake activities. Critics have pointed out that no data exists from the national organizations that support the claims that membership intake is successful.[16] This approach could quantify the successes and provide leaders with hard data to make informed decisions.

The final initiative needed by national organizations is to hire and train field staff to service chapters. This model has been employed for years by most NIC and NPC organizations. Field consultants may visit chapters within regions generally once a year, providing assessments of the chapters and filing reports. They may also do some programming with the chapter, focusing on areas of weakness in an effort to improve the chapter. Field staff provide an outside assessment, from the national organization, of the chapter that can be used to improve chapter operations.

These field staff members can supplement the work of the regional and state volunteers that technically provide some leadership for the organizations. Yet, most of these volunteers never visit the chapters on the campuses let alone provide any assessment of chapter effectiveness. A trained, paid, national staff member could provide additional support that Black Greek–lettered organizations have not benefited from, while predominantly White organizations have utilized these to the fullest extent.

The creation of field staff positions again is a paradigm shift for Black Greek–lettered organizations. Kappa Alpha Psi Fraternity created the prototype of this program for Black Greeks in the late 1990s. The organization used educational leadership consultants, men who were older than traditional NIC and NPC consultants just out of college, to travel and visit their chapters. This program was short-lived, but a good first attempt at such a program.[17] One of the issues with this type of program is that it is costly to support traveling field staff. However, if Black Greek–lettered organizations are serious about their commitment to undergraduate members, the respective budgets will be adjusted to support this kind of activity—one necessary for the future survival of college chapters.

The National Pan-Hellenic Council, the umbrella body for the nine largest Black Greek–lettered organizations, must play a more important role in the advising of undergraduate chapters. The organization, while founded in 1930, really spent much of its history developing an identity and a purpose. As an umbrella body with no power over individual councils, the NPHC has had difficulty establishing a meaningful role within Black Greek life. This differs from the North American Interfraternity Conference (NIC), which has a tremendous amount of influence on member organizations and college IFCs given that the leadership is made up of past presidents of member organizations. This also differs from the National Panhellenic Conference (NPC), which actually sets rules and guidelines for college Panhellenics to follow, especially with regard to membership recruitment (formerly known as rush).

The NPHC has no power or influence similar to these two umbrella bodies. In reality, the NPHC has really been reborn within the last decade. During many conversations with Dr. Michael V. W. Gordon, recently retired executive director of the NPHC, one learns that the organization was basically nonexistent in the late 1980s. With aggressive leadership through Daisy Wood, a multiple-term national president, the organization was resurrected in the 1990s. One of the first major initiatives was to establish a partnership with Indiana University through the help of Dr. Gordon (who was a faculty member there and past Dean of Students) to create a national headquarters in 1992. With that action, the NPHC developed the infrastructure to begin offering services to member councils, services that had not been provided prior to that time.

During the 1990s the organization made small steps to begin servicing councils. These included instituting national collegiate leadership summits, the first being in 1993, and a national think tank on collegiate issues held in 1994. Yet the flux in national leadership, with NPHC national presidents holding two-year terms, and three different persons holding the office of president from 1995 through 2001, has hindered a consistent approach to working with councils, particularly collegiate ones. Challenges are magnified by the fact that the organization, now made up of five regions, is often led by regional directors who have no experience working in higher education or student affairs and are often viewed as out of touch by collegiates.

However, the National Pan-Hellenic Council should be viewed as a tremendous opportunity for providing support to collegiate councils. Using the model adopted by the NIC for many years, the NPHC should investigate and establish a full national office staff which includes member service consultants. These field staff members would function similarly to individual organization field staffers, but they would provide services to the entire council as well as determine what issues are challenging the students on the campus by meeting with campus Greek advisers and related administrative staff.

These traveling consultants would ideally be persons who have completed training in student affairs and higher education, and would travel to campuses to help establish stronger councils. They would also provide support in the national office when not traveling, and help plan and implement national and regional conferences. The current national office is staffed by an executive director and an assistant (a graduate student). A membership services consultant staff of five to ten persons would make the national office a more viable organization.

But on a more substantive level, the National Pan-Hellenic Council is in need of complete reorganization. It is obvious that there is no firm commitment by any of the member organizations to make an NPHC that is a functioning, effective body. While a constitutional change ratified at the 1999 national conference held in Atlanta required all chapters of affiliate organizations to form councils on the campuses and in the cities, only a fraction actually have done so.[18] This lack of commitment was apparent during the fall 2000 conference season as each of the five regions held conferences. No region had a conference attendance of more than one hundred, with the average being closer to sixty persons per conference.

The organization should reconsider its structure. One idea would be to completely downsize the board of directors, which includes three vice presidents, five regional directors, and every organization's executive director. If membership services consultants could be employed, regional directors could be abolished completely as well as the regional conventions. The "business" conducted at these meetings is minimal, and at the overwhelming majority of conventions where there are elections, most are uncontested, which does not always guarantee the best or most qualified person to be responsible for the success of a region and the related councils. The NPHC is structured like its member organizations, but it does not have the commitment to make such a structure work. A structure more like that of NIC or NPC would be much more efficient and effective.

One of the criticisms of the NPHC, especially by college members, is that it doesn't do anything. There is some truth to this assertion, as member councils don't receive regular publications or services. And while national leaders of the organizations would like to think they help college chapters work with school administrations, administrators more often contact their colleagues with expertise in Black Greek life to assist the chapters on their campuses. Very rarely is the NPHC sought to provide programming or services to college councils, mainly because the organization does not have persons trained to work with college chapters. A new NPHC as outlined here, along with these organization-specific recommendations, would be a positive step in the challenge of eradicating the underadvisement of college chapters.

MINORITIES: VISIBLE AND INVISIBLE

The third area that Black Greek life must face is the issue of minority members. Initially, one might think that the minorities most often discussed with regard to historically Black fraternities and sororities are those members who are not Black. Any controversy on this topic is not geared so much toward other persons of color, such as Latinos and Asians, but rather Whites who go against the grain of societal norms and seek membership in groups founded to serve the Black community. This is a definitely a controversial subject.

But there is a minority within Black fraternities and sororities that is not even discussed publicly. While there have probably always been gay and lesbian fraternity and sorority members, their presence is much more noticed today and is a greater source of controversy. While many closed-door meetings probably take place with regard to admitting or not admitting persons based on their sexuality, at the writing of this book no national Black Greek–lettered organization has offered any type of formal statement with regard to homosexuality within its membership. This invisible minority is also one that organizations must address in the future.

As indicated, the first minority group, specifically Whites who join Black fraternal organizations, is the source of controversy to this day. As described in the history of the Black fraternal movement through chapter 1, race was an important factor during the early 1900s when Black fraternal organizations were founded on campuses, both Black and White. The founders of all the organizations explicitly and directly experienced racism in many forms during a time when, roughly thirty years after the abolition of slavery, Blacks were still routinely lynched. Historian E. Franklin Frazier directly attributed the founding of these organizations to the refusal of predominantly White fraternities and sororities to allow Black students to gain membership.[19]

Based on societal restrictions, Black Greek–lettered organizations grew on their own.[20] There would be over forty years between the founding of the major Black fraternal organizations and the massive integration of major, southern universities beginning in the 1960s. Two separate Greek systems developed during this time, one White and one Black, and each with specific ways of operating that in many instances were completely different. While predominantly White groups selected students right out of high school, Black groups decided that prospective members would need to have accumulated college credits and a respectable grade point average. Black groups also tapped into a preformed pool of recruits who grew up wanting to join specific organizations, while Panhellenic sororities, for example, operated on a system where women would accept a bid to any sorority in which she was offered membership, even if the offer was a second or third choice.

Black and White Greek organizations, while philosophically similar, are functionally different. The recruiting of members as described, the ways in which service is performed (philanthropy versus hands-on community service), and even the ways the groups "party" have led to separate systems. Some have been concerned about the segregated Greek systems as late as the 1990s. At the University of Alabama a professor threatened to sue the university for "subsidizing segregation" if it did not develop a plan for integrating the Greek system. In 1997 the professor, who is White, wanted to see at least one Black student gain membership in a White organization and was disappointed that it had not occurred.[21]

University officials claimed that the professor was threatening to create a lawsuit that had no defendants. One of his colleagues assisting him indicated that some of the fiercest opponents were members of Black fraternities and sororities. That included faculty and staff, including one faculty member who in 1986, as president of her sorority, remembered a cross being burned on its yard shortly after the chapter became the first Black group on sorority row. Some students indicated that they should not join White groups now because the groups were not welcoming before.[22]

The university's solution was to create a committee to study the integration of the system, even though many agreed that the challenge would be great. Others acknowledged that change would be dependent upon students forming friends within other races. In the story reported by the *Chronicle of Higher Education*, the issue of minorities in Black Greek organizations was clearly articulated.

> But the odds are long against Dr. Hermann's witnessing his dream of integration before he retires. Resistance remains strong in both Greek systems. "I don't know what the climate would be like in a predominantly black fraternity for a white student," says Dr. Stallworth, the education professor. "The motives would be questioned: 'What things do we have in common? Why do you want to do this? We don't understand.'"[23]

In the very few articles that discuss Whites who have joined Black Greek–lettered organizations, these questions were real for those who made that decision. In a 1994 *Rolling Stone* article, author Laurence Stains posed more blunt questions in an article entitled "Black Like Me."

> Fad or not, it's got some people in an uproar. Why are white guys joining? Are they wannabe's? Do they want to cheese off their parents? Do they think they'll get to date black women? Are they filled with pity or guilt? Suspicion exists on both sides, says Brodey Milburn, a white student who joined Kappa Alpha Psi at Indiana University. "There are black people who don't appreciate my presence in a black fraternity, just as there are white people who can't understand why I did it in the first place."[24]

And yet, national officials contacted for the article estimated that 10 to 15 percent of their members were White, Latino, or Asian. But White members are still viewed as an anomaly.

This article, written three years before the concerns expressed by the professor at the University of Alabama, focused heavily on Everett Whiteside, a White man who joined Phi Beta Sigma at the University of Alabama. His thoughts about White fraternities provided a sensible explanation as to why many students, including Whites, would be interested in the Black fraternal experience. Stains wrote, "It's been estimated that black fraternities devote five times as many man-hours to community service than do white fraternities. And the very nature of black frats' service, which involves less money raising and more hands-on help, is an attraction in itself to some students."[25]

Whiteside was clear about what his impressions of Greek life were and knew the typical options for White students.

> When Everett Whiteside got to the University of Alabama, he took a good look around. "It was real easy to see what the white fraternities were all about," he says: two or three parties before Thursday—when the weekend began. Some kind of serious money was required, because those weekend parties hired $1,000 bands. "What I saw," recalls Everett, "was a lot of clones and cliques and 'My Daddy makes this much money, so I can be in this fraternity.'"[26]

He chose to join Phi Beta Sigma in 1990 and was part of a minitrend on that campus, as three Whites joined NPHC organizations on that campus between 1986 and 1990. But Everett maintained that he was White, and had no intentions of trying to "act Black" as some would imagine. He added in the interview, "One of my friends told me the other day I sound very white on the radio. I go, 'Well, that's good. 'Cause I am.' I don't want to fake the funk. I don't want to pretend that I'm something I'm not."[27]

A recent *Ebony* magazine article also addressed the issue, providing the sorority point of view as well. The article bluntly stated, "If you're envisioning a bunch of Eminem- and Teena Marie-look-alikes, get ready for the real. These White members fit no easy stereotypes."[28] As with the *Rolling Stone* article, those interviewed agreed that the Black fraternal experience was appealing to Whites, especially because the organizations provide perpetual membership as well as community service. Cassandra Black, president of the NPHC, indicated, "We have a moral fabric that is more desirable to some people. Historically, White fraternities have reputations for drinking and other behaviors, and some people don't want to be associated with that."[29]

One White member of Delta Sigma Theta indicated that she was attracted to the organization because of the sisterhood and service. She indicated that she felt accepted immediately, and has been challenged only once as a White member. She did acknowledge a degree of curiosity from some members. Martha Riley, a White Sigma Gamma Rho interviewed for the article, said, "I've never been challenged by a soror. . . . Quite a few sorors have asked me my reasons for joining, but that's it. I've had to earn respect the same way any other soror has to earn respect. . . . I'm just another soror."[30]

It seems plausible based on the history and legacy of Black fraternal organizations that persons of many racial backgrounds would be attracted to the ranks of membership. As indicated in these two articles, Whites have been attracted to the community service and commitment to sisterhood and brotherhood that are hallmarks of the Black Greek experience. Consequently, it may appear that more Whites, more so than Asians and Latinos who are rapidly developing fraternal organizations similar to NPHC groups, will continue to seek Black Greek membership as an option to the predominantly White fraternity system. This influx, despite the challenges facing Black Greek–lettered organizations, is thought to be a significant boost to the ranks of membership.[31]

But this probably won't lead to a more integrated Greek system. In the book *Torn Togas,* Esther Wright noted that before the civil rights movement, "most fraternities and sororities had rules forbidding them to pledge any member who wasn't white."[32] She noted several racial incidents that continue to deter Blacks from seeking membership. As late as 2000 a highly publicized racial incident involving a White University of Georgia sorority that denied a Black student membership emphasized the value of mostly Black fraternal organizations.[33]

At the same time, Whites are finding their niches in the ranks of Black fraternities and sororities. While many members shudder at the thought of having a sizable number of White members within their ranks, the organizations must understand and recognize that their history, traditions, and practices are very appealing to many non-Blacks. It should be anticipated that more Whites will seek membership, and all organizations should begin to mentally prepare their members for an influx of more White members. While the prevalent racism in America will always minimize the number of Whites seeking Black Greek membership, Whites will continue to join the organizations and play active roles. In fact, many will be more active than their Black brothers and sisters in an effort to prove the sincerity of their membership. Sadly for some Black members, they have noticed that Whites are more active and committed than their Black brothers and sisters.

If Whites joining Black fraternities and sororities is a controversial idea, the acknowledgment of gay and lesbians within the ranks Black fraternal organizations is culture shock. Many will admit that Black America is one of, if not the most homophobic group in the country. With most Blacks being deeply religious, they challenge the issues of homosexuality on the most fundamental levels. Generally stated, Blacks do not endorse homosexuals and homosexuality as a legitimate lifestyle.

The high levels of homophobia within Black America are only exaggerated within the context of the Greek system, a community built along gender lines and that fosters heterosexual family values. Wright further discussed how the Greek system breeds sexism and sexual harassment, particularly through fraternities that were described as objectifying women. She noted activities that exploited women sexually, including rape, and making them function in a subservient role through little sister organizations. She indicated that women played their roles as well, from catering to fraternity men as little sisters (which included sexual favors) to attending sorority functions designed to match women with men in hopes of finding a husband as a part of the college experience.[34]

While Wright described her experiences as a White sorority woman who attended a California school, there are both similarities and differences with regard to Black Greek organizations. A study by Berkowitz and Padavic suggested that Black women didn't look at the sorority as a means to find a man, as their White counterparts did, but as a means to get ahead. The researchers suggested,

> While white sororities are structured to largely ignore the career message and concentrate on the more traditional goal of pairing ("getting a man"), black sororities are organized to facilitate economic self-sufficiency ("getting ahead," in the words of these women) and to contribute to the betterment of the black community.[35]

Yet, Black sororities and fraternities do uniquely emphasize heterosexual pairings. Zeta Phi Beta and Phi Beta Sigma maintain a constitutional alliance as a brother-sister alliance, with numerous dating and marriage couples modeling this union. Alpha Phi Alpha and Alpha Kappa Alpha have united under the "First Family" motto as a pairing of what are acknowledged as the first collegiate Black Greek organizations. And Delta Sigma Theta and Omega Psi Phi have created brother-sister bonds, following a history of founders of Omega who dated Delta founders.

The strong heterosexual structure of the Greek system, along with the homophobia of Black America, created an interesting dynamic. It would, on the surface, seem reasonable that the Black Greek system would be the last place where one would expect to find gays and lesbians. The activities would be organized along traditional gender lines with traditional gender roles, presumably uncomfortable for homosexuals. However, an unanticipated outcome occurred. Many gays and lesbians realized that a way to hide their sexuality within an unforgiving Black community was as a member of a Black fraternal organization. In essence, this was the perfect way to live an "invisible life."

In 1991, novelist E. Lynn Harris self-published *Invisible Life,* the story of a young man who explores his sexuality beginning with his college years. The lead character, Raymond Winston Tyler Jr., was a member of the fictional Black fraternity Kappa Alpha Omega, a group that chased freshmen girls in an effort to make them their sweethearts as well as persuaded men to pledge the organization. He was dating a Delta who was a cheerleader. And while living a seemingly heterosexual life, in the early stages of the novel he finds himself attracted to another man and they engage in a sexual encounter.[36]

Raymond struggled after his first homosexual experience. In the novel, he says to himself,

> What if Kevin had me set up and now everybody on campus knew about last night's escapade. What if he told one of Sela's sorority sisters or, even worse, one of my fraternity brothers. I would have to drop out of school or transfer to A-State or Auburn in my senior year. I thought about the humiliation my parents and fraternity would feel. I would probably be kicked out.[37]

The story follows Raymond through his professional life. Throughout the story he is involved sexually with both men and women, but struggled with acceptance. He indicated that he did not "bother to affiliate with the graduate chapter of my fraternity because of my gayness."[38]

Through conversation with a friend, Raymond realizes that he is living an invisible life, unseen by everyone except the man he was involved with, a man who was married and had children. The story ends with the death of a woman due to AIDS, suspected to be given to her by the man that Raymond has his first homosexual experience with. He was troubled as well that the woman he was involved with, the best friend of the deceased (and her sorority sister), reacted angrily to his admission of bisexuality *after* they engaged in sex. He questioned himself, acknowledging, "I was part of a secret society that was endangering black women like Candance to protect our secret desires. Would this have happened if society had allowed Kelvin and I to live free from ridicule? Was it our fault for hiding behind these women to protect our futures and reputations?"[39]

Raymond's thoughts seem to speak for a more visible, yet largely invisible minority within Black fraternities and sororities as well as in Greek life as a whole. In writing an introduction for the book *Out on Fraternity Row*, Douglas Case presents a sobering message about the realities of gay men in fraternities. Using data from the Kinsey studies, Case indicates that 10 percent of the population can be classified as predominantly homosexual. Case conducted studies on his own and determined that the gay population in fraternities was at least as high as the general campus population, and likely higher.[40]

He also tried to determine why gay men joined fraternities. They gave responses expected of any man: friendship, social activities, and a sense of belonging. Very few joined to find sex partners, and Case indicated that most gay fraternity men are terrified (as is the fictional character Raymond) of being exposed as gay. In fact, through the stories of the writers for *Out on Fraternity Row*, Case noted many "mentioned that they joined a fraternity as a way of hiding or denying their sexual orientation."[41]

And more than just joining, the men worked extra hard within the organizations. Through Case's research, he found that gay fraternity men were high achievers, with 80 percent of his sample having held executive-level positions within their chapters, and 20 percent of the sample having held the office of president. Case explained that while some would argue that gay people have greater leadership abilities, "a more likely explanation is that the tendency toward overachievement is actually a coping mechanism. Subconsciously fearing rejection from the group, gay men strive to gain acceptance and respect by demonstrating their commitment and contribution to the group through leadership roles."[42]

The stories within the book provide excellent insight into the invisible life that many gay men lead through fraternities. The vast majority of the writers are White men. Yet, one writer spoke of his experience as a member of Phi Beta Sigma Fraternity. In a chapter entitled "Silent Rituals, Raging Hearts," R. Derrick Thomas discussed his experiences that he asserts include "inner turmoil and stress." He builds his story by describing the pledging he endured, pledging he acknowledged was illegal in 1992, but necessary for him to feel the full fraternal experience.[43]

Within eight months after pledging, Thomas decided to explore life as a gay man. He wrote,

> It was not an easy decision to make. I faced many trials and confrontations because of my choice. I knew the possible consequences of my fraternity

brothers' learning of my homosexuality. Many brothers made many antigay remarks during the pledgeship and had even joked that I was gay, but several others stuck up for me. In some ways, I was threatened and tested during the pledgeship to make sure I was not gay. It did not do any good.[44]

He noted that the conflict he felt caused him to withdraw from the organization. In an effort to ease the tension, he offered as an excuse a want to become involved in outside organizations.

At the same time he fought off rumors about being gay. One of the reasons was that he was hanging around his boyfriend (unbeknownst to his fraternity brothers) as well as another male student rumored to be gay. But he was also questioned because he did not participate in the sexist rituals of fraternity life, those that resembled ones described by Esther Wright. Thomas explained,

During this early time of exploration and my first boyfriend, rumors started to surface among the girls of a particular sorority. They were known for sleeping with my brothers. When I did not follow the custom of having sex with someone the night we "went over" (were initiated by secret ritual into the fraternity), they became suspicious. They really started tearing me apart when I actually took one of the girls on a date and did not jump her bones. That sorority was not our official sister organization, but they often provided some kind of entertainment.[45]

Thomas described the challenges he faced by his fraternity brothers who wanted to know about the rumors circulating about his sexuality. While he wrestled with how to handle his situation, he began to learn that men also engaged in same-sex relationships had challenged him. Thomas finally had the opportunity to openly discuss his sexuality with at least one member, but for the most part felt that he had been suppressed by the fraternity that fostered a type of individuality-restricting uniformity. Even though a state leader called a meeting for members about homosexuality in the organization, Thomas realized that the leader was not an advocate for gay members.[46]

Thomas ended his essay with very strong words about gays and lesbians within the Black Greek community.

All the national black Greek-letter organizations fiercely resist pressure to openly accept their homosexual members. . . . They fight a losing battle to hold on to the status quo, which does not even serve their own interests. In the end, though, they will find themselves outdated and struggling to survive. There are gay members in every organization. They serve in leadership positions, as loyal members, and are often the most respected.[47]

He further asserts that gays endure the harassment to hide their true identities. In essence, Thomas suggests that the "invisible life" phenomenon is a reality, not just fiction.

Having studied gay student culture as a part of a master's project at Miami University, I was able to learn a great deal about a lifestyle I was naive of, one that was invisible to me. But now, the lessons learned from the students have made me more aware of a reality of Black Greek life. Thomas is very true in his assertions. Some persons in leadership positions within Black Greek–lettered organizations are gay. My personal observations from my own fraternity conventions, to attendance at National Pan-Hellenic Council meetings, clearly show me numerous homosexual members who seem to be the backbone of organizations, ironically, built on traditional sexual roles.

I fully expect a major national leader of a Black Greek–lettered organization to publicly "come out" in the near future, creating a level of cognitive dissonance previously not experienced by the members of these organizations. While many members will openly criticize these gay members, hurling slurs their way, homophobic members must begin to accept the fact that they are (ironically) a cause of the gay members joining the organizations. The harsh level of homophobia existing in Black America has essentially encouraged homosexuals to find refuge, and cover, as a member of a fraternity or sorority, public statements of heterosexuality.

In the larger context, though, the organizations will have to come to recognize that in the end, those members who join the organizations and truly believe in lifetime commitment through their membership must be supported and encouraged, no matter what their orientation. While many members would love to have completely heterosexual brothers or sisters, there will never be a time when gays and lesbians are not fraternity and sorority members. Rather, they should strive to create a world where gays and lesbians do not seek Greek membership in order to hide and live "invisibly," so that those who join do so for the friendship, the service, and the commitment to African-American communities.

THE LATIN EXPLOSION

The 1990s became a time in American popular culture when the country experienced a Latin explosion. The emergence of popular stars Ricky Martin and Jennifer Lopez brought a new awareness of Latin culture, primarily through music. This popular culture awareness signaled the much-anticipated advent of a Latino population explosion. Demographers reasserted claims that within a short period of time Latinos would surpass Blacks as the largest minority group in America.

Predictably, higher education has started to see increases in the number of Latinos attending. Latinos began entering higher education in earnest in the 1960s and 1970s.[48] In 1976, 383,800 Latinos attended college, representing about 3.5 percent of all students. By 1995 the Latino college population had multiplied threefold to 1,166,100, representing 8.2 percent of college students. In contrast, the Black student college population only increased about 400,000 in total during that time, from 1,033,000 to 1,473,700.[49]

As the Latino college population increased, students sought to form college fraternities and sororities similar to those founded by White and Black students. Actually there were indications that Latinos flirted with fraternalism prior to the 1900s. In the late 1800s some Latino students formed secret societies similar to fraternities. However, these students were the privileged class and attended schools such as MIT and the University of California at Berkeley.[50]

The first significant founding was Phi Iota Alpha, but several theories exist on its founding. According to official fraternity information, including websites, the fraternity was founded 26 December 1931 at Rensselaer Polytechnic Institute. In an article published in *Black Issues in Higher Education*, the date 1888 was given as a founding date for Phi Iota Alpha.[51] Another article, "Greeks Empowering Hispanics" in *Hispanic Outlook,* says that Phi Iota Alpha "was developed by Latin American exchange students as a club in 1889 and then, after disappearing from the scene in 1973, reemerged as a fraternity for Hispanic Americans in 1984."[52] And in a *Boston Globe* interview, a fraternity member communicated that the organization was founded in 1901 as the Union Hispano-Americana, a secret society at RPI, and through mergers with other Latino fraternities nationwide it became Phi Iota Alpha.[53] These variances indicate that much more research must be done on Latino fraternal organizations as the history, while recent, is already sketchy. All accounts indicate that the fraternity had an extended period of dissolution and was completely inactive by 1973, but it resurfaced in 1984.

But not until the mid-1970s would the Latino Greek movement begin in earnest. At Kean College (now University), students founded both Lambda Theta Alpha Sorority and Lambda Theta Phi Fraternity. From that point in time until today, over seventy-five Latin fraternal organizations have been started on college campuses across the nation.[54] This number too is difficult to firmly establish, as many local Latin fraternal organizations are suspected to exist but have not been recognized by any large national body.[55] A listing of Latin fraternal organizations is found in Table 12.

Similar to reasons for the establishment of Black fraternal organizations, Latinos have sought to engage in significant out-of-class experiences that offered a sense of security. In an interview with *Link* magazine, Monica Miranda of the University of Rochester pointed out,

A lot of Latinos are first-generation college students. College is an unfamiliar environment for them. They need a greater level of support—a home away from home. They have a real understanding of how difficult life can be in economically deprived areas, and the need to give back to their communities. All this finds expression in Latino Greek life.[56]

TABLE 12
Latin Greek Timeline

Date	Organization	Founding Location
late 1800s	Secret Latino societies founded	
	Lasted until the 1930s	
	Union Hispano Americana	
	First association of Latin American	
	students founded in the US	
1931	Fraternidad Phi Iota Alpha	Rensselaer Polytechnic Institute
1969	Hostos Community College	Bronx, NY
	1st Puerto Rican college in the U.S.	
1973	Boricua College	Brooklyn, NY
	1st four-year Hispanic Serving Institution (HSI)	
1975	Lambda Theta Alpha Latin Sorority, Inc.	Kean College
1975	Lambda Theta Phi Latin Fraternity, Inc.	Kean College
	1st to join NIC (1992)	
1979	Lambda Sigma Upsilon Fraternity	Rutgers University
	From Latinos Siempre Unidos Latino Social Fellowship	
1980	Chi Upsilon Sigma Latin Sorority, Inc.	Rutgers University
	Also known as Corazones Unidos Siempre	
1982	La Unidad Latina, Lambda Upsilon	
	Lambda Fraternity, Inc.	Cornell University
1985	Alpha Psi Lambda	Ohio State University
	1st coed Latina/o coed interest fraternity	
	Lambda Alpha Upsilon Fraternity, Inc.	SUNY Buffalo
1986	Sigma Lambda Beta Fraternity	University of Iowa
	Lambda Theta Nu Sorority	Cal State Chico
	Lambda Sigma Gamma Sorority	Sacramento State University
1987	Gamma Zeta Alpha Fraternity	Cal State Chico
	Omega Delta Phi Fraternity	Texas Tech University
	Sigma Lambda Upsilon/	
	Senoritas Latinas Unidas Sorority, Inc.	Binghamton University
	Kappa Delta Chi Sorority	Texas Tech University
1988	Nu Alpha Kappa Fraternity	Cal Poly, San Luis Obispo
	Latinas Promoviendo Comunidad,	
	Lambda Pi Chi Sorority, Inc.	Cornell University
	Lambda Phi Delta Sorority	SUNY Buffalo

continued

1989	Omega Phi Beta Sorority, Inc.	University of Albany
Early 90s	National Council of Latino Fraternities and Sororities (Concilio Nacional de Hermandades Latinas) founded	
	Represented about 40 groups (7 national fraternities, 8 national sororities, and 1 national coed group included)	
1990	Sigma Lambda Gamma Sorority	U. of Iowa
	Hermandad de Sigma Iota Alpha Sorority	SUNY Albany, SUNY Stony Brook, College at New Paltz, Rensselaer Polytechnic Institute
	Alpha Pi Sigma Sorority	San Diego State University
1991	Sigma Theta Psi Sorority	San Jose State University
	Kappa Alpha Rho Sorority	University of Texas
	Gamma Phi Omega Sorority	Indiana University
1992	Gamma Phi Sigma Fraternity, Hermanos Unidos	Temple University
	Sigma Delta Alpha Fraternity	USC
	Sigma Lambda Alpha Sorority	Texas Women's University
	Lambda Pi Upsilon Sorority	SUNY Geneseo
1993	Gamma Alpha Omega Sorority	Arizona State
	Alpha Rho Lambda Sorority/ Alianza de Raices Latinas	Yale University
	Phi Lambda Rho Sorority	Cal State Stanislaus
	Sigma Lambda Sigma Sorority	Johnson and Wales (RI)
	Beta Lambda Delta Fraternity	Johnson and Wales (RI)
1994	Lambda Pi Upsilon Sorority	SUNY Geneseo
	Lambda Kappa Kappa	Ft. Worth, TX
	Pi Lambda Chi Sorority	University of Colorado
1996	Sigma Omega Nu Sorority	Cal Poly, San Luis Obispo
	Sigma Delta Lambda	Southwest Texas University
1997	National Association for Latino Fraternal Organizations (NALFO) founded	
2000	NALFO and CNHL merge under the NALFO umbrella	

Some have even suggested that since Latinos have trouble adjusting to college, the Latin Greek organizations have sold the benefits of brother-hood and sisterhood to potential members.[57]

The growth of Latin fraternal organizations in and of themselves may not appear to be an issue for historically Black fraternal organizations. While some Latinos have (and still seek) membership in Black Greek–lettered organizations, it does not appear that their numbers are significant enough to impact overall Black Greek membership should a new wave of students seek membership in Latino fraternal organizations. As previously

indicated, only Malik Sigma Psi Fraternity had experienced some challenges, as their founders included Latinos, and members of Latino organizations may sometimes challenge peers who join groups such as Malik
Sigma Psi. More of these challenges could appear with regard to Latinos
joining Black and White fraternal organizations, just as Black students
have been labeled as "sellouts" for joining White fraternities.

The real issue will be the pledging practices of Latin fraternal organizations. While there is relatively little written about these organizations, some
of the articles indicate that Latin fraternal organizations are experimenting
with pledge programs that clearly mimic those established by Black fraternal organizations in the 1920s. An article in *Latina* magazine discussed
pledging at Yale.

> This spring, seven student pledges of Sigma Lambda Upsilon Senoritas Lati-
> nas Unidas Sorority drew fire at Yale for what the campus newspaper called
> their "seemingly strange" practices. No one died from paddling or alcohol
> poisoning, but the rituals were unique. The pledges were required to march
> in line around the campus—which the paper likened to the African Ameri-
> can slave marches. They were also required to wear red armbands that some
> students compared with Nazi armbands. . . . Pledges may be required to wear
> similar clothes or "gear" T-shirts, with the sorority's Greek letters. They may
> also have to speak in code or answer the phone with a sorority phrase.[58]

In the article, Lupita Temiquel, national president of Sigma Lambda
Gamma Sorority and a university administrator, indicated that there were
concerns about hazing. In language that parallels that of Black fraternities
and sororities, Temiquel noted, "There's a pervasive opinion that you have
to earn your letters. We have to start clearly identifying the term 'earn' in
the best possible sense so that there's no confusion."[59]

Other cultural artifacts displayed by Black Greeks have also accompanied
the pledging by some Latino organizations. Pledges, as indicated in the article, march in single file line while wearing similar or identical clothing.
Accordingly, the organizations have developed elaborate jackets with line
names and numbers along with the term the member pledged. Hand signs
and calls have also been adopted by many Latin fraternal organizations. In
an effort to add cultural significance to many of these activities, Latin fraternal organizations have called upon their heritage to provide a twist to Greek
life. Some refer to themselves as Hermandades, meaning brothers and sisters, or use other Spanish phrases reflected in the official names of some
organizations (such as Latinas Promoviendo Communidad, Lambda Pi Chi
Sorority, and La Unidad Latina, Lambda Upsilon Lambda Fraternity).

Both of these activities sometimes ruffle the feathers of Black Greeks.
The Latino's use of calls, hand signs, and stepping is seen by many undergraduates as nothing more than blatant copying of Black Greek customs.

Latin Greek members claim that the practices are part of their culture and heritage as well. These competing forces for the rightful "ownership" of these traditions appear to be a point of future tension as the Latin fraternal organizations continue to grow and develop.

The final related area, which leads to tension, is the proper way for Latin fraternities and sororities to be represented under an umbrella organization. Predominantly White fraternities are unified under the North-American Interfraternity Conference (NIC), an organization founded in 1909 that represents the interests of almost seventy fraternities. It is noted that two historically Black fraternities, Kappa Alpha Psi and Iota Phi Theta, are members of the NIC as well as the NPHC. Additionally, several Latin fraternities, including Sigma Lambda Beta and Lambda Theta Phi, are members of the NIC. Twenty-six predominantly White sororities are unified under the National Panhellenic Conference (NPC). Established in 1902, the NPC has not added any members since the twenty-six current members were admitted.

These umbrella organizations and their campus counterparts (generally called IFC and Panhellenic) are geared toward the interests of organizations that function like predominantly White Greek organizations, with emphasis on rush (recruitment) activities and discussions about social policies that regulate alcohol usage. Most Latino organizations do not function in this manner and are therefore hesitant to join an IFC or Panhellenic. It is important to note that there are Latin organizations that do function within these systems as well.

The similarities between Black and Latin Greek–lettered organizations have caused the Latin organizations to work under an umbrella body with Black Greeks. On some campuses, multicultural Greek councils or similarly named organizations serve as umbrella bodies for all culturally based fraternal organizations, which could also include Asian-American organizations. On some campuses Latin fraternal organizations are members of the local NPHC council, especially since their operations are essentially the same as those of Black Greek–lettered organizations.

For many campuses this was a viable solution. However, during the 1990s, conversations were held at NPHC conferences that discussed future expansion of the organization. This was significant because the question of admitting Iota Phi Theta was at hand. The National Pan-Hellenic Council had to begin developing policies that would govern the selection of new members. While some were in favor of limited admissions, others vehemently opposed a mass influx of both Black and Latino fraternal organizations.[60]

Prior to this time, during the late 1980s, efforts were made by several Latin fraternal organizations to establish an umbrella body. The Concilio Nacional de Hermandades Latinas (National Council of Latino Fraternities and Sororities) evolved as a means to provide an umbrella body as well as a support system for those organizations on predominantly White campuses. By 1995 the organization boasted a membership of forty organizations, including seven national fraternities, eight national sororities, and a coed organization.[61]

But the organization was not able to serve as an effective national voice for Latin Greeks. In 1997 the National Association of Latino Fraternal Organizations (NALFO) was formed in an effort to unite the widely spread Latin fraternal organizations.[62] While the Concilio focused more on groups in the East and Midwest, NALFO sought to become a national force. Beginning in 1997 the organization began conducting annual meetings to facilitate networking opportunities.[63]

Predictably, the rapidly growing Latin fraternal movement produced two umbrella bodies. The exponential growth of new organizations made it difficult for one group to meet all the needs, particularly at a time when there was no clear picture as to how many organizations existed. A step to provide an overall direction for the Latino fraternal movement occurred in October 2000. In a NALFO news release, the organizations indicated,

> The National Association of Latino Fraternal Organizations, Inc. and Concilio Nacional de Hermandades Latinas (CNHL) made history as they approved a proposal to merge and unite Latino sororities and fraternities under one national umbrella organization. The NALFO membership endorsed the proposal at their Third National Convention in Tempe on October 12–14, 2000. CNHL had approved the recommendation at a meeting earlier that week. The two organizations will work out the details of the merger over the next several months, however, the immediate effect is the unification of the two councils under the NALFO banner.[64]

The growth and maturity of NALFO will probably alleviate some of the tension caused by NPHC members who are leery of Latin Greek organizations seeking membership. However, strong local NALFO councils on campuses will provide logistical challenges for university administrators trying to advise four umbrella bodies, each with different needs. However, if NALFO is unable to establish itself as a strong national force, it is foreseeable that Latin fraternal organizations will reinvestigate membership in the NPHC as a viable means of survival.

These four large-scale issues will be prominent in the next century of Black fraternalism. The pledging dilemma is by far the most pressing, as the potential for hazing deaths remains a distinct possibility every time membership intake is conducted (and even when it is conducted without the approval of the national organization, increasing the risk). The ability to adequately advise chapters also will continue to be an issue, but is one that should be easily remedied if the organizations are willing to rethink how they are structured, and make difficult decisions in terms of which chapters should be recognized and which must be culled.

The last two issues, while not pressing in the sense of threatening the existence of the organizations, are significant enough to cause turmoil. The ability of Black America to address homosexuality will inevitably impact the quality of life for gay and lesbian Black Greeks. Likewise, the rapid growth of the Latino population will produce fraternal organizations that may become larger and more prominent—initially on college campuses, but by the end of the next century in the community—than the historically significant Black Greek–lettered organizations. All four of these issues must be closely watched, and studied, as they evolve in the near future.

Afterword

I GUESS I AM AMAZED THAT NO BOOK BEFORE NOW HAS SOUGHT TO provide a thorough understanding and history of Black fraternal organizations. Almost one hundred years after the founding of Sigma Pi Phi, the first Black Greek–lettered organization to remain in continuous existence, there are very many questions that should have sparked a curiosity in the members that never materialized. I guess members were comfortable using folklore and old wives tales, if you will, to define the Black Greek experience.

This book should provide all persons interested, especially members of Black Greek–lettered organizations, with a solid foundation concerning their organizations, their beginnings, their customs and traditions, and the history of their most sacred event (pledging). It should also enlighten people about the numerous Black fraternal organizations that are and have been in existence as well as preview four hot topics for consideration in the twenty-first century that will undoubtedly continue to affect Black Greek life.

But after pulling together the ten years of research I've conducted, and attempting to gather it into one volume to provide the foundation for further inquiry on Black fraternalism (and hopefully, Latin and Asian fraternalism as well), I think I have more questions than I have provided answers for, and hopefully I can begin a quest to unravel these new mysteries. I find myself puzzled as to how Charles Harris Wesley, historian extraordinaire, could write histories of Sigma Pi Phi and Alpha Phi Alpha and never mention the existence of Gamma Phi at Wilberforce. Wesley was literally across the street from the birthplace of Gamma Phi, as he served as president of Central State University.

I find myself wondering why undergraduate Black Greeks began practices that mirror practices of their African ancestors. Was there a concerted effort to research African customs and systematically introduce them into Black Greek life, or did these practices evolve biologically? Was it their innate nature as Africans that caused them to create plots that resemble Moletji shrines, or have pledges carry symbolic items as did members of tribes who carried lamps and fertility dolls? I am still struggling to find some kind of documentation that shows proof either way.

At the time of the writing of this book I caught a PBS special entitled "Gumboots," which aired on Georgia Public Television.[1] I had seen the troop perform about two weeks prior to this special on the *Tonight Show*, and through my research I knew that many linked the origins of stepping to gumboot dancing. Indeed, this current troop exhibited a dance style where they slapped their boots while stomping to rhythmically made music. But unlike stepping, the gumboot dancers sang beautifully and maintained tight, a cappella harmonies. With stepping not really coming into being until the 1970s, I wonder why we adopted an art form that clearly is related to gumboot dancing, and why it took almost seventy years for it to enter the Black Greek culture.

My musings are leading me to one point that has to be my parting shot: There is an urgent need for many more people to engage in serious research regarding the Black fraternal experience. As I reflect upon my career, I realize that in thirteen years I have created a knowledge base on Black fraternal life that is probably unrivaled. I guess the nerd in me has pushed me to keep asking questions that lots of people had, but for which no one really sought to determine the answers. This perpetual questioning and inquisition has caused me to begin and end numerous research projects that are reflected in this volume.

And yet, I look around and I don't see others following in my footsteps, or taking my research to a new, higher, and more sophisticated level. Most important, I don't see others initiating research outside of the scope I have only begun to investigate. Admittedly, I am thrilled to be viewed as a national expert on Black fraternal organizations. It would be "misleading" not to acknowledge that my ego is fed by this unofficial title. Deep down, I think we all want and need this kind of informal recognition by our peers as a sign that we have made some kind of impact in our field of study. So I must say that I am truly honored to have many of my colleagues feel this way.

But I also am not so selfish and arrogant to believe that I am the only one who is able to conduct and present interesting research on Black Greek–lettered organizations. Realistically, there is no way that I am able to currently accept every invitation I receive to speak at a conference or on a campus. I figure that I could easily make my living by traveling and speaking full-time on these issues due to the vacuum of speakers on this topic. However, this has been something I've done because it is simply fun for me. I don't think I'll ever claim to be the best or most knowledgeable speaker in the area of Black Greek life, but I think I will always argue that I have the most fun doing these kinds of presentations.

The point is that others must begin to view this as a legitimate area for inquiry. In reviewing the roughly ten dissertations that have focused exclusively on Black Greek life, only two have seen the light of day in a journal article (mine and Andre McKenzie's). Future doctoral studies must be converted to research articles so that they inspire others to read in the area, and conduct additional studies. For that matter, numerous masters' theses also have potential for publication in research journals. Faculty must begin to encourage graduate students to view the study of Black fraternal organizations as a legitimate area of inquiry, and push them to submit their studies for possible publication in refereed journals.

Professionals who work in Greek affairs are the most qualified to begin these types of studies. Their day-to-day activities should spur numerous questions about the nature of these organizations. When problems are solved on campuses, the question of why the problem even arose should always be asked. I hope that my colleagues who read this book will begin to dedicate themselves to engage in some form of scholarly activity. It may not be in Greek life. In reality, it should be in something that they are truly interested in so that they can make the commitment to carry out the research.

Some of this should be quantitative research, using formal assessment tools to understand the Black fraternal experience. But some of this has to be qualitative. I still feel that there is a jackpot out there of historical information on Black Greek life that is hidden on some obscure campus, and someone is going to be blessed enough to find it and reveal something special to the world. My personal gold mine thus far was the finding of Gamma Phi Fraternity at Wilberforce. I don't think I can accurately describe with words the amazement I experienced when I realized that this was truly the oldest Black collegiate fraternity that had any longevity. Who is to say that there isn't another such group out there?

Once these research projects are completed, it is the duty of researchers to present this information. I have found in over a decade of lecturing on Black fraternal life that undergraduates are excited to learn about their organizations. They are starved for a better understanding of organizations they love so dearly. In some regards I think my research validates the love that they espouse. I think it is extremely difficult to love and value something you don't fully understand and appreciate. So when I lecture and I see students furiously taking copious notes, I not only have hope for our organizations, but I have hope for Black students and their commitment to scholarly pursuits. The trick, with anything, is to find something they are interested in, and use that as a vehicle for greater learning. I've been able to educate students on many aspects of Black history through my presentations (as well as teach myself a thing or two).

Those of us who have successfully done some research and given presentations have a duty to mentor others. I don't think I've been as successful in this regard. Sometimes I felt that those being mentored just want me to do the work for them, and I am sure there have to be times when they feel that I'm not doing enough to help them. But it is my responsibility to keep working at this role. I have to intentionally help colleagues learn how to give good presentations (all presentations are not good, not entertaining nor informative). This includes using the broad spectra of media available and not relying solely on the standard overhead projector and screen. I am confident that I have been successful as a presenter by using slides of pictures that clearly illustrated my points and by actively engaging the audience with my words. Others have to find a style that suits them and develop it.

So I hope this book will inspire more seasoned colleagues, even if they have never done any research in this area, to help those who might want to begin a research agenda in Black Greek life. I have included an appendix as a part of this volume. This is an annotated bibliography of research and articles on the Black Greek experience. The careful reader will note that most of the articles are from newspapers and magazines. For me this is a problem, in that they often reflect mere opinions and contain inaccurate information. I hope the short list of research-based studies will also inspire new efforts.

Finally, I would love to see each national organization begin a serious research agenda. As each major group ends its first century of existence, a significant milestone in American history, now is the time to recap the first century and set a research agenda for the next. Their educational foundations should follow the lead of some NIC and NPC groups that have provided scholarship monies to encourage research on Greek life. Admittedly, we, the Black Greek–lettered organizations, have not espoused a need for this kind of work. But we must see this as valuable, as there may be some studies done that could help us address the issues that keep the organizations at peril. I'm convinced that sociological and psychological studies must be intensified if we are ever to fully understand hazing and figure out how we can eradicate it. As I made painfully clear in an earlier chapter, pledging and hazing (cultures) cannot be legislated, and anyone who thinks otherwise is simply being foolish!

My hope is that this book is a catalyst for research. I met Lawrence Ross out in Long Beach in November 1999. After giving a presentation, he told me I should write a book. Admittedly, I never seriously considered writing a book, thinking I didn't have time for such an arduous task. But I began giving it serious consideration, and finally completed the book.

Just as Lawrence inspired me to complete this book, I hope others are inspired to write additional books on the subject. The foundation has been set. "The Divine Nine" was the logical first step, in that it provided the basic, historical information that only true scholars of Black fraternalism would have known. This book hopefully is the next logical step in that progression of research. But hopefully, now there will be several books that come into existence that further shed light on a culture that is expanding into mainstream Americana.

In the process of finishing the book draft, I was watching *Who Wants To Be a Millionaire* with host Regis Philbin. The show was a special edition featuring college students. A question posed to a White student from the University of Arkansas at Fayetteville was, "What is the name of the rhythmic dance form performed by Black fraternities and sororities?" The student thought he had seen it, but asked the audience for help. An overwhelming 72 percent of the audience knew that the answer was "stepping."[2] While I was shocked that this overwhelmingly White audience knew what stepping was, it provided me with further proof that Black fraternalism is an important culture within higher education and the country. Hopefully, others will agree and really create a push to research Black fraternal organizations.

Chronology of Hazing Incidents: 1989–2001

1989	Morehouse College, Alpha Phi Alpha
	• Joel Harris dies
	• fraternity pays $500,000+ in lawsuit; college pays $500,000
	• chapter members face $13M lawsuit—settled out for maximum value of parents' home insurance policy
1989	Clark Atlanta University, Omega Psi Phi
	• hospitalized: severe kidney damage
	• ten arrested for hazing
1990	Clark Atlanta University, Phi Beta Sigma
	• suspended for hazing: beaten in buttocks, kidney damage
1991	University of Georgia, Omega Psi Phi
	• chapter caught hazing by judicial director, fraternity adviser, and student activities director
1992	Norfolk State University, Omega Psi Phi
	• one hospitalized: broken jaw
1993	University of Maryland-College Park, Omega Psi Phi
	• six hospitalized: fractured ankle, bruised buttocks, bruised ribs, blood clot in spleen, broken ribs, liver damage, ruptured eardrum
	• fraternity lost court case—paid out $375,000 (1997)
1993	University of Georgia, Kappa Alpha Psi
	• one hospitalized: severely infected buttocks- required surgery
1993	University of North Texas, Alpha Kappa Alpha
	• suspended for hazing: paddling, assault
	• five arrested
1994	University of Southern Mississippi, Phi Beta Sigma
	• five arrested for hazing
1994	Southeast Missouri State University, Kappa Alpha Psi
	• Michael Davis dies
	• fraternity settles for $2.25M (1997)—includes $1.4—by National organization and $850,000 by members/advisers
	• students expelled from school; several arrested
1994	Georgia Tech, Kappa Alpha Psi
	• one hospitalized: abdominal injuries from being stood on
	• seven arrested
1994	Indiana University, Omega Psi Phi
	• one hospitalized: injured kidneys, face, neck, and chest

• three arrested, including adviser
• $1M lawsuit—fraternity paid $774,500 in damages

1995   Purdue University, Alpha Phi Alpha
        • ten undergraduates, two alums arrested

1996   West Virginia University, Omega Psi Phi
        • one hospitalized: kidney damage

1996   University of Georgia, Phi Beta Sigma
        • one hospitalized: bruises to buttocks and torn blood vessels
          (paddled seventy times)
        • three arrested (including adviser)—hazing and battery charges
        • students suspended from school

1996   University of Pittsburgh, Kappa Alpha Psi
        • one hospitalized: on kidney dialysis machine after being
          beaten with a paddle and cane
        • five members arrested

1997   University of Louisville, Omega Psi Phi
        • one hospitalized: kidney damage

1997   University of Georgia, Delta Sigma Theta
        • chapter suspended for mental hazing and harassment

1997   Georgia State University, Alpha Kappa Alpha
        • one hospitalized: beaten by "line sisters"
        • five students arrested, four suspended for two quarters

1997   Georgia State University, Phi Beta Sigma
        • aspirant pushed through a wall
        • chapter suspended; student body president (Sigma) resigns
          under pressure

1998   University of Maryland-Eastern Shore, Kappa Alpha Psi
        • five hospitalized: surgery for cuts and infections on buttocks

1998   Kansas State University, Kappa Alpha Psi
        • one hospitalized: kidney damage (dialysis)

1998   Southern Illinois University-Carbondale, Phi Beta Sigma
        • one hospitalized: chest injuries
        • chapter suspended for four years for hazing

1998   Bennett College, Alpha Kappa Alpha
        • chapter suspended four years for hazing
        • two graduating seniors were initially barred from graduating,
          but a judge forced the college to allow the two to graduate, say-
          ing they would suffer irreparable injury to their careers and
          public embarrassment if not allowed to graduate

1999   Lincoln University, Alpha Phi Alpha
        • one hospitalized: colostomy performed

1999   Georgia State University, Kappa Alpha Psi
        • one hospitalized: serious injuries to buttocks, stomach, and
          legs; blood in urine

• five members arrested

1999   Grambling State University, Kappa Alpha Psi
• one treated on campus for bruises from paddling and cane beatings
• three members arrested for hazing

1999   West Virginia University, Phi Beta Sigma
• seven arrested for hazing (including one former student) due to criminal charges filed by one aspirant

1999   University of Missouri, Kappa Alpha Psi
• student came forward to indicate he was hazed; later attempted to retract statements
• chapter suspended four years

1999   University of Florida, Alpha Phi Alpha
• chapter suspended for hazing: alcohol and paddling

1999   University of South Florida, Zeta Phi Beta
• chapter suspended for four years for paddling
• rush/intake chair suspended from school for one year; former members banned from campus

1999   Michigan State University, Phi Beta Sigma
• chapter suspended and investigated for hazing after student was hospitalized for six days and placed on kidney dialysis
• initial incident described as "trading wood"

1999   Western Illinois University, Delta Sigma Theta
• chapter suspended for hazing
• one hospitalized: torn skin on lower back and buttocks
• suit pending against sorority and two members
• reported in May 1999 *The Source* magazine

1999   Norfolk State University, Delta Sigma Theta
• one hospitalized: intensive care
• school expelled nine students; the seniors were not permitted to graduate

1999   Mississippi State University, Omega Psi Phi
• one treated at campus health center: injuries on buttocks
• two members identified as responsible for the hazing

1999   Illinois State University, Kappa Alpha Psi
• suspended from university after members were photographed hazing pledges

1999   University of Georgia, Omega Psi Phi
• chapter suspended for hazing of three students

1999   Georgia Institute of Technology, Kappa Alpha Psi
• found guilty of minor physical abuse and personal servitude by IFC judicial board
• placed on suspended suspension, meaning the chapter would be on probation for one year, and if it had further violations it would be suspended for not less than five years

1999   Old Dominion University, Alpha Kappa Alpha
                • chapter alumni and several undergraduates began an unsanc-
                  tioned intake program
                • chapter suspended for five years by the university
2000   University of Memphis, Omega Psi Phi
                • new initiate claimed hazing by alumni and chapter members,
                  but student withdrew complaint after an investigation
2000   Ball State University, Zeta Phi Beta
                • new member alleged mental abuse, personal servitude, and
                  mild physical abuse
                • chapter found in violation and suspended by university for
                  three years
2000   University of Arkansas-Monticello, Phi Beta Sigma
                • student suffered broken ribs, internal bleeding, and lost con-
                  sciousness
2000   Georgia Tech, Kappa Alpha Psi
                • chapter received a three-year sentence, only to be imposed if
                  chapter violated IFC policy again
                • evidence of hitting, coerced calisthenics that occurred outside
                  of the regulated intake program
2001   Ohio State University, Alpha Phi Alpha
                • suspended two years by university and fraternity
                • reported by a student's academic adviser, who noticed that his
                  appearance changed and grades were falling
                • several pledges needed medical attention, including one who
                  required extensive dental work
2001   Louisiana State University, Kappa Alpha Psi
                • student paddled so severely that blood seeped through his
                  jeans; wound was seven inches round and one-half inch deep
                  and required two surgeries, including a skin graft
2001   Old Dominion University, Kappa Alpha Psi
                • student with asthma sought medical attention and was treated
                  for numerous bruises to his hands and buttocks
2001   Tennessee State University, Omega Psi Phi
                • Joseph Green died while prepledging
                • died from an overheated body, with a temperature of 103 degrees
2001   Western Kentucky University, Kappa Alpha Psi
                • suspended five years and fined $1,000 for hazing
                • chapter allowed members not in good standing participate in
                  intake as well
2001   University of Maryland, Kappa Alpha Psi
                • investigated for hazing

Black Greek 101 Dictionary

Alpha Kappa Alpha

First Black Greek–lettered sorority, founded in 1908 by sixteen students at Howard University.

Alpha Phi Alpha

First collegiate Black Greek–lettered organization, founded in 1906 by seven students at Cornell University.

Brand

Organizational symbol(s) burned into members, usually on the arms or chest. Relates to scarification practiced by African tribes. Most associated with Omega Psi Phi, but appearing more in other fraternities, as well as in sororities. Branding is a voluntary process, not a requirement for membership.

Call

Audible sounds used by members to acknowledge or gain the attention of other members. Calls may vary regionally within organizations, and some organizations may use more than one call.

Club

Persons sharing the same number, regardless of organization. Sometimes referred to simply as **Number**.

Delta Sigma Theta

Black Greek–lettered sorority founded in 1913 by twenty-two students at Howard University.

Go Over

To be initiated into the organization. Also referred to as **Crossing** or **Crossing the Sands.**

Graduate Chapter

College graduates who are members of a particular organization and who operate similarly to a collegiate chapter. Members may have been initiated as undergraduates or through a graduate chapter. Also referred to as **Grad Chapter**.

Grooves

Members of **Groove Phi Groove** Social Fellowship (S.F.), a Black social/ fraternal organization popular on historically Black college campuses in the 1960s and 1970s. Another such organization is **Swing Phi Swing** S. F. (women), also known as Swings.

Hand Sign

Symbol or gesture made with the hand(s) that signify membership in a particular organization. Referred to as a **Hailing Signal** by older members (initiated prior to 1970).

Informational

A meeting to provide membership information to prospective members. Also referred to as an **Interest Meeting**, or a **Rush**. Replaced **Smokers** that fraternities held and **Teas** that sororities held for potential members prior to pledging (up until 1990).

Ism

Person going through intake who shares the number of an initiated member. Same concept as **Special** or **Personal**.

Iota Phi Theta

Black Greek–lettered fraternity that gained membership in the NPHC in November of 1996. Prior national affiliation was through the National Interfraternity Conference (NIC). The fraternity was founded in 1963 at Morgan State University in Baltimore, by twelve nontraditional students—being older, married, service veterans, or having full-time jobs.

Kappa Alpha Psi

Black Greek–lettered fraternity founded in 1911 by ten students at Indiana University.

Line

The persons who were pledging or had pledged together (1990 and before). The phrase is still used by undergraduates initiated together through membership intake.

Made

When and/or where a person was initiated.

Membership Intake

Process by which interested persons become members of most Black Greek–lettered organizations. Generally characterized by an Informational Meeting, an application process, an interview or series of interviews, and an intensive educational process. Membership intake formally replaced pledging for NPHC groups in February of 1990. The educational phase may be referred to as **Intake.**

National Pan-Hellenic Council

The umbrella organization of the major, historically Black Greek-lettered organizations. Commonly referred to as **NPHC**, it was established in 1930.

Neophyte

1. In some regions of the country, a new member during his/her first year of membership.

2. In some regions of the country, a member that has not initiated a group since his/her initiation. Also known as **Neos**.

Neophyte Show

Step show to introduce new members to the campus. Replaced in some instances **Probate Shows** (also referred to as **Pro Shows**) that were performed by pledges before initiation. The term Probate Show is still widely used as it notes the end of a pledge process.

Nupe

Nickname for a member of Kappa Alpha Psi, used primarily by members of the organization.

Old School

Refers to a person(s) or practice(s) of an earlier era. A very relative term, occupying different meanings based on the membership longevity. Older members may simply be referred to as **Old Heads**.

Omega Psi Phi

First Black Greek–lettered fraternity founded on a historically Black college campus, by three students and a professor at Howard University.

On Line

A person that was in the process of pledging. The phrase is still used in relation to underground pledging.

Que; Que Dog

Nicknames for members of Omega Psi Phi. Nationally, the organization does not condone the canine reference, but it is still commonly used.

Parallel

Persons initiated in the same organization at different chapters, but initiated during the same term; a California variation of the term **Sands**.

Paper

Derogatory term for a person who does not participate in underground pledging; simply indicates that the person completed the paperwork and then was initiated. Also known as **Skaters**, **Sign-ins,** or **Sign-ons**.

Phi Beta Sigma

Black Greek–lettered fraternity founded in 1914 by three students at Howard University.

Plot

Designated area on campus where a sorority or a fraternity decorates with the letters and colors of their organization. It serves as a gathering place on campus for members, visiting sisters/brothers, and friends. The plot also serves as a gathering place during major events such as homecoming. Plots are more commonly seen on historically Black college and university campuses. Known as the **Stone** on some campuses and, in other cases, **Trees**.

Real

Person who participates and completes an underground pledge program.

Sands

1. Persons that were initiated together at the same time and chapter. Also referred to as **Line Brother(s)** or **LB(s)**, **Line Sister(s)** or **LS(s)**, and **Ship(s)** or **Shippee(s)**.

2. Persons who were initiated during the same term at different chapters. Sometimes used for persons in different organizations.

Ship/ Shippee

Persons initiated together. Historical reference to slaves traveling from Africa to America in the tight confines of a slave ship. The symbolism is carried out further in referring to the first person in the line as the **Captain,** and the last in line as the **Anchor.** There are sometimes exceptions to this rule of naming. These terms are used almost exclusively in parts of the Midwest, particularly Illinois, Iowa, Michigan, and Kansas.

Showing

Persons participating in a step show. The group of participants is known as a **Step Team**.

Sigma Gamma Rho

Black Greek–lettered sorority founded in 1922 by seven educators at Butler University, a teachers' college at the time.

Sigma Pi Phi (The Boule)

Secretive Black fraternity founded in 1904 by Black doctors and dentists in Philadelphia. Technically the first Black Greek–lettered organization, it now maintains in its ranks national Black leaders. *Boule* is a Greek word signifying a legislative council or advisory council.

Soror(s)	Member(s) of the same sorority. Sometimes used in NPHC functions to refer to any sorority woman (and men are referred to as **Frater** or **Fraters**).
Special	An acknowledged mentor relationship between a new member and an established chapter member, usually selected while the new member is going through the intake (or pre-1990 pledge) process. The shortened and more popular usage of the term is **Spec** (pronounced "Spesh"). Some regions of the country use the term **Personal** (or **Pers**) to signify the same relationship during the intake (or pre-1990 pledge) process.
Step Master	Person that organizes the step show, and usually the best stepper. Also referred to as the **Point**.
Step Show	A Black Greek function characterized by synchronized hand and foot movements, along with singing, dancing, chanting, and acting. Also referred to as **Blocking** or **Stepping**.
Surfacing	The first public appearance of a line, often at a party. More widely used post-1990 by Latino fraternal organizations that maintain an aboveground pledge program.
Underground	1. Term used to note persons participating in a pre-pledge process that was not sanctioned (prior to 1990).
	2. Term used to note that persons are or have participated in a pledge program although pledging was abolished in 1990.
Viewing	An opportunity for members of other organizations to watch a line pledge underground. This is mostly a Northeastern activity, and may be done with both Black and Latin fraternal organizations in attendance since the processes are similar.
Walk	A series of steps that members do, usually during dances or as a part of step shows. Differ from regular stepping because the walks are generally performed to music. Also referred to as **Party Walks**, **Struts** or **Halos**.

Week   Period of time when a Black Greek–lettered
                                  organization sponsors a variety of events for
                                  the campus. May include educational pro-
                                  grams, discussions or debates, variety
                                  shows, parties, and step shows. Sometimes
                                  they are referred to as **Founders' Week**.

Zeta Phi Beta   Black Greek-lettered sorority founded in
                                  1920 by five students at Howard University.

Notes

CHAPTER 1. THE FOUNDATION ERA OF BLACK FRATERNALISM

1. Alan Axelrod, *The International Encyclopedia of Secret Societies and Fraternal Orders* (New York: Facts On File, Inc., 1997).

2. Ibid.

3. W. L. Wilmshurst, *The Meaning of Masonry* (New York: Gramercy Books, 1980), 10.

4. Axelrod, *International Encyclopedia*; Richard T. Watkins, "Black Social Orders," *Black Enterprise*, July 1975, 26–28.

5. Lawrence O. Graham, *Our Kind of People* (New York: HarperCollins, 1999), 129.

6. Axelrod, *International Encyclopedia*.

7. Rayford L. Logan, "Hall, Prince," Microsoft Encarta Africana 2000 [CD-ROM] (Cambridge, MA).

8. Frederick Rudolph, *The American College and University: A History* (Athens: University of Georgia Press, 1990), 147.

9. Axelrod, *International Encyclopedia*.

10. Helen Horowitz, *Campus Life* (New York: Alfred A. Knopf, 1987), 36.

11. Herman Mason, Jr., *The Talented Tenth: The Founders and Presidents of Alpha* (Winter Park, FL: Four-G Publishers, 1999).

12. Thomas Clark, *Indiana University: Midwestern Pioneer,* vol. 1 (Bloomington: Indiana University Press, 1970).

13. Ibid.

14. Ibid., 119.

15. Thomas Clark, *Indiana University: Midwestern Pioneer*, vol. 2 (Bloomington: Indiana University Press, 1973).

16. Ibid.

17. William Crump, *The Story of Kappa Alpha Psi*, 3d ed. (Philadelphia: Kappa Alpha Psi Fraternity, 1983), 4.

18. Charles H. Wesley, *History of Sigma Pi Phi: First of the Negro-American Greek-Letter Fraternities* (New York: Sigma Pi Phi Fraternity, 1954), 23–24.

19. Carrington L. Davis, *A Brief History of Sigma Pi Phi Fraternity* (Xenia, OH: The Aldine Publishing Co., 1947), 1.

20. Wesley, *History of Sigma Pi Phi*.

21. Graham, *Our Kind of People*, 130.

22. Ibid.

23. E. Franklin Frazier, *Black Bourgeoisie* (New York: Free Press Paperbacks, 1957).

24. W. E. B. Du Bois, "The Talented Tenth Memorial Address," in Henry L. Gates Jr. and Cornel West, *The Future of the Race* (New York: Alfred A. Knopf, 1996).

25. Ibid.

26. Ibid.

27. Ibid., 174.

28. Karen G. Bates, "Elite Fraternity Widens Agenda for Black Men," *Los Angeles Times*, 18 July 1990, E1–2.

29. Hobart S. Jarrett, *The History of Sigma Pi Phi*, vol. 2 (Philadelphia: Quantum Leap Publisher, Inc., 1995).

30. Ibid.

31. Ibid.

32. Graham, *Our Kind of People.*

33. Jarrett, *The History of Sigma Pi Phi.*

34. Du Bois, "The Talented Tenth Memorial Address."

35. James Anderson, "Training the Apostles of Liberal Culture: Black Higher Education, 1900–1935," in Lester F. Goodchild and Harold S. Wechsler, eds., *ASHE Reader on the History of Higher Education* (Needham Heights, MA: Ginn Press, 1989), 474.

36. Charles F. Porter, "Gamma Phi Fraternity," *The Forcean*, 1923, 136.

37. Morris Bishop, *Early Cornell, 1865–1900* (Ithaca: Cornell University Press, 1962).

38. Charles H. Wesley, *The History of Alpha Phi Alpha* (Chicago: Foundation Publishers, 1961).

39. Rayford L. Logan, *Howard University: The First Hundred Years, 1867–1967* (New York: New York University Press, 1969).

40. Marjorie H. Parker, *Alpha Kappa Alpha: Through the Years* (Chicago: Mobium Press, 1990), 11.

41. Robert L. Gill, *The Omega Psi Phi Fraternity and the Men Who Made Its History* (Washington, DC: Omega Psi Phi, 1963), 3.

42. Paula Giddings, *In Search of Sisterhood: Delta Sigma Theta and the Challenge of the Black Sorority Movement* (New York: Quill, 1988), 48.

43. Ibid.

44. Jaqui Malone, *Steppin' on the Blues: The Visible Rhythms of African American Dance* (Urbana: University of Illinois Press, 1996).

45. Lawrence Ross Jr., *The Divine Nine: The History of African American Fraternities and Sororities* (New York: Kensington Books, 1999); P. S. White, *Behind These Doors—A Legacy: The History of Sigma Gamma Rho Sorority* (Chicago: Sigma Gamma Rho Sorority, 1974).

46. Malone, *Steppin' on the Blues.*

47. Crump, *The Story of Kappa Alpha Psi.*

48. Wesley, *The History of Alpha Phi Alpha.*

49. *Initium*, 1922.

50. *The Bison*, 1945, 75.

51. Wesley, *The History of Alpha Phi Alpha*, 300.

52. Giddings, *In Search of Sisterhood.*

53. *The Bison*, 1945, 75.

CHAPTER 2. THE HISTORY OF PLEDGING

1. Hank Nuwer, *Wrongs of Passage: Fraternities, Sororities, Hazing, and Binge Drinking* (Bloomington: Indiana University Press, 1999).

2. Ibid., 94.

3. Nuwer, *Wrongs of Passage*; Frank Kershner Jr., "History of Greek Hazing," *The Bulletin of Interfraternity Research and Advisory Council*, 1 May 1978.

4. Kershner, "History of Greek Hazing."

5. Ibid.

6. Nuwer, *Wrongs of Passage*, 100.

7. Bishop, *Early Cornell.*

8. Ibid.

9. Clark, *Indiana University*, vol. 2.

10. Andre McKenzie, "Fraters: Black Greek-Letter Fraternities at Four Historically Black Colleges, 1920–1960" (Ph.D. diss., Teachers College, Columbia University, 1986), 18.

11. Ibid.

12. Nuwer, *Wrongs of Passage.*

13. *Enopron*, Howard Yearbook 1921.

14. McKenzie, "Fraters."

15. *The Ayeni*, 1939, 47.

16. *The Bison*, 1945, 81.

17. *The Forcean*, 1923, 122.

18. *The Bison*, 1923.

19. "Delta Sigma Theta," *The Bison*, 1923.

20. McKenzie, "Fraters," 19.

21. Ibid., 20.

22. *The Bison*, 1930.

23. *The Bison*, 1931, 89.

24. McKenzie, "Fraters," 21.

25. Ibid.

26. Marjorie Parker, *Alpha Kappa Alpha: In the Eye of the Beholder* (Washington, DC: Alpha Kappa Alpha Sorority, 1979).

27. Semi-Annual Meeting Minutes, Hampton Institute Board of Trustees, 27 April 1951, 20.

28. Ibid., 21.

29. McKenzie, "Fraters."

30. Ibid.

31. "Greekdom on CSC's Campus," *The Gold Torch*, December 1954, 8.

32. Ibid.

33. "Fraternities and Sororities: A Dramatic Comeback on Campus," *Ebony*, December 1983, 93.

34. Charlayne Hunter-Gault, *In My Place* (New York: Farrar, Straus and Giroux, 1992).

35. Jeanne Noble, "A Sense of Place," *Essence*, May 1985, 131.

36. Parker, *Alpha Kappa Alpha: In The Eye of the Beholder*, 122.

37. *The Brownite*, 1961.

38. *The Bison*, 1965, 135.

39. "Hell Week or Plain 'Hell,'" *The Gold Torch*, 12 November 1965, 2.

40. Parker, *Alpha Kappa Alpha: Through the Years.*

41. "Fraternities and Sororities," *Ebony*, December 1983, 96.

42. Giddings, *In Search of Sisterhood,* 284.

43. Ibid.

44. Michelle Collison, "Serious Issues, Touchy Subject: New Film Pokes Fun at Black Fraternities," *Chronicle of Higher Education*, 10 February 1988, A34.

45. Ibid.

46. Spike Lee with Lisa Jones, *Uplift The Race: The Construction of School Daze* (New York: Simon and Schuster, 1988).

47. Lee, *Uplift The Race,* 83.

48. Michelle Freeman and Tina Witcher, "Stepping Into Black Power," *Rolling Stone*, 24 March 1988, 143.

49. Collison, "Serious Issues," A35.

50. Larry Copeland, "Black Frats May End Tradition of Pledging," *Atlanta Journal-Constitution*, 14 March 1988, 8A.

51. Ibid.

52. "Pledging a Brother, Not Intaking a 'Paper Brother,'" *Black Issues in Higher Education*, 12 June 1997, 26–27.

53. I served on the Board of Directors as the Southern Region Assistant Vice President from 1988 to 1989, just prior to the Morehouse incident. I was privy to numerous discussions about the case due to my status as a former board member, and was also considered as a candidate to replace the Assistant Vice President at that time, who was a student at

Morehouse and was in the apartment when the hazing took place. The event was a major discussion item at the 1989 regional convention held in Tampa, Florida.

54. Margaret Usdansky, "Frat Brothers Remorseful, Frustrated," *Atlanta Journal-Constitution*, 5 November 1989, D1, D6.

55. Ibid., D6.

56. Ibid.

57. Walter M. Kimbrough, "The Membership Intake Movement of Historically Black Greek-Letter Organizations," *NASPA Journal* 34, no. 3 (1997) : 229–239; David Mills, "The Wrongs of the Rites of Brotherhood," *Washington Post*, 18 June 1990, B1, 6.

CHAPTER 3. THE MEMBERSHIP INTAKE MOVEMENT

1. Ullysses McBride, then Grand Polemarch of Kappa Alpha Psi Fraternity, interview by Michelle Collison, "8 Major Black Fraternities and Sororities Agree to End the Practice of Pledging" *Chronicle of Higher Education*, 28 February 1990, A31.

2. Jonathan Brandt, then executive director of the National Interfraternity Conference, interview by Collison, in ibid., A31.

3. Moses Norman, then Grand Basileus of Omega Psi Phi Fraternity, interview by Collison, in ibid., A31.

4. Lybroan James, then vice president of Phi Beta Sigma Fraternity at UCLA, interview by Collison, in ibid., A31.

5. Nicole Webb, then president of the Rutgers University Minority Greek Council, interview by Collison, in ibid., A31.

6. Heather S. Keets, "Greek Philosophy," *YSB*, April 1996, 48–51; Collison, "8 Major Black Fraternities and Sororities," A31.

7. John Blake, "Black Fraternities Feel Loss of Pledging Rite," *Atlanta Constitution*, 8 October 1990, E1, E4; Ernie Suggs, "The Rise of the Black Greek Empire," *The (Durham) Herald-Sun* [article online]; available from http://www.herald-sun.com/hbcu/docs/whyhbcu_3.html; Internet; accessed 11 March 1997.

8. Ed Wiley III, Ed and Angela Clarke, "Recent Death Rekindles Concern About Fraternity Hazing," *Black Issues in Higher Education*, 9 November 1989.

9. Collison, "8 Major Black Fraternities and Sororities," A31.

10. Mills, "The Wrongs of the Rites of Brotherhood," B1, B6.

11. Michel Marriott, "Black Fraternities and Sororities End a Tradition," *New York Times*, 3 October 1990, Education, 8.

12. Mills, "The Wrongs of the Rites of Brotherhood."

13. Ibid., B6.

14. Ibid.

15. Some predominantly White institutions took early stands against the old pledge program as well, although they were criticized sharply by undergraduates. See "University Softens on Some Aspects of Hazing Policy," *New York Times*, Campus Life Section I, 4 March 1990, 37.

16. Napoleon Moses, "Membership Intake: A Time For Decision," *Sphinx*, summer 1990, 10.

17. Mills, "The Wrongs of the Rites of Brotherhood."

18. Blake, "Black Fraternities Feel Loss of Pledging Rite," E4.

19. Copeland, "Black Frats May End Tradition of Pledging," 8A; Kimbrough, "The Membership Intake Movement," 229–39.

20. Blake, "Black Fraternities Feel Loss of Pledging Rite," E4.

21. Kimbrough, "The Membership Intake Movement."

22. Ibid.

23. John A. Williams, "Perceptions of the No-Pledge Policy for New Member Intake by Undergraduate Members of Predominantly Black Fraternities and Sororities" (Ph.D. diss., Kansas State University, 1992).

24. Ibid.

25. Ibid.

26. Ibid.

27. Ibid., 94.

28. Ibid., 103–4.

29. Williams, "Perceptions of the No-Pledge Policy."

30. Mills,"The Wrongs of the Rites of Brotherhood," B6.

31. Lisa Leff, "24 Students at U-Md. Charged with Hazing," *Washington Post*, 27 May 1993, C3.

32. Nuwer, *Wrongs of Passage.*

33. Courtland Milloy, "The Gang Called Frats," *Washington Post*, 5 May 1993, C1, C10.

34. Paul Ruffins, "Greek Tragedy," *Washington City Paper*, 18 June 1999, 16–27.

35. Ibid., 17.

36. Christopher Shea, "U. of Maryland Fraternity Chapter Is Suspended for Abusive Hazing," *Chronicle of Higher Education*, 3 November 1993, A38.

37. Rebecca McCarthy, "UGA Closes Fraternity While Alleged Hazing Investigated," *Atlanta Constitution*, 27 May 1993, B7.

38. "Black Greek Fraternities in the '90s: Are They Still Culturally Relevant?" *Ebony Male*, August 1993, 44, 51.

39. Kim Bell, "Two Post Bond in Death of Fraternity Pledge," *St. Louis Post-Dispatch*, 20 February 1994, 11D.

40. Tim O'Neil and Marianna Riley, "Student Dies in Hazing," *St. Louis Post-Dispatch*, 17 February 1994, 1A.

41. Christopher Shea, "Brutal Hazing Death Shocks Missouri Campus," *Chronicle of Higher Education*, 2 March 1994, A37–38.

42. William E. Cox, "Joining a Fraternity Should Not Result in Death," *Black Issues in Higher Education*, 10 March 1994, 88.

43. Erika D. Neal, "Search for Brotherhood Ends in Death," *St. Louis Post-Dispatch*, 23 February 1994, 7B.

44. Paul Ruffins, "Fratricide: Are African American Fraternities Beating Themselves to Death?" *Black Issues in Higher Education,* 12 June 1997, 19.

45. Ibid., 20.

46. Soraya Gage (producer) and Sarah Karlson (editor), "Blood Brothers," *Dateline NBC*, 24 May 1995.

47. Ibid.

48. Ibid.

49. Ibid.

50. Ibid.

51. Ibid.

52. Doug Payne, "Seven Students Face Hazing Charges," *Atlanta Constitution*, 2 March 1994, D6.

53. Kassia Cato and Bill Greve, "ΚΑΨ Fraternity Investigated for Hazing," *(Georgia Tech) Sting*, 8 March 1994, 1, 16.

54. J. R. Ross, "More Arrests Expected in Hazing Attack," *Indiana (University) Daily Student*, 2 March 1994, 1.

55. Andrew Welsh-Huggins, "IU Student Talks About Alleged Fraternity Hazing," *Bloomington (IN) Herald-Times*, 5 March 1994, A1.

56. Shea, "Brutal Hazing Death Shocks Missouri Campus."

57. Eleena De Lisser, "Violent Hazing Threatens Black Fraternities," *Wall Street Journal*, 18 November 1994, B1.

58. Joe Gerrety, "12 Face Hazing Charges," *Lafayette (IN) Journal and Courier*, 3 August 1995, A1.

59. Angela Townsend, "Hazing Lives Despite Crackdown," *Lafayette (IN) Journal and Courier*, 4 August 1995, A10.

60. Mary Geraghty, "5 Fraternity Members Charged in Beating of Student at Pitt; His Condition Is Serious," *Chronicle of Higher Education*, 19 April 1996, A47.

61. Duane Stanford and Doug Cumming, "Police Probe UGA Hazing," *Atlanta Journal-Constitution*, 12 September 1996, B1.

62. Duane Stanford, "Frat Pledges Describe UGA Player's Paddling," *Atlanta Journal-Constitution*, 27 September 1996, B2.

63. Rebecca McCarthy, "Suspension of UGA Fraternity To Be Appealed," *Atlanta Journal-Constitution*, 30 October 1996, C6.

64. "Fraternity Pays Millions to Settle Hazing Suit," *Chronicle of Higher Education*, 24 January 1997, A6.

65. While lecturing in Ohio in 1996, a graduate member of Kappa Alpha Psi discussed with me a letter he received from the national organization asking for a donation to support their defense of the lawsuit.

66. Karla Haworth, "U. of Louisville Student Hospitalized After Beating in Fraternity Ritual," *Chronicle of Higher Education*, Daily News, 14 April 1997.

67. Sarah Carr, "National Fraternity Is Told to Pay Nearly $1-Million in Beating of Pledge," *Chronicle of Higher Education*, Daily News, 3 August 1999.

68. Kim Wessel, "Hazing Victim to Get $1 Million," *Louisville Courier-Journal*, 7 April 2000, C1.

69. "Fraternity Suing Students Involved in Hazing Incident," *Associated Press*, 25 May 2000.

70. Brian Brick, "You Just Can't Beat Those Sorority Sisters at U. of North Texas," *U Magazine*, December 1993, 6.

71. Sherrell Evans, "Georgia State Sorority Pledge Alleges Attack," *Atlanta Journal-Constitution*, 30 April 1997, C4.

72. Alexandra Pharnor, "Breaking the Code," *The Source*, May 1999, 72.

73. "Accused Students Get To Graduate," *Associated Press*, 18 May 1998.

74. Philip Walzer, "Judge Lets Stand NSU Expulsions over Hazing," *Virginian-Pilot*, 4 May 1999, B1, 4.

75. Tom Lasseter, "SGA President Shawn Mitchell Resigns Temporarily in Lieu of Fraternity's Turmoil," *Georgia State University Signal*, 22 April 1997, 1, 4.

76. Paul Ruffins, "The Persistent Madness of Greek Hazing," *Black Issues in Higher Education*, 25 June 1998, 14–18.

77. Todd Spangler, "Md. Police Probe Alleged Hazing," *Associated Press*, 13 April 1998.

78. *BET Tonight with Tavis Smiley*, April 1998.

79. Ibid.

80. Ibid.

81. Stephen Sweet, "Understanding Fraternity Hazing: Insights from Symbolic Interactionist Theory," *Journal of College Student Development* 40, no. 4 (1999): 355.

82. Walter M. Kimbrough and Michael Sutton, *The Persistent Pledging of Black Greeks: A Student Development Approach for Understanding and Challenging the Culture* (Washington, DC: National Association of Student Personnel Administrators, 1998).

83. Michael Rothfield and Christina Asquith, "Lincoln Suspends 7 In Hazing of Student," *Philadelphia Inquirer*, 9 March 1999, B1; Michael Rothfield, Christina Asquith, and Angela Galloway, "Lincoln Suspends All Greek Intake Events," *Philadelphia Inquirer*, 19 February 1999, B1; Michael Rothfield, "Hazing at Lincoln Put One in Hospital," *Philadelphia Inquirer*, 18 February 1999, B1.

84. Christina Aquith, "Del. Pair Charged in Feb. Hazing," *Philadelphia Inquirer*, 7 April 1999, B1.

CHAPTER 4. WAS EIGHT ENOUGH?

1. I attended the San Diego NPHC convention, and was in attendance at the meetings where the issue of expansion was discussed in full. In addition, I sat at the banquet table at the 1995 AFA conference with the members of Iota Phi Theta during the discussions of expansion.

2. Letter by Melvin M. Slater, then NPHC graduate member at large, to the NPHC National Board on 26 July 1996.

3. "Alpha Phi Literary Society," *NIKH*, 1915, 61.

4. "Student Council," *The Bison*, 1924.

5. *The Forcean*, 1928, 122.

6. *Encyclopedia Britannica online*, "Swastika."

7. *The Ayeni*, 1939.

8. *The Jacksonian*, 1948.

9. "Social Organizations," *Tuskeana*, 1941.

10. Charles D. Houston, "Bout the Greeks," *The (Tuskegee University) Campus Digest*, September 1948, 3.

11. Daniel Dixon, "Beta Tau Sigma," *The Golden Book*, 1950, 42.

12. Cora Williams, "Presenting Pi Beta Sigma," *The Golden Book*, 1950, 41.

13. John Hope Franklin and Alfred A. Moss Jr., *From Slavery to Freedom*, 6th ed. (New York: McGraw-Hill, 1988), 458.

14. Darius James, *That's Blaxploitation* (New York: St. Martin's Griffin, 1995).

15. Nelson George, *Hip Hop America* (New York: Viking, 1998), 104–5.

16. Ross, *The Divine Nine*, 134.

17. *Promethean*, 1971, 229.

18. Elquemedo Alleyne, also known as Malik Lukman Khalfani, phone interview by author, Atlanta, GA, 1 October 1996.

19. Elquemedo Alleyne, "Malik Sigma Psi Fraternity Inc." (unpublished pamphlet), 1994, 2.

20. Ibid., 3

21. Ibid., 5

22. "Alpha Beta Sigma," [website]; available from http://www.angelfire.com/ny/AlphaBetaSigma/faqs1.html.

23. "Pi Psi Fraternity" [website]; available from http://www.msu.edu/user/pipsi/questions.html.

24. "Delta Phi Upsilon Fraternity" [website]; available from http://www.delta-phi-upsilon.org/page3.html.

25. Lacy Burrell, Durix Paloade, and Royal Thompson, members of Gamma Alpha Chi fraternity and students at the University of Southwestern Louisiana, interview by author, Hammond, LA, 3 November 1996. Also participating was Shawn Wilson, Assistant Dean of Students at the institution and member of Alpha Phi Alpha.

26. Ibid.

27. Walter M. Kimbrough, "Was Eight Enough? New Trends in Black Fraternal Life," *(AFA) Perspectives,* summer 1997, 4–6.

28. I worked at Georgia State University from March 1995 to December 1996. While there, one of the students joined Kemet and provided me with an opportunity to learn a great deal about the fraternity. This included attending his "Resurrection March," which was done prior to his initiation.

29. Abiona Irungu Baruti Kemet, interview by author, Atlanta, GA, 27 November 1996. He legally changed his name after initiation into the fraternity. The name of the fraternity, Kemet or KMT, has an emphasis on the first syllable (KEM-et), while his name has emphasis on the second syllable (ke-MET). The name Abiona is Yoruba and means one who is

born while on a journey. The name Irungu is Ibo, meaning one who takes things and places them in order. The name Baruti is Tswana, meaning several teachers. And Kemet means black face, black land, or land of black face.

30. I thought the first presenter was synonymous to a dean of pledges, but Baruti indicated that all of the members were very involved in the process.

Chapter 5. That Thing You Do

1. *The Ayeni,* 1939, 47.

2. Crump, *Kappa Alpha Psi,* 46.

3. *The Bison,* 1945, 34.

4. *The Bison,* 1930.

5. *The Bison,* 1931, 87.

6. *The Forcean,* 1923, 122

7. *The Jacksonian,* 1959.

8. I first encountered the use of the word "ship" with regards to a line in 1992 while speaking at Bradley University. While visiting the Alpha Phi Alpha house, I noticed paddles that had the prefix "S.S." and then the name of a line. I asked the brothers about the meaning and was given the entire explanation of the symbolism.

9. Ishmail Conway, "It's More Than Just Steppin': An Exploration of African-American Fraternities and Sororities," *PROfile Newsletter for NACA Professional Members,* June 1991, 8.

10. *The Centralian,* 1956.

11. Conway, "It's More Than Just Steppin'," 8.

12. *The Bison,* 1931, 89.

13. Walter M. Kimbrough, "Why Pledging Died," *The Sphinx,* spring 1994, 7, 9.

14. Andrew Selsky, "Circumcision Still Rite of Manhood in Africa," *Virginian Pilot,* 23 February 1997, A17, A22. Quote from page A22.

15. Ibid., A22.

16. *The Forcean,* 1962.

17. The national organization passed a resolution on the canine reference, indicating that they did not approve nor condone the usage of the reference in regard to the fraternity.

18. *The Tennesseean,* 1954, 128.

19. *The Bison,* 1955, 78.

20. *The Jacksonian,* 1958, 76.

21. Conway, "It's More Than Just Steppin'," 8.

22. Burnel Coulon, "The Lampados Club," *The (Tuskegee University) Campus Digest,* 11 November 1950, 3.

23. *The Heritage,* 1950, 116.

24. *The Jacksonian,* 1958, 76.

25. Marcella McCoy, "African American Fraternities and Sororities and African Communities: Cultural Parallels among Selected Public Rituals" (Ph.D. diss., Bowling Green State University, 1998).

26. *Archiviste,* 1920.

27. John Wilson, "Lampados Club," *The Ayeni,* 1939, 53.

28. *The Bison,* 1951, 60.

29. "Omega Psi Phi," *Tuskeana,* 1957.

30. *The Bison,* 1945, 75.

31. *The Bison,* 1951, 52.

32. Wesley, *History of Alpha Phi Alpha.*

33. Peter Becker, *Inland Tribes of Southern Africa* (London: Granada, 1979).

34. I was informed by an Alcorn State alumnus that the plotlike areas were actually called the trees. The different groups would tell members to meet at the "tree" just as other campuses would tell members to meet at the "plot."

35. Sandra A. Posey, "The Body Art of Brotherhood: Branding in an African American Fraternity" (Ph.D. diss., UCLA, 1999).

36. Ibid.

37. Matt Melucci, "Brothers in Scars," *San Francisco Examiner*, 26 March 1997, C1.

38. Posey, "The Body Art of Brotherhood."

39. Ibid., 77–78.

40. Ibid., 83–84.

41. Ibid., 85.

42. Ibid., 82.

43. Ibid., 70.

44. Ibid., 85.

45. "H.U. Sorority Paddlers and Mob Called Strangely Akin," *Afro-American*, 19 May 1935, p. B1.

46. McCoy, *African American Fraternities,* 51.

47. Ibid., 48.

48. Ibid.

49. Melucci, "Brothers in Scars."

50. Lisa Faye Kaplan, "Beyond Piercing: Branding Heats Up as the Ultimate Way to Send a Message with Your Body," *Detroit News*, 28 July 1997. Available at http://detnews.com/1997/accent/9707/28/07280008.htm

51. Dana Snider, "Burning for a Brand," *Indiana Daily Student*, 20 April 1999. Available at http://www.idsnews.com/news/042099/campus/042099brand.html.

52. Lonnae O'Neal Parker, "Brand Identities," *Washington Post*, 11 May 1998, D10.; The woman interviewed was one of my students while I was director of student activities at Old Dominion University. She was the first female student I personally knew who had a brand.

53. Asra Q. Nomani, "Steeped in Tradition, 'Step Dance' Is Central to Black Campus Life," *Wall Street Journal*, 10 July 1989, A4.

54. Ibid.

55. Jill Nelson, "Stepping Lively: At Black Frats and Sororities, the Dance that Unites," *Washington Post*, 29 May 1990, C1, C8.

56. Ibid., C8.

57. Linda Jones, "Stepping Up: Ritual of Black Fraternities and Sororities Is Moving into the Mainstream." *Dallas Morning News*, 10 April 1997; Deborah Peeples-Salah, "Clap Your Hands and Do a Little Steppin', *Flint Journal*, 29 January 1994, C1–2.

58. John Blake, "Steppin' It Up," *Atlanta Journal-Constitution*, 3 April 1996, D1.

59. Tonya Jameson, "Tradition, Pride and Footwork," *Charlotte Observer*, 19 November 1999, 3E.

60. Nelson, "Stepping Lively," C8.

61. Blake, "Steppin' It up," D1.

62. Tamara Hill, "Step for Pride," *Corpus Christi Caller-Times*, 19 March 2000, H3.

63. Malone, *Steppin' on the Blues*, 189.

64. Ibid.

65. Ibid.

66. Ibid., 192.

67. Conway, "It's More than Just Steppin'."

68. Elizabeth Fine, "Stepping, Saluting, Cracking, and Freaking: The Cultural Politics of African-American Step Shows," *Drama Review* 35, no. 2:39.

69. Ibid., 40.

70. Ibid., 47–48.

71. Ibid., 56.

72. Ibid.

73. Malone, *Steppin' on the Blues,* 195.

74. As a collegian in the late 1980s, "your mamma" jokes were an entertaining way for many students to relax. Examples of jokes heard around this time included, "Your mamma so Black she sweats coffee," "Your mamma so dumb she studied for a drug test and failed," and "Your mamma's hair is so short she rolls it with rice." In my particular fraternity chapter, Calvin Grier was the expert in this arena, as he incorporated both verbal and visual aspects to his snaps.

75. McCoy, "African American Fraternities," 90.

76. Malone, "Steppin' on the Blues."

77. *The Tuskeana*, 1961.

78. *The Heritage*, 1961, 201.

79. *The Hornet*, 1969, 198.

80. "Greek Show Turns 'Em On," *The Tennesseean*, 1968, 91.

81. Ibid.

82. *The Bison,* 1969, 221.

83. Malone, "Steppin' On The Blues."

84. *The Bison,* 1970, 187.

85. *The Tennesseean*, 1969.

86. Ibid., 1970.

87. "Greek Presentation Day," Ibid., 1973, 114.

88. McCoy, "African American Fraternities."

89. *Reflections*, 1979.

90. Malone, "Steppin' on the Blues."

91. Hill, "Step for Pride," H3.

92. I did not actually see church step groups until I moved to Norfolk, Virginia, in 1997, where I learned that the church where I joined sponsored a step team, as did many of the local congregations. High school step teams were also very prevalent in the Hampton Roads region of Virginia.

Chapter 6. The Future of Black Greek Life

1. Walter Kimbrough, "Notes from Underground: Despite Ban, Pledging Remains," *Black Issues In Higher Education*, 11 May 2000, 88.

2. Arthur Levine and Jeanette S. Cureton, *When Hope and Fear Collide* (San Francisco: Jossey-Bass, 1998).

3. Athur W. Chickering and Linda Reisser, *Education and Identity*, 2nd ed. (San Francisco: Jossey-Bass, 1993).

4. Williams, "Perceptions of the No-Pledge Policy."

5. Mason, *The Talented Tenth,* 33.

6. Edward T. Hall, *Beyond Culture* (New York: Anchor Books, 1981).

7. Ibid.

8. Nuwer, *Wrongs of Passage.*

9. John A. Williams, "Hazing In Black Fraternities" [website]. Available at http://www.stophazing.org/fraternity_hazing/blackfrat.htm

10. The National Pan-Hellenic Conference instituted a National Leadership Summit in 1993, first held in Pittsburgh, Pennsylvania. A third was held in Indianapolis in 1997, but the decision was made to combine the summit with the national convention in 1999 held in Atlanta. At that convention the revision of the constitution and bylaws dominated the ses-

sions, so much so that numerous educational sessions were canceled, and in essence, there was no undergraduate leadership summit.

11. I was invited to participate in the inaugural academy and served as assistant academy director in 1998. I was able to participate in 1999, 2000 and 2001 and have watched the program develop as well as seen the participants move into substantive leadership positions with the fraternity.

12. Walzer, "Judge Lets Stand NSU Expulsions over Hazing," B1, B4.

13. Nuwer, *Wrongs of Passage, 207–8.*

14. William Raspberry, "Brothers? Time to Treat Frat Hazings as Assaults," Virginian-Pilot, 24 April 1998, B11.

15. I was interviewed by Africana.com and pushed for this kind of program (Tamu Henry, "Black Greeks Out of Step?" Africana.com, 24 July 2000; http://www.africana.com/index_20000724.htm; Internet; accessed 2 October 2000).

16. Comments by John Williams on *BET Tonight* with Tavis Smiley, April 1999.

17. The Kappa Alpha Psi educational leadership consultants were generally in their mid to late twenties. While I was working at Georgia State University from 1995–96, the program was implemented and our consultant worked with students on the campus.

18. National Pan-Hellenic Council constitution and bylaws.

19. Frazier, *Black Bourgeoisie.*

20. R. A. Pickett, "Black Greeks Were Born out of Segregation," *Mobile Register,* 6 May 2000.

21. Ben Gose, "U. of Alabama Studies Why Its Fraternities and Sororities Remain Segregated By Race," *Chronicle of Higher Education,* 5 December 1997, A54–A55.

22. Ibid.

23. Ibid., A55.

24. Laurence Stains, "Black Like Me," *Rolling Stone,* 24 March 1994, 69–72. Quote is from p. 70.

25. Ibid., 70.

26. Ibid., 70.

27. Ibid., 72.

28. "Whites in Black Sororities and Fraternities," *Ebony,* December 2000, 172–75. Quote is from pp. 172–73.

29. Ibid., 174.

30. Ibid., 75.

31. Ernie Suggs, "Black Greeks Face Challenge of Change," *Atlanta Journal-Constitution,* 4 August 2000, E5.

32. Esther Wright, *Torn Togas* (Minneapolis: Fairview Press, 1996), 157; While working at Old Dominion University from 1997–2000, I remember a conversation before I left in January 2000 with a former university dean of students and longtime adviser of one of the White fraternities. He indicated that he remembered when his fraternity first voted in 1965 to allow Blacks to join. He said that vote failed. It would not be until 1967 that the fraternity voted to allow Blacks to join. That conversation had a profound impact on me given that I was born in 1967.

33. Rebecca McCarthy, "UGA Suspends Sorority for Race-Based Rejection," *Atlanta Journal and Constitution,* 7 September 2000, B1; Rebecca McCarthy, "Sorority Racial Snub a 'Wake-Up Call,'" *Atlanta Journal and Constitution,* 8 September 2000, A1; Rebecca McCarthy, "Diversity on Campus: UGA Sorority Case Spotlights Role of Race in Greek System," *Atlanta Journal and Constitution,* 10 September 2000, B2; "Sorority Members Agree to Racial Sensitivity Training," *Associated Press,* 19 September 2000.

34. Wright, *Torn Togas.*

35. Alexandra Berkowitz and Irene Padavic, Getting A Man or Getting Ahead: A Comparison of White and Black Sororities. *Journal of Contemporary Ethnography,* vol. 27 (4), January 1999, 530–57. Quote from page 532.

36. E. Lynn Harris, *Invisible Life,* Fifth Anniversary Edition (New York: Doubleday, 1999).

37. Ibid., 17.

38. Ibid., 184.

39. Ibid., 240–41.

40. Douglas N. Case, "Breaking the Cycle of Invisibility," in Shane L. Windmeyer and Pamela W. Freeman, eds., *Out On Fraternity Row* (Los Angeles: Alyson Books, 1998).

41. Ibid., xxx.

42. Ibid., xxxii.

43. R. Derrick Thomas, "Silent Rituals, Raging Hearts," in Shane L. Windmeyer and Pamela W. Freeman, eds., *Out On Fraternity Row* (Los Angeles: Alyson Books, 1998).

44. Ibid., 16.

45. Ibid., 16.

46. Ibid.

47. Ibid., 19.

48. Ennio L. Quevedo-Garcia, "Facilitating the Development of Hispanic College Students," in D. J. Wright ed., "Responding to the Needs of Today's Minority Students," *New Directions for Student Services,* no. 38 (San Francisco: Jossey-Bass, summer 1987), 49–63.

49. *Chronicle of Higher Education, Almanac,* 1 September 2000, 24.

50. Roberto Rodriguez, "Hermandades on Campus," *Black Issues in Higher Education,* 14 December 1995, 26–29.

51. Ibid.

52. Michelle Adam, "Greeks Empowering Hispanics," *Hispanic Outlook,* 26 February 1999, 17–19. Quote is from page 17.

53. Vanessa E. Jones, "The New Greeks: At Fraternities and Sororities Such as Lambda Phi Epsilon and Sigma Iota Alpha, Latinos and Asian-Americans Can Find Their Niche," *Boston Globe,* 8 February 2000.

54. Jeff Howe, "The New Latin Explosion," *Link,* April 2000, 16–17.

55. Jones, "The New Greeks."

56. Ibid., 17.

57. Deborah DiClementi, "Latinas Rush In," *Latina,* August 1999, 86–92.

58. Ibid., 90.

59. Ibid., 90.

60. I attended the 1995 NPHC conference in San Diego where the issue was raised, and several members expressed concerns about specifically allowing Latin fraternal organizations to join. The main point was that the expansion could possibly dilute the purpose of NPHC and the affiliate organizations, which was articulated as being to serve the African-American community.

61. Rodriguez, "Hermandades on Campus."

62. Jones, "The New Greeks."

63. Adam, "Greeks Empowering Hispanics."

64. "NALFO and CNHL Make History: Approve Merger to Unite Under One Organization," National Association of Latino Fraternal Organizations, 25 October 2000. News release.

Afterword

1. "Gumboots." Aired on Georgia Public Television, a PBS station, Tuesday, 5 December 2000.

2. *Who Wants To Be a Millionaire.* ABC Television, 19 December 2000.

Works Cited

"Accused Students Get to Graduate." *Associated Press*, 18 May 1998.

Adam, Michelle. "Greeks Empowering Hispanics." *Hispanic Outlook*, 26 February 1999, 17–19.

Alleyne, Elquemedo. "Malik Sigma Psi Fraternity Inc." Unpublished pamphlet, 1994.

"Alpha Beta Sigma" [website]. Available from http://www.angelfire.com/ny/AlphaBetaSigma/faqs1.html.

"Alpha Phi Literary Society." *NIKH Yearbook*. Howard University, 1915, 61.

Anderson, James. "Training the Apostles of Liberal Culture: Black Higher Education, 1900–1935." In eds. *ASHE Reader on the History of Higher Education,* Lester F. Goodchild and Harold S. Wechsler, Needham Heights, MA: Ginn Press, 1989.

Archiviste Yearbook. Wilberforce University, 1920.

Asquith, Christina. "Del. Pair Charged in Feb. Hazing." *Philadelphia Inquirer*, 7 April 1999, B1.

Axelrod, Alan. *The International Encyclopedia of Secret Societies and Fraternal Orders.* New York: Facts On File, 1997.

The Ayeni Yearbook. Tennessee State University, 1939.

Bates, Karen G. "Elite Fraternity Widens Agenda for Black Men." *Los Angeles Times*, 18 July 1990, E1–E2.

Becker, Peter. *Inland Tribes of Southern Africa.* London: Granada, 1979.

Bell, Kim. "Two Post Bond in Death of Fraternity Pledge." *St. Louis Post-Dispatch*, 20 February 1994, 11D.

Berkowitz, Alexandra, and Irene Padavic. "Getting a Man or Getting Ahead: A Comparison of White and Black Sororities." *Journal of Contemporary Ethnography* 27, no. 4 (January 1999): 530–57.

BET Tonight with Tavis Smiley, April 1998.

Bishop, Morris. *Early Cornell, 1865–1900.* Ithaca: Cornell University Press, 1962.

The Bison Yearbook. Howard University, 1923, 1930, 1931, 1945, 1951, 1955, 1965, 1969, 1970.

"Black Greek Fraternities in the '90s: Are They Still Culturally Relevant?" *Ebony Male*, August 1993, 44, 51.

Blake, John. "Black Fraternities Feel Loss of Pledging Rite." *Atlanta Constitution,* 8 October 1990, E1, E4.

————. "Steppin' It Up." *Atlanta Journal-Constitution*, 3 April 1996, D1.

Brick, Brian. "You Just Can't Beat Those Sorority Sisters at U. of North Texas." *U Magazine*, December 1993, 6.

The Brownite. Morris Brown College, 1961.

Carr, Sarah. "National Fraternity Is Told to Pay Nearly $1-Million in Beating of Pledge." *Chronicle of Higher Education*, Daily News, 3 August 1999.

Case, Douglas N. "Breaking the Cycle of Invisibility." In *Out on Fraternity Row,* edited by Shane L. Windmeyer and Pamela W. Freeman. Los Angeles: Alyson Books, 1998.

Cato, Kassia, and Bill Greve. "ΚΑΨ Fraternity Investigated for Hazing." *(Georgia Tech) Sting*, 8 March 1994, 1, 16.

The Centralian. Central State University, 1956.

Chickering, Arthur, and Linda Reisser. *Education and Identity.* 2nd ed. San Francisco: Jossey-Bass, 1993.

Chronicle of Higher Education, Almanac. 1 September 2000.

Clark, Thomas. *Indiana University: Midwestern Pioneer.* Vol. 1. Bloomington: Indiana University Press, 1970.

———. *Indiana University: Midwestern Pioneer.* Vol. 2. Bloomington: Indiana University Press, 1973.

Collison, Michelle. "Serious Issues, Touchy Subject: New Film Pokes Fun at Black Fraternities." *Chronicle of Higher Education,* 10 February 1988, A34.

———. "8 Major Black Fraternities and Sororities Agree to End the Practice of Pledging." *Chronicle of Higher Education,* 28 February 1990, A31.

Conway, Ishmail. "It's More than Just Steppin': An Exploration of African-American Fraternities and Sororities." *PROfile Newsletter for NACA Professional Members,* June 1991.

Copeland, Larry. "Black Frats May End Tradition of Pledging." *Atlanta Journal and Constitution,* 14 March 1988, 8A.

Coulon, Burnel. "The Lampados Club." *(Tuskegee University) Campus Digest,* 11 November 1950, 3.

Cox, William E. "Joining a Fraternity Should Not Result in Death." *Black Issues in Higher Education,* 10 March 1994, 88.

Crump, William. *The Story of Kappa Alpha Psi.* 3rd ed. Philadelphia: Kappa Alpha Psi Fraternity, 1983.

Davis, Carrington L. *A Brief History of Sigma Pi Phi Fraternity.* Xenia, OH: Aldine Publishing, 1947.

De Lisser, Eleena. "Violent Hazing Threatens Black Fraternities." *Wall Street Journal,* 18 November 1994, B1.

"Delta Phi Upsilon Fraternity" [website]; available from http://www.delta-phi-upsilon.org/page3.html

"Delta Sigma Theta." *The Bison Yearbook.* Howard University, 1923.

DiClementi, Deborah. "Latinas Rush In." *Latina,* August 1999, 86–92.

Dixon, Daniel. "Beta Tau Sigma." *The Golden Book Yearbook,* Coppin State University, 1950, 42.

Du Bois, W. E. B. "The Talented Tenth Memorial Address." In Henry L. Gates Jr. and Cornel West. *The Future of the Race.* New York: Alfred A. Knopf, 1996.

Enopron Yearbook. Howard University, 1921.

Evans, Sherrell. "Georgia State Sorority Pledge Alleges Attack." *Atlanta Journal-Constitution,* 30 April 1997, C4.

Fine, Elizabeth. *Soulstepping: African American Step Shows.* Urbana: University of Illinois Press, 2003.

———. "Stepping, Saluting, Cracking, and Freaking: The Cultural Politics of African-American Step Shows." *Drama Review* 35, no. 2:39.

The Forcean Yearbook. Wilberforce University, 1923, 1928, 1962.

Franklin, John Hope, and Alfred A. Moss Jr. *From Slavery to Freedom.* 6th ed. New York: McGraw-Hill, 1988.

"Fraternities and Sororities: A Dramatic Comeback on Campus." *Ebony,* December 1983, 93.

"Fraternity Pays Millions to Settle Hazing Suit." *Chronicle of Higher Education,* 24 January 1997, A6.

"Fraternity Suing Students Involved in Hazing Incident." *Associated Press,* 25 May 2000.

Frazier, E. Franklin. *Black Bourgeoisie.* New York: Free Press Paperbacks, 1957.

Freeman, Michelle, and Tina Witcher. "Stepping Into Black Power." *Rolling Stone,* 24 March 1988.

Gage, Soraya (producer), and Sarah Karlson (editor). "Blood Brothers." *Dateline NBC,* 24 May 1995.

George, Nelson. *Hip Hop America.* New York: Viking, 1998.

Geraghty, Mary. "5 Fraternity Members Charged in Beating of Student at Pitt; His Condition Is Serious." *Chronicle of Higher Education*, 19 April 1996.

Gerrety, Joe. "12 Face Hazing Charges." *Lafayette (IN) Journal and Courier*, 3 August 1995, A1.

Giddings, Paula. *In Search of Sisterhood: Delta Sigma Theta and the Challenge of the Black Sorority Movement.* New York: Quill, 1988.

Gill, Robert L. *The Omega Psi Phi Fraternity and the Men Who Made Its History.* Washington, DC: Omega Psi Phi, 1963.

Gose, Ben. "U. of Alabama Studies Why Its Fraternities and Sororities Remain Segregated By Race." *Chronicle of Higher Education*, 5 December 1997, A54–A55.

Graham, Lawrence O. *Our Kind of People.* New York: HarperCollins, 1999.

"Greek Presentation Day." *Tennesseean Yearbook.* Tennessee State University, 1973, 114.

"Greek Show Turns 'Em On." *Tennesseean Yearbook.* Tennessee State University, 1968, 91.

"Greekdom on CSC's Campus." *The Gold Torch newspaper.* Central State College, December 1954, 8.

"H.U. Sorority Paddlers and Mob Called Strangely Akin." *Afro-American*, 19 May 1935, B1.

Hall, Edward T. *Beyond Culture.* New York: Anchor Books, 1981.

Harris, E. Lynn. *Invisible Life.* Fifth Anniversary Edition. New York: Doubleday, 1999.

Haworth, Karla. "U. of Louisville Student Hospitalized After Beating in Fraternity Ritual." *Chronicle of Higher Education*, Daily News, 14 April 1997.

"Hell Week or Plain 'Hell'." *The Gold Torch*, 12 November 1965, 2.

Henry, Tamu. "Black Greeks Out of Step?" [website]. Africana.com [cited, 24 July 2000]. Available from http://www.africana.com/index_20000724.htm

The Heritage Yearbook. Alabama A&M University, 1950, 1961.

Hill, Tamara. "Step for Pride." *Corpus Christi Caller-Times*, 19 March 2000, H3.

The Hornet Yearbook. Alabama State University, 1969.

Horowitz, Helen. *Campus Life.* New York: Alfred A. Knopf, 1987.

Houston, Charles D. "Bout the Greeks." *(Tuskegee University) Campus Digest*, September 1948, 3.

Howe, Jeff. "The New Latin Explosion." *Link*, April 2000, 16–17.

Hunter-Gault, Charlayne. *In My Place.* New York: Farrar, Straus and Giroux, 1992.

Initium Yearbook. Howard University, 1922.

The Jacksonian Yearbook. Jackson State University, 1948, 1958, 1959.

James, Darius. *That's Blaxploitation.* New York: St. Martin's Griffin, 1995.

Jameson, Tonya. "Tradition, Pride and Footwork." *Charlotte Observer*, 19 November 1999, 3E.

Jarrett, Hobart S. *The History of Sigma Pi Phi.* Vol. 2. Philadelphia: Quantum Leap Publisher, Inc., 1995.

Jones, Linda. "Stepping Up: Ritual of Black Fraternities and Sororities Is Moving into the Mainstream." *Dallas Morning News*, 10 April 1997.

Jones, Vanessa E. "The New Greeks: At Fraternities and Sororities Such as Lambda Phi Epsilon and Sigma Iota Alpha, Latinos and Asian-Americans Can Find Their Niche." *Boston Globe*, 8 February 2000.

Kaplan, Lisa Faye. "Beyond Piercing: Branding Heats Up as the Ultimate Way to Send a Message with Your Body." *Detroit News*, 28 July 1997. Available from http://detnews.com/1997/accent/9707/28/07280008.htm

Keets, Heather S. "Greek Philosophy." *YSB*, April 1996, 48–51.

Kershner, Frank, Jr. "History of Greek Hazing." *Bulletin of Interfraternity Research and Advisory Council,* 1 May 1978.

Kimbrough, Walter M. "Why Pledging Died." *The Sphinx*, spring 1994, 7, 9.

———. "Was Eight Enough? New Trends in Black Fraternal Life." *(AFA) Perspectives,* summer 1997, 4–6.

———. "The Membership Intake Movement of Historically Black Greek-Letter Organizations." *NASPA Journal* 34, no. 3 (1997): 229–39.

———. "Notes from Underground: Despite Ban, Pledging Remains." *Black Issues In Higher Education*, 11 May 2000, 88.

———, and Michael Sutton. *The Persistent Pledging of Black Greeks: A Student Development Approach for Understanding and Challenging the Culture*. Washington, DC: National Association of Student Personnel Administrators, 1998.

Lasseter, Tom. "SGA President Shawn Mitchell Resigns Temporarily in Lieu of Fraternity's Turmoil." *Georgia State University Signal*, 22 April 1997, 1, 4.

Lee, Spike, with Lisa Jones. *Uplift the Race: The Construction of School Daze*. New York: Simon and Schuster, 1988.

Leff, Lisa. "24 Students at U-Md. Charged with Hazing." *Washington Post*, 27 May 1993, C3.

Levine, Arthur, and Jeanette S. Cureton. *When Hope and Fear Collide*. San Francisco: Jossey-Bass, 1998.

Logan, Rayford L. *Howard University: The First Hundred Years, 1867–1967*. New York: New York University Press, 1969.

———. "Hall, Prince," Microsoft Encarta Africana 2000 [CD-ROM] (Cambridge, MA).

Malone, Jacqui. *Steppin' on the Blues: The Visible Rhythms of African American Dance*. Urbana: University of Illinois Press, 1996.

Marriott, Michel. "Black Fraternities and Sororities End a Tradition." *New York Times*, 3 October 1990, Education, 8.

Mason, Herman, Jr. *The Talented Tenth: The Founders and Presidents of Alpha*. Winter Park, FL: Four-G Publishers, 1999.

McCarthy, Rebecca. "Diversity on Campus: UGA Sorority Case Spotlights Role of Race in Greek System." *Atlanta Journal and Constitution*, 10 September 2000.

———. "Sorority Racial Snub a 'Wake-Up Call.'" *Atlanta Journal and Constitution*, 8 September 2000, A1.

———. "UGA Suspends Sorority for Race-Based Rejection." *Atlanta Journal and Constitution*, 7 September 2000, B1.

———. "UGA Closes Fraternity While Alleged Hazing Investigated." *Atlanta Constitution*, 27 May 1993, B7.

———. "Suspension of UGA Fraternity To Be Appealed." *Atlanta Journal-Constitution*, 30 October 1996, C6.

McCoy, Marcella. "African American Fraternities and Sororities and African Communities: Cultural Parallels among Selected Public Rituals." Ph.D. diss., Bowling Green State University, 1998.

McKenzie, Andre. "Fraters: Black Greek–Letter Fraternities at Four Historically Black Colleges, 1920–1960." Ph.D. diss., Teachers College, Columbia University, 1986.

Melucci, Matt. "Brothers in Scars." *San Francisco Examiner*, 26 March 1997, C1.

Milloy, Courtland. "The Gang Called Frats." *Washington Post*, 5 May 1993, C1, C10.

Mills, David. "The Wrongs of the Rites of Brotherhood." *Washington Post*, 18 June 1990, B1, B6.

Moses, Napoleon. "Membership Intake: A Time For Decision." *The Sphinx*, summer 1990, 10.

"NALFO and CNHL Make History: Approve Merger to Unite under One Organization." National Association of Latino Fraternal Organizations, 25 October 2000. News release.

Neal, Erika D. "Search for Brotherhood Ends in Death." *St. Louis Post-Dispatch*, 23 February 1994, 7B.

Nelson, Jill. "Stepping Lively: At Black Frats and Sororities, the Dance that Unites." *Washington Post*, 29 May 1990, C1, C8.

Noble, Jeanne. "A Sense of Place." *Essence*, May 1985, 131.

Nomani, Asra Q. "Steeped in Tradition, 'Step Dance' Is Central to Black Campus Life." *Wall Street Journal*, 10 July 1989, A4.

Nuwer, Hank. *Wrongs of Passage: Fraternities, Sororities, Hazing, and Binge Drinking*. Bloomington: Indiana University Press, 1999.

"Omega Psi Phi." *Tuskeana Yearbook*. Tuskegee University, 1957.

O'Neal Parker, Lonnae. "Brand Identities." *Washington Post*, 11 May 1998, D10.

O'Neil, Tim, and Marianna Riley. "Student Dies in Hazing." *St. Louis Post-Dispatch*, 17 February 1994, 1A.

Parker, Marjorie H. *Alpha Kappa Alpha: In the Eye of the Beholder*. Washington, DC: Alpha Kappa Alpha Sorority, 1979.

————. *Alpha Kappa Alpha: Through the Years, 1908–1988*. Chicago: Mobium Press, 1990.

Payne, Doug. "Seven Students Face Hazing Charges." *Atlanta Constitution*, 2 March 1994, D6.

Peeples-Salah, Deborah. "Clap Your Hands and Do a Little Steppin'. *Flint Journal*, 29 January 1994, C1–C2.

Pharnor, Alexandra. "Breaking the Code." *The Source*, May 1999, 72.

Pickett, R. A. "Black Greeks Were Born out of Segregation." *Mobile Register*, 6 May 2000.

"Pi Psi Fraternity" [website]. Available from http://www.msu.edu/user/pipsi/questions.html.

"Pledging a Brother, Not Intaking a 'Paper Brother.'" Black Issues in Higher Education, 12 June 1997, 26–27.

Porter, Charles F. "Gamma Phi Fraternity." *The Forcean Yearbook*. Wilberforce University, 1923, 136.

Posey, Sandra A. "The Body Art of Brotherhood: Branding in an African American Fraternity." Ph.D. diss., UCLA, 1999.

Promethean Yearbook. Morgan State University, 1971, 229.

Quevedo-Garcia, Ennio L. "Facilitating the Development of Hispanic College Students." In D. J. Wright, ed., "Responding to the Needs of Today's Minority Students." *New Directions for Student Services*, no. 38 (San Francisco: Jossey-Bass, summer 1987), 49–63.

Raspberry, William. "Brothers? Time to Treat Frat Hazings as Assaults." *Virginian-Pilot*, 24 April 1998, B11.

Reflections Yearbook. Norfolk State University, 1979.

Rodriguez, Roberto. "Hermandades on Campus." *Black Issues in Higher Education*, 14 December 1995, 26–29.

Ross, J. R. "More Arrests Expected in Hazing Attack." *Indiana (University) Daily Student*, 2 March 1994, 1.

Ross, Lawrence, Jr. *The Divine Nine: The History of African American Fraternities and Sororities*. New York: Kensington Books, 1999.

Rothfield, Michael. "Hazing at Lincoln Put One in Hospital." *Philadelphia Inquirer*, 18 February 1999, B1.

Rothfield, Michael, and Christina Asquith. "Lincoln Suspends 7 in Hazing of Student." *Philadelphia Inquirer*, 9 March 1999, B1.

Rothfield, Michael, Christina Asquith, and Angela Galloway. "Lincoln Suspends All Greek Intake Events." *Philadelphia Inquirer*, 19 February 1999, B1.

Rudolph, Frederick. *The American College and University: A History*. Athens: University of Georgia Press, 1990.

Ruffins, Paul. "Fratricide: Are African American Fraternities Beating Themselves to Death?" *Black Issues in Higher Education*, 12 June 1997, 19.

————. "The Persistent Madness of Greek Hazing." *Black Issues in Higher Education*, 25 June 1998, 14–18.

————. "Greek Tragedy." *Washington City Paper*, 18 June 1999, 16–27.

Selsky, Andrew. "Circumcision Still Rite of Manhood in Africa." *Virginian Pilot*, 23 February 1997, A17, A22.

Semi-Annual Meeting minutes. Hampton Institute Board of Trustees, 27 April 1951.

Shea, Christopher. "U. of Maryland Fraternity Chapter Is Suspended for Abusive Hazing." *Chronicle of Higher Education*, 3 November 1993, A38.

————. "Brutal Hazing Death Shocks Missouri Campus." *Chronicle of Higher Education*, 2 March 1994, A37–A38.

Snider, Dana. "Burning for a Brand." *Indiana Daily Student*, 20 April 1999. Available from http://www.idsnews.com/news/042099/campus/042099brand.html

"Social Organizations." *TuskeanaYearbook*. Tuskegee University, 1941.

"Sorority Members Agree to Racial Sensitivity Training." *Associated Press*, 19 September 2000.

Spangler, Todd. "Md. Police Probe Alleged Hazing." *Associated Press*, 13 April 1998.

Stains, Laurence. "Black Like Me." *Rolling Stone*, 24 March 1994, 69–72. Quote is from p. 70.

Stanford, Duane. "Frat Pledges Describe UGA Player's Paddling." *Atlanta Journal-Constitution*, 27 September 1996, B2.

Stanford, Duane, and Doug Cumming. "Police Probe UGA Hazing." *Atlanta Journal-Constitution*, 12 September 1996, B1.

"Student Council." *The Bison Yearbook*. Howard University, 1924.

Suggs, Ernie. "Black Greeks Face Challenge of Change." *Atlanta Journal-Constitution*, 4 August 2000, E5.

———. "The Rise of the Black Greek Empire." *(Durham) Herald-Sun* [article online]. Available from http://www.herald-sun.com/hbcu/docs/whyhbcu_3.html; accessed 11 March 1997.

Sweet, Stephen. "Understanding Fraternity Hazing: Insights from Symbolic Interactionist Theory." *Journal of College Student Development* 40, no. 4 (1999): 355.

The Tennesseean Yearbook. Tennessee State University, 1954, 1969, 1970.

Thomas, R. Derrick. "Silent Rituals, Raging Hearts." In *Out on Fraternity Row,* edited by Shane L. Windmeyer and Pamela W. Freeman, Los Angeles: Alyson Books, 1998.

Townsend, Angela. "Hazing Lives Despite Crackdown." *Lafayette (IN) Journal and Courier*, 4 August 1995, A10.

The Tuskeana, 1961.

"University Softens on Some Aspects of Hazing Policy." *New York Times*, Campus Life Section I, 4 March 1990, 37.

Usdansky, Margaret. "Frat Brothers Remorseful, Frustrated." *Atlanta Journal-Constitution*, 5 November 1989, D1, D6.

Walzer, Philip. "Judge Lets Stand NSU Expulsions over Hazing." *Virginian-Pilot*, 4 May 1999, B1, B4.

Watkins, Richard T. "Black Social Orders." *Black Enterprise*, July 1975, 26–28.

Welsh-Huggins, Andrew. "IU Student Talks About Alleged Fraternity Hazing." *Bloomington (IN.) Herald-Times*, 5 March 1994, A1.

Wesley, Charles H. *History of Sigma Pi Phi: First of the Negro-American Greek-Letter Fraternities.* New York: Sigma Pi Phi Fraternity, 1954.

———. *The History of Alpha Phi Alpha.* Chicago: Foundation Publishers, 1961.

Wessel, Kim. "Hazing Victim to Get $1 Million." *Louisville Courier-Journal*, 7 April 2000, C1.

White, P. S. *Behind These Doors—A Legacy: The History of Sigma Gamma Rho Sorority.* Chicago: Sigma Gamma Rho Sorority, 1974.

"Whites in Black Sororities and Fraternities." *Ebony*, December 2000, 172–75.

Wiley III, Ed, and Angela Clarke. "Recent Death Rekindles Concern About Fraternity Hazing." *Black Issues in Higher Education*, 9 November 1989, 13.

Williams, Cora. "Presenting Pi Beta Sigma." *The Golden Book Yearbook*. Coppin State University, 1950, 41.

Williams, John A. "Hazing In Black Fraternities" [online]. http://www.stophazing.org/fraternity_hazing/blackfrat.htm

———. "Perceptions of the No-Pledge Policy for New Member Intake by Undergraduate Members of Predominantly Black Fraternities and Sororities." Ph.D. diss., Kansas State University, 1992.

Wilmshurst, W. L. *The Meaning of Masonry.* New York: Gramercy Books, 1980.

Wilson, John. "Lampados Club." *The Ayeni Yearbook*. Tennessee State University, 1939, 53.

Wright, Esther. *Torn Togas*. Minneapolis: Fairview Press, 1996.

Black Greek Bibliography

Argetsinger, A. "Fraternity Pledges Beaten, Police Say; At Least 5 on Eastern Shore Hospitalized." *Washington Post* 14 April 1988, B3.

> Discusses the pledges hospitalized pledging Kappa Alpha Psi at UMES.

Bates, K. G. "Elite Fraternity Widens Agenda for Black Men." *Los Angeles Times* 18 July 1990, E1–E2.

> Provides a general overview of Sigma Pi Phi Fraternity, including history, famous members, changes in philosophy to serve the Black community, and membership demographics.

Benbow, L. P. "It's Time To Stop 'The Dance'." *Ebony* October 1976, 52.

> Editorial by immediate past president of Delta Sigma Theta who urges Black Greeks to end formal dances, which are expensive. Estimates how much the groups spend and how the beneficiaries are generally White businesses. Suggests the groups take a collective vow of abstinence and use the money and energy for the more serious needs of Blacks.

Berkowitz, A., and Padavic, I. "Getting A Man or Getting Ahead: A Comparison of White and Black Sororities." *Journal of Contemporary Ethnography* 27, no. 4 (1999): 530–57.

> Compares attitudes of White and Black sorority members, particularly in reference to their attitudes toward finding men, engaging in community service, and enhancing careers.

"Black Sorority Boom." *Ebony* 53, no. 12, 68–75.

> Article discusses how membership in the four largest Black sororities is growing, and shows that sorority members are taking an active role in improving society. Discusses both political and financial power.

Blake, J. "Steppin' it up: Combining Dance, Drills, Black College Ritual Gains Mass Appeal, Wows Crowds." *Atlanta Journal-Constitution*, 13 April 1996, D1.

> Discusses stepping as an art form, mentioning a performance by the group Stomp on the Academy Awards. Interviews include Frank Mercado-Valdes, producer of the show STOMP.

Blake, J. "Black Fraternities Feel the Loss of Pledging Rite." *Atlanta Constitution* 8 October 1990, E1, E4.

> Discusses undergraduate reactions to the end of pledging that year, noting the Morehouse incident. Interviews include Carter Womack (Phi Beta Sigma), Jonathan Brandt (NIC), and several Clark Atlanta University students.

Brick, C. "You Just Can't Beat Those Sorority Sisters at U. of North Texas." *U. Magazine* December 1993, 6.

> Reports hazing perpetrated by five alumni members of Alpha Kappa Alpha sorority at the school. Included paddling and assaults with eggs. Denton County court gave the women probated sentences of ninety days in jail, with two receiving five-hundred-dollar fines.

Campbell, K. "Phi Beta Sigma's Charter Revoked by National Office, Is Suspended by GSU, Pending Investigation into Alleged Hazing Incident. *The Signal* 64 no. 23 (22 April 1997): 1, 4.

Documents hazing investigation of fraternity involving an Emory University student pledging at Georgia State University. Interviews include Lawrence Miller (Phi Beta Sigma), James Scott, and Kurt Keppler (Georgia State University).

Carr, S. "National Fraternity Is Told to Pay Nearly $1- Million in Beating of Pledge." *Chronicle of Higher Education,* 3 August 1999.

Reports on the Kentucky jury that awarded $931,428 to Shawn Blackston for being hazed by Omega Psi Phi at the University of Louisville in 1997. The award included $750,000 in punitive damages and $181,428 for medical expenses, lost wages, and mental and physical suffering.

Cato, K., and Greve, B. "Kappa Alpha Psi Fraternity Investigated for Hazing." *The Sting* 47, no. 4 (8 March 1994): 1, 16.

Report on the suspension of the fraternity by Georgia Tech and Southern Tech pending the outcome of a Georgia Bureau of Investigation inquiry into hazing. Notes the state law, university policy, and a fraternity executive order reiterating the outlaw of pledging.

Childs, R. "Black Greek Fraternities in the '90s: Are They Still Culturally Relevant?" *Ebony Man*, August 1993, 44, 51.

Challenges the existence of these groups based on a litany of hazing cases described by the author. Suggests that there are more important issues for these groups to address. Quotes a speech by Dick Gregory given at Grambling State University where he challenges the groups to use their collective power, or have it taken by him and people like him.

Chura, K. "Greeks Kicked Off Campus for Hazing." *Kentucky Kernel*, 11 June 1998.

Delta Sigma Theta was suspended from the University of Kentucky following charges of physical and mental abuse. A three-year suspension was the result of the two-month investigation.

Cohen-Vrignaud, G. "Step Show Helps Unify Black Greek Association." *Daily Michigan*, 16 February 1998.

Discusses the step show at the University of Michigan, with a discussion of what stepping is and its origins.

Collison, M. N-K. "8 Major Black Fraternities and Sororities Agree to End the Practice of Pledging." *Chronicle of Higher Education*, 28 February 1990, A31.

Reports the decision from the Council of Presidents meeting in St. Louis, which ended pledging. Mentions ZBT and TKE no-pledge initiative as well as Joel Harris incident. Interviews include Ulysses McBride (Kappa Alpha Psi), Moses Norman (Omega Psi Phi), Raymond Archer (Howard University), and Teresa Loser (Rutgers University).

Collison, M. N-K. "Serious Issues, Touchy Subject: New Film Pokes Fun at Black Fraternities." *Chronicle of Higher Education*, 10 February 1988, A34–A35.

Discusses the debate surrounding the movie *School Daze*. Addresses the positive aspects and the hazing incidents. Describes Lee's difficulties filming at Morehouse, issues of racial division, and the problems associated with pledging. Interviews include Spike Lee, Michael Price (Alpha Phi Alpha), and Gerald Smith (Phi Beta Sigma).

Collison, M. N-K. "Black Fraternities on White Campuses, Accused of Separatism, Say They Are Just Misunderstood." *Chronicle of Higher Education,* 22 April 1987, 35, 38.

Reports on a two-day conference at Michigan State University between college and university administrators and officers of the eight national Black Greek groups. Participants discuss the perceptions of the groups by White administrators and students to Black Greek culture, especially around pledging and step shows. Interviewed numerous participants.

Conway, I. "It's More than Steppin': An Exploration of African-American Fraternities and Sororities." *Profile* 14 (June 1991):1–11.

Analysis of the customs of Black Greek organizations and their link to African customs and traditions. Discussion includes pledging and stepping.

Copeland, L. "Black Frats May End Tradition of Pledging." *Atlanta Constitution*, 14 March 1988, 1A, 8.

Reports on Phi Beta Sigma's new initiative to ban pledging and the trend it might set. Georgia State University is the backdrop, where the Sigma Chapter follows the new rules. Interviews include Ted Smith (Kappa Alpha Psi), and John Day (GSU/Phi Beta Sigma adviser).

Cox, W. E. "Joining a Fraternity Should Not Result in Death." *Black Issues in Higher Education* 11, no. 1 (10 March 1994): 88.

Editorial on the death of Michael Davis from a member of the fraternity.

Crump, W. L. *The Story of Kappa Alpha Psi,* 3rd ed. Philadelphia: Kappa Alpha Psi Fraternity, 1983.

House history of Kappa Alpha Psi.

Cumming, D. "School Says Worst Offenses Now a Thing of the Past." *Atlanta Journal-Constitution*, 12 September 1996, B3.

Provides a brief history of hazing at UGA and efforts to solve problems. Mentions Omega Psi Phi and Delta Sigma Theta.

Davis, C. L. *A Brief History of Sigma Pi Phi Fraternity.* Xenia, Ohio: Aldine Publishing, 1947.

Short house history of Sigma Pi Phi Fraternity.

De Lisser, E. "Violent Hazing Threatens Black Fraternities." *Wall Street Journal*, 18 November 1994, B1, B14.

Discusses the potential threats to Black fraternities based on recent hazings at Indiana University, Paine College, and the death at SEMO. Interviews include Robert Harris (Kappa Alpha Psi), Michael Gordon (NPHC), and Darryl Matthews (Alpha Phi Alpha).

Fine, E. C. "Stepping, Saluting, Cracking, and Freaking: The Cultural Politics of African-American Step Shows." *Drama Review* 35, no. 2 (1991): 39–57.

An ethnographic study of the culture around stepping. Detailed analysis of how it is done, including notations of rhythm and chants. Emphasis of the researcher is on the use of African-American folk traditions and communication patterns including call and response, rapping, the dozens, etc.

Fox, E., Hodge, C., and Ward, W. "A Comparison of Attitudes Held by Black and White Fraternity Members." *Journal of Negro Education* 54, no. 6 (1987): 521–34.

Authors conducted a study of five White and four Black fraternities at a public institution of 6,000 students in the southwestern US. The students completed the CSQ, part II. Concluded that fraternity men were more dependent on family and peers. White fraternity men were less involved with social issues, less satisfied with faculty and the student body, and less involved with studying than White nonfraternity students. Black fraternity members scored higher than White fraternity members for liberalism and social consciousness, and were the most active group (Greek and non-Greek) in extracurricular activities. Black fraternity men scored significantly higher on cultural sophistication than any of the other three groups.

"Fraternities and Sororities: A Dramatic Comeback On Campus." *Ebony*, December 1983, 93–98.

Indicates that the groups were irrelevant during the sixties. "Enthusiasm was for picket lines, not pledge lines." Identifies Ozell Sutton as chair of the Council of Presidents (defines that the group was founded in 1981). Article indicates total NPHC membership is about 500,000. Interviews with various national presidents.

"Fraternity sued again over hazing." *Daily Southtown*, 25 March 1998.

Student at Northern Illinois University sued Kappa Alpha Psi for $150,000 in damages due to hazings that gave him a bruised kidney, a concussion, and cigarette burns. Five members were expelled from the university and two suspended.

"Fraternity Suspended at Mississippi State for Hazing Incident." *Black Issues in Higher Education* 16, no. 1, 14–15.

Omega Psi Phi was suspended after a student was treated by the university health center for injuries sustained from paddling.

Freeman, M., and Witcher, T. "Stepping into Black Power." *Rolling Stone*, 24 March 1988.

Provides an explanation of some of the culture of Black fraternity life. Includes an emphasis on stepping. Provides detailed information on the alumni experience in these organizations, providing a list of influential Blacks who are members and their experiences in the organizations. Also provides criticism by Spike Lee of the groups, as evidenced in the film *School Daze*. Interviews include Lee, John Lewis (congressman- GA), Ben Hooks (NAACP), Julian Bond (civil rights leader), and David Dinkins (NYC official).

Geraghty, M. "5 Fraternity Members Charged in Beating of Student at Pitt; His Condition Is Serious." *Chronicle of Higher Education* 42, no. 32 (19 April 1996): A47.

Reports a University of Pittsburgh student is placed on a kidney dialysis machine after being beaten with a wooden paddle and a cane. The men were arrested, but only one of the five was a current student.

Gerrety, J. "12 Face Hazing Charges." *Indianapolis Journal and Courier*, 3 August 1995, A1.

Reports on court appearances of twelve members of Alpha Phi Alpha Fraternity at Purdue University in response to hazing of nine pledges in February of that year. Three of the members received felony charges, including one who was a university employee. The others faced multiple misdemeanor charges.

Giddings, P. "Sorority Sisters." *Essence* 19, no. 3 (July 1998): 36.

Short article describing the historical origins of Black sororities and their impact on Black communities.

Giddings, P. *In Search of Sisterhood: Delta Sigma Theta and the Challenge of the Black Sorority Movement.* New York: William Morrow and Company, 1988.

House history of Delta Sigma Theta.

Goodner, J. (1992). "Comparison of Hazing Attitudes of Black and White Fraternity Members at Colleges in the State of Alabama" (doctoral dissertation, University of Alabama, 1992). *Dissertation Abstracts International* 54, no 1: 104.

Dissertation seeking to determine differences in attitudes toward hazing between black and white fraternity members at six schools (public and private, PWI and

HBCU) in the state of Alabama. Survey covered areas dealing with hazing and the Alabama law against it, the tradition of hazing in fraternities, hazing on the respondent's campus, and hazing in the respondent's fraternity. Study revealed that there is a statistically significant difference between fraternity members based on race, regardless of school type.

"Greek Tragedies." *U.S. News and World Report*, 29 April 1996, 26.

Short article that reports Alpha Phi Alpha suing its own members who participated in hazing.

Hackett, D. "The Greeks." *The Crisis* 92, no. 10 (December 1985): 42–47, 59–62.

A description of Black fraternities and sororities. Includes a brief overview of each NPHC organization, the activities of the organizations, and community efforts. Emphasis is placed on graduate members and their activities.

Hendricks, M. L. "Racial Identity Development of African-American Male Fraternity Members and Nonmembers at Historically Black Colleges and Universities and Predominantly White Campuses" (doctoral dissertation, Texas A&M University–Commerce, 1996). *Dissertation Abstracts International* 58, no. 3 (1997): 752.

Dissertation explored the relationship between stages of racial identity development and membership in African-American fraternities on Historically Black College and University (HBCU) campuses and predominantly White campuses (PWIs) in Texas. Two hundred subjects completed the Racial Identity Attitude Scale and a Student Information Form. No significant differences in racial identity development found between African-American male students at HBCUs and those at PWIs; members of African-American fraternities and non-members; members of African-American fraternities and non-members at HBCUs; members of African-American fraternities and non-members on PWIs; or members of African-American fraternities at HBCUs and those on PWIs. Significant numbers of non-members at HBCUs demonstrated higher levels of Racial Identity Development than did non-members at PWIs.

Hill, T. "Step for Pride." *Corpus Christi Caller-Times*, 19 March 2000, H1, H3

Discusses stepping by a youth organization and how the form links to Black Greeks. Interviews include Walter Kimbrough.

Hinkel, J. "Kappa Alpha Psi Found Guilty of Hazing Violations." *The Technique*, 2 June 2000.

Discusses the three-year suspension of Kappa Alpha Psi at Georgia Tech by the IFC, but the fraternity received a suspended sentence, indicating that the penalty would not be enacted unless a future incident occurred.

Hurla, J. "Hazing Suspected in Injury." *Kansas State Collegian*, 20 April 1998.

Details police investigation of a student taken to the KU medical center for extensive back and kidney damage. Kappa Alpha Psi fraternity was being investigated, as the victim was linked to the organization.

Jameson, T. "Tradition, Pride, and Footwork." *Charlotte Observer*, 19 November 1999, 3E.

Previews the Battle of the Greeks Step Show by explaining stepping. Interviews include Elizabeth Fine (Virginia Tech) and Walter Kimbrough.

Jarrett, H. B. *The History of Sigma Pi Phi. First of the African American Greek-Letter Fraternities (Vol. 2)*, 1999.

House history of Sigma Pi Phi fraternity.

Jones, L. "Stepping Up: Ritual of Black Fraternities and Sororities Is Moving into the Mainstream." *Dallas Morning News*, 10 April 1997, C1–2C.

Previews an upcoming step show at the Dallas Convention Center, providing a historical perspective of the art form. Interviews include Walter Kimbrough and Adrian Drake (Kappa Alpha Psi consultant).

Jones, R. "The Historical Significance of Sacrificial Ritual: Understanding Violence in the Modern Black Fraternity Pledge Process." *Western Journal of Black Studies* 24, no. 2 (2000): 112–24.

Discusses the traditional pledge process of Black fraternities in relation to the violence that occurs via hazing. The article also views the process of pledging in terms of a sacrificial rite. The author compares African initiation systems to draw comparisons between that process and fraternity pledging. The article concludes that the process must be understood in order to eliminate the violence that occurs.

Keets, H. "Greek Philosophy: Weakened by Slander and Scandal, Black Greek Letter Organizations Need Rehabilitation." *YSB*, April 1996, 49–51.

Reviews the problems facing Black Greeks related to pledging activities that continue to exist despite the end of pledging in 1990. Interviews include Darryl Matthews (Alpha Phi Alpha).

Kimbrough, W. M. "Notes from Underground: Despite a Ban, Pledging Remains." *Black Issues in Higher Education* 17, no. 6 (2000): 88.

Summarizes the results of a replication of Williams's dissertation and challenges the logic of membership intake.

Kimbrough, W. M., and Hutcheson, P. A. "The Impact of Membership in Black Greek-Letter Organizations on Black Students' Involvement in Collegiate Activities and Their Development of Leadership Skills." *Journal of Negro Education* 67, no. 2 (1998): 96–105.

Despite numerous recent events that have cast collegiate Black Greek–letter organizations (BGOs) in a negative light, many view these and other Greek organizations as important leadership development vehicles. This article reports on a study that examined the impact of BGO membership on Black students' involvement in campus-related activities and their leadership development.

Kimbrough, W. M., and Sutton, E. M. *The Persistent Pledging of Black Greeks: A Student Development Approach for Understanding and Challenging the Culture.* Washington, D.C.: National Association of Student Personnel Administrators, 1998.

White paper on the continued pledging within Black Greek organizations, emphasizing the problem from a cultural standpoint, and suggestions through use of student development to change the culture of pledging.

Kimbrough, W. M. "The Membership Intake Movement of Historically Black Greek-Letter Organizations." *NASPA Journal* 34, no. 3 (1997): 229–39.

Critical essay reviews the history of pledging and movements to reform the practice among historically Black fraternities and sororities. Describes the membership intake process and suggests that the national leadership should emphasize the founding ideas of the organizations as a means of overcoming resistance to change.

Kimbrough, W. M. "A Comparison of Involvement, Leadership Skills and Experiences For Black Students Based On Membership In A Black Greek-Lettered Organization and Institutional Type" (doctoral dissertation, Georgia State University, 1996). *Dissertation Abstracts International* 57, no. 9 (1997): 3844.

Dissertation determined the impact of membership in a historically Black fraternity or sorority on Black student involvement and leadership development, based on the campus type. Three hundred ninety-one students participated from seven Southeastern states. Greek members were significantly more likely to be members of six selected student groups than non-Greek members, as well as hold more elected and appointed positions. For leadership skill assessment, Greek members scored higher on all eight leadership roles, and for thirty-one of the thirty-two skill areas. Greek and non-Greek members differed in their views of student organizations ability to develop leadership. Similar results occurred based on campus type, although to a greater degree for Black campuses. It was concluded that Greek members are more involved than non-Greek members and have a higher degree of confidence in their leadership skills. Furthermore, the impact of Greek membership was more significant on a historically Black campus.

Kimbrough, W. M. "Self-Assessment, Participation, and Value of Leadership Skills, Activities, and Experiences for Black Students Relative to Their Membership in Historically Black Fraternities and Sororities." *Journal of Negro Education* 64, no. 1 (1995): 63–74.

This study reports on the views held by Black students about Black Greek–letter organizations (BGOs) and their role in leadership development. Leadership was found to be an important attribute among students, and BGO membership, valued overwhelmingly among members, provided them with more and earlier opportunities for leadership development than did White-dominated student groups.

Kimbrough, W. M. "Why Pledging Died." *The Sphinx* 79, no. 1 (1994): 7, 9.

Offers an analysis of the events and mentality that led to the change in the pledge program of Black fraternities and sororities. Provides cultural explanation of the customs of these organizations.

Leff, L. "U-Md. College Park Bans Social Fraternity." *Washington Post,* 23 October 1993, B1, 5.

Reports the banning of Omega Psi Phi fraternity at the university until 1998 for hazing incidents. Details the hazing that took place.

Leff, L. "24 Students at U-Md. Charged with Hazing." *Washington Post,* 27 May 1993, C3.

Reports on hazing of six students pledging Omega Psi Phi fraternity at the University of Maryland, College Park. Describes that pledges were punched, kicked, whipped, and beaten with paddles over a two-month period, and some required hospitalization. Notes two other Omega hazing-related deaths in the 80s.

Logan, C. "Bonds of Brotherhood." *Upscale,* September/October 2000, 128.

Opinion piece on the divisions within the Black Greek system.

Malone, D. V. "A Cultural and Social Perspective on Black Greek-Letter Organization Membership: Perceptions of Power and Influence through Affiliation" (Master's thesis, Florida Atlantic University, 1999). *Masters Abstracts International* 37, no. 4 (1999): 1061.

This research investigated "Black Greek" culture, its social impact, the influence of its members, and member and nonmember perceptions of the Black Greek experience. Ethnographic interviews and a questionnaire revealed that: (1) members and nonmembers showed familiarity with black Greek culture, and that (2) members and nonmembers believed membership in Black Greek–letter organizations is a conduit for power and influence among African-Americans.

Malone, J. "Stepping: Regeneration through Dance in African American Fraternities and Sororities." In *Steppin' on the Blues: The Visible Rhythms of African American Dance.* Urbana: University of Illinois Press, 1996.

Chapter 11 provides a thorough analysis of stepping in Black Greek organizations as a form of dance. Provides some comparison to African dance forms and provides some historical information on the evolution of stepping.

Marriott, M. "Black Fraternities and Sororities End a Tradition." *New York Times* 3 October 1990, B8.

Documents reaction to the changes in the pledge process approved that February. Interviews Darryl Matthews (Alpha Phi Alpha), Daisy Wood (NPHC), Mary Shy Scott (Alpha Kappa Alpha), and Moses Norman (Omega Psi Phi).

Mason, H. Jr. "Historically Speaking: Sisterhood in Atlanta." *Atlanta Metro*, March 1995, 38.

Pictorial sketch that indicates the development of Black sororities in Atlanta.

Matuszewski, K. "Black Greek Groups Face New Criticisms." *The Daily Orange* 36, no. 117 (3 April 1998): 1, 4.

Reviews presentation on Black Greeks by Walter Kimbrough at Syracuse University.

Maxwell, B. "To Black Frats: Grow Up." *New York Times*, 11 May 1991, 23–24.

Columnist from the *Gainesville Sun* writes about the negative actions of Phi Beta Sigma and Kappa Alpha Psi on the campus. Author reveals he dropped line for Omega Psi Phi because of the hate taught of other groups, and how he continues to see it now in graduate ranks.

McCarthy, R. "Hazing probe says 11 witnesses were innocent." *Atlanta Constitution*, 13 November 1996, C4.

Reports that the pledges associated with an illegal process were found guilty of hazing as it related to a UGA football player. Student reported to have been paddled seventy times.

McCarthy, R. "2 More Found Guilty in UGA Hazing Case." *Atlanta Constitution*, 25 October 1996, C2.

Reports on sanctions against students involved in hazing a UGA football player trying to join Phi Beta Sigma fraternity.

McCarthy, R. "UGA Closes Fraternity While Alleged Hazing Investigated." *Atlanta Journal-Constitution*, 27 May 1993, B7.

Reports closing of Kappa Alpha Psi temporarily following the hospitalization of a student. The student had severely infected buttocks. The incident was initially reported to the university by a friend of the victim.

McCoy, M. L. "African American Fraternities and Sororities and African Communities: Cultural Parallels Among Selected Public Rituals" (doctoral dissertation, Bowling Green State University, 1998). *Dissertation Abstracts International* 59, no. 12 (1999): 4465.

Dissertation to examine selected public rituals of Black fraternities and sororities and selected African pubilc rituals to determine what, if any, function these traditions serve for their practitioners. In-depth interviews were conducted with organizations members to discuss the meanings, origins, and functions of the public rituals. Author concluded that while the introduction of the public rituals to the fraternities and sororities varied in time and circumstance, over the years members have come to practice them as an expression of pride in and affirmation of their affiliation with the groups.

McKenzie, A. "Community Service and Social Action: Using the Past to Guide the Future of Black Greek-Letter Fraternities." *NASPA Journal* 28, no. 1 (1990): 30–36.

The author examines Black fraternities from a historical perspective, focusing particularly on their founding and the impact of social action and community service on their development. Discusses founding principles, the Talented Tenth, and the early service programs of the national groups. Four thematic themes are offered to redefine the organizations through more active involvement in campus community: campus service, community service, program advisement and administration, and participation in Greek/student life activities.

McKenzie, A. "Fraters: Black Greek–Letter Fraternities At Four Historically Black Colleges, 1920–1960" (doctoral dissertation, Teachers College, Columbia University, 1986). *Dissertation Abstracts International* 47, no. 6 (1986): 2055.

Dissertation to trace the origin and evolution of Black Greek–letter fraternities at four historically Black colleges (Howard, Lincoln, Fisk, and Clark) and to examine the effect and impact these student societies had on the extracurriculum, the campus culture, and the members themselves over a forty-year period, 1920–1960. The study revealed that fraternities were seen as: serving the personal needs of their members, addressing the social needs of their fellow students, and acting as agents of social change. These organizations were found to be influential in the development and maintenance of out of class experiences at their institutions.

Melucci, M. "Brothers in Scars." *San Francisco Examiner*, 26 March 1997.

Discusses the branding practices of Black fraternities, with broader explanations through body art professionals.

Milloy, C. "The Gang Called Frats." *Washington Post*, 5 May 1993, C1, C10.

Editorial critiquing the organizations based on the hazings at the University of Maryland-College Park involving Omega Psi Phi. Mentions other hazing incidents and discusses concerns about the pledge process and its imitation of slavery.

Mills, D. "The Wrongs of the Rites of Brotherhood: Leaders of Black Fraternities Move to End a Cruel Tradition of Violent Hazing." *Washington Post*, 18 June 1990, B1, B6.

Documents rationale for changing the pledge process with focus on the undergraduate experience. Discusses the Morehouse incident, hazing deaths as reported by C.H.U.C.K, individual tales, plus historical and future trends. Interviews include Carter Womack (Phi Beta Sigma), Charles Wright (Coppin State College/past president of Phi Beta Sigma), and Andrew Young (former Atlanta mayor).

Mitchell, C. "College Hazing Fails Every Test: Black Greek-Letter Groups Meet, Vow End to Violence." *Atlanta Constitution and Journal*, 14 July 1990, A1, A5.

Recaps the Council of Presidents meeting to end pledging, with emphasis on the Joel Harris case at Morehouse College.

Nelson, J. "Stepping Lively: At Black Frats and Sororities, the Dance That Unites." *Washington Post*, 29 May 1990, C1, C8–9.

Describes the details of a recent step show in Washington DC, "Step Fest '90." A historical explanation is provided by Maurice Henderson, author of a book on the topic.

Nelson, J. C. "Comparison of Members and Non-Members of Greek Letter Social Fraternities and Sororities at Virginia State College" (doctoral dissertation, Indiana University, 1959). *Dissertation Abstracts International* 20, no. 9 (1967): 3579.

Dissertation to determine if Greeks at Virginia State differed from non-Greeks in selected characteristics. Among the issues investigated were: academic success, participation in extracurricular activities, adjustment to college, academic load, and general health. Students who participated were initiated into their organizations between 1954 and 1958. The dissertation identified numerous differences between the two groups, with the greatest difference found in the level of participation in extracurricular activities. The second greatest difference was in the scholastic averages of the two groups, which was determined to be a result partly due to the attraction of stronger students academically to Greek organizations.

Noble, J. (1985, May). "A Sense of Place." *Essence*, May 1985, 131+.

Discussion of Black sororities from a historical perspective. Describes the political and community clout the organizations have developed. Charlayne Hunter-Gault is used as an example.

Nomani, A. Q. "Step Dance Unites Blacks on Campus: Its Synchronized Movements Are a Fraternity Ritual and a Focus on Social Life." *Wall Street Journal*, 10 July 1989, A1, A4.

Discusses stepping, including the growing appeal and the cultural/historical foundations. Background is Northwestern University, where several students are interviewed. Interviews include Maurice Henderson (Temple University).

Nuwer, H. "Violence in Historically African American Groups." In *Wrongs of Passage: Fraternities, Sororities, Hazing, and Binge Drinking*. Bloomington: Indiana University Press, 2000.

Nuwer offers chapter 8, "Violence in Historically African American Groups," to discuss hazing in Black Greek organizations. The chapter highlights some of the hazing incidents, particularly that of Joseph Snell at Maryland. Interviews include Tony Williams (Tennessee State), Jason DeSousa (Alabama State), and Michael Gordon (NPHC).

O'Reilly, A. R. "The Impact of Membership in Black Greek–Letter Organizations on the Identity Development of Black Students on Predominantly White Residential Campuses" (Doctoral dissertation, Ohio University, 1990). *Dissertation Abstracts International* 52, no. 2 (1991): 439.

Dissertation examined the impact of membership in Black Greek–letter organizations on the identity development of Black students at two predominantly White residential colleges in Ohio. The data were collected using the Erwin Identity Scale (EIS). For the 158 participants, no significant differences appeared based on affiliation and gender for the Confidence subscale, no significant differences based on affiliation and gender for the Sexual Identity subscale, and no difference based on affiliation and class rank for the Conceptions About Body and Appearance and Sexual Identity subscales. There were differences based on gender for the Conceptions About Body and Appearance subscale, with males scoring higher than females, and class rank for the Confidence subscale. The study suggested that affiliation may not be a significant factor in the development of identity in Black students on predominantly White campuses, but that gender and class rank differences exist for certain subscales.

Parker, L. O. "Brand Identities: Some Call Burning Flesh a 'Rite of Passage.' Others Say It's an Ugly Throwback to Slavery." *Washington Post*, 11 May 1998, D1, D10.

Debates the merits and drawbacks of branding for Black fraternity and sorority members and includes discussion on the prevalence of the fad as seen in gangs. Interviews include Walter Kimbrough, and students at Howard and Old Dominion.

Parker, M. H. *Alpha Kappa Alpha: Through The Years*. Chicago: Mobium Press, 1990.

House history of Alpha Kappa Alpha.

Parker, M. H. *Alpha Kappa Alpha: In the Eye of the Beholder.* Washington, D. C: Alpha Kappa Alpha Sorority, Inc., 1979.

House history of Alpha Kappa Alpha.

Patton, L., and F. A. Bonner II "Advising the Historically Black Greek Letter Organization (HBGLO): A Reason for Angst or Euphoria?" *NASAP Journal,* 4, no. 1 (2001): 17–30.

Provides insight into advising HBGLOs through an overview of history, followed by discussion of current issues. The authors offer recommendations for all constituencies serving in an advisory capacity to these organizations.

Payne, D. "Seven Students Face Hazing Charges." *Atlanta Journal-Constitution*, 2 March 1994, D6.

Reports on students from Georgia Tech and Southern Tech that placed a Southern Tech student in the hospital. The victim indicated his injuries were the result of attempting to join Kappa Alpha Psi Fraternity.

Peeples-Salah, D. "Clap Your Hands and Do a Little Steppin'." *Flint Journal*, 29 January 1994, C1–C2.

Previews an upcoming show in Flint, Michigan, by providing a background of the art form. Interviews include Walter Kimbrough and several community members in Flint.

Pharnor, A. "Breaking the Code: A Delta Sues Her Own Sorority for Hazing." *The Source* 116, (May 1999): 72.

Short article in hip-hop magazine about Delta member at Western Illinois who has sued the organization for hazing.

Pickett, R. A. "Black Greeks Were Born out of Segregation." *Mobile Register*, 6 May 2000.

Discusses the development of Black Greek organizations, referencing E. Franklin Frazier, and then goes on to discuss the activities of the organization in Mobile, Alabama.

"Pledging a Brother, Not Intaking a 'Paper Brother.'" *Black Issues in Higher Education* 14, no. 8 (12 June 1997): 26–27.

Anonymous account of personal experiences with hazing as a part of a Black fraternity.

Posey, S. A. "The Body Art of Brotherhood: Branding in an African American Fraternity" (doctoral dissertation, University of California, Los Angeles, 1999). *Dissertation Abstracts International* 60, no. 8 (2000): 3074.

Dissertation studied branding practices among members of the fraternity Omega Psi Phi Fraternity, and the varied thoughts about its history, purpose, and meaning in the culture of the organization.

Raspberry, W. "Time to Treat Frat Hazings as Assaults." *Virginian-Pilot*, 24 April 1998, B11.

Syndicated editorial by a member of Kappa Alpha Psi who comments on the recent hazings related to his fraternity at Kansas State and the University of Maryland-Eastern Shore.

Reese, P. L. "Applying Organizational Development to Enhance the Culture of Black, Greek-Letter Organizations." *Profile,* 17, no. 2 (June 1994): 1–4.

Author examines problems of Greek misbehavior and the use of organizational development, which was recommended by an earlier study on Greek life and can also be used for Black Greeks. Provides a detailed description of organizational development and offers suggestions as to how the process of OD might be applied.

Reese, P. "Addressing Hazing in Black Greek Organizations through an Awareness of Organizational Culture." *Campus Activities Programming*, December 1993, 37–39.

Author discusses the problems of hazing in Greek organizations, using organization development techniques to diagnose the problems and institute change in fraternities and sororities. Describes the culture of the organizations and the culture of hazing, with emphasis on organizational symbolism and stories that perpetuate hazing.

Rice-Mason, J. "An Assessment of Black Fraternities' and Sororities' Goals on Predominantly White Campuses" (Doctoral dissertation, Southern Illinois University, 1989). *Dissertation Abstracts International* 50, no. 12 (1990): 3928.

Dissertation to investigate administrators' perceptions of Black Greek-letter organizations. The survey measured by opinion of administrators regarding the achievements of Black Greek–letter organizations in community involvement, social and cultural participation, involvement in governance, and scholarship and academic participation on campus. Major findings were that administrators perceived Black Greek–letter organizations achieving these goals: community service and social action, recruitment of members, and involvement in fund raising activities in support of the national organizations' goals. Administrators perceived Black Greek–letter organizations to be achieving their goals at a level significantly less than espoused in promoting political causes and issues, race relations, scholarship and academic preparation, governance, retention of members, and providing a mechanism for fund raising activities in support of the local organizations' goals.

Rodriguez, R. "Pledging Relevance: From the Million Man March to Educational Budget Cuts, Black and Latino Fraternities and Sororities Lock Step with Their Communities." *Black Issues in Higher Education* 12, no. 20 (30 November 1995): 32–34.

Provides an overview of the community action emphasis of Black Greeks. Includes historical perspectives on the purpose of these organizations. Interviews include Jason DeSousa (Kappa Alpha Psi), and Michael Gordon (NPHC).

Ross, J. More arrests expected in hazing attack. *Indiana Daily Student,* 2 March 1994, 1, 14.

Reports on arrests related to the hazing of a student attempting to pledge Omega Psi Phi Fraternity. The chapter was suspended until receipt of criminal reports.

Ross, L. *The Divine Nine*. New York: Kensington, 1999.

A compilation of historical information, most generated from house histories, of the nine largest Black Greek organizations. Interviews with one undergraduate and one graduate chapter of each organization provide a contemporary view of the organizations. Famous members of each organization are interviewed in the final section providing accounts of their membership and thoughts about the Divine Nine.

Rowland, D. "Service Joins Status at Black Fraternities." *Chicago Tribune*, 12 November 1990, D1–D2.

Discusses more active role groups are playing in the Black community. Discusses several local community programs of the groups. Discusses some of the famous members and the misunderstood nature of the groups.

Ruffins, P. "Greek Tragedy." *Washington City Paper* 19, no. 24 (18–24 June 1999): 1, 16–25.

The detailed story of the hazing of Joseph Snell at the University of Maryland by Omega Psi Phi. It further discusses the state of hazing in Black fraternities and sororities in depth. Interviews include Anthony Hill (Province Polemarch, Kappa Alpha Psi), Doug Fierberg (DC attorney who tried the Snell case), and Dr. William Cox (co-owner of *Black Issues in Higher Education*).

Ruffins, P. (1998, June 25). "The Persistent Madness of Greek Hazing." *Black Issues in Higher Education* 15, no. 9 (25 June 1998): 14–18.

Discusses reasons for the continued pledging and hazing within NPHC organizations. Interviews with psychologists explored themes of slavery, abuse, and homoeroticism.

Ruffins, P. "Fratricide. Are African American Fraternities Beating Themselves to Death?" *Black Issues in Higher Education* 14, no. 8 (12 June 1997): 18–25.

Discusses the problems of hazing since the death of Michael Davis. Emphasis on underground pledge activities, sociological aspects of hazing, which includes gangs, and national efforts to end hazing. Also discusses implications of the lack of housing, HBCU concerns, and the issue of rape. The financial implications of hazing are also discussed. Interviews include Jason DeSousa (Alabama State University), John Williams (Tennessee State University), Douglas Richmond (attorney-Missouri), and Antonio McDaniel (sociologist-University of Pennsylvania).

Scales, M. E. "Relationship of Membership in Fraternities and Sororities and Academic Achievement in Four Historically Black Colleges in North Carolina, 1974–1979" (Doctoral dissertation, University of North Carolina at Greensboro, 1982). *Dissertation Abstracts International* 43, no. 7 (1983): 2192.

Dissertation to investigate the comparative relationship between members and non-members of fraternities and sororities in academic achievement at four historically Black schools in North Carolina during the period 1974–79. The results indicated there was no significant difference in year-to-year variation of members and nonmembers over the four years. The data indicated that there was no relationship between membership status and academic achievement.

Schuh, J. H., Triponey, V. L., Heim, L. L., and Nishimura, K. "Student Involvement in Historically Black Greek Letter Organizations." *NASPA Journal* 29, no. 4 (1992): 274–82.

The authors present results of a study designed to examine the experiences of members of NPHC organizations at Witchita State University. The study used qualitative methods, interviewing twenty-two students (of a possible forty-five NPHC members) and reported five themes from the study: bonding, service projects, role modeling, lifelong commitment, and cooperation. Suggestions were offered for staffs who work with NPHC fraternities and sororities to increase support for the groups.

Shea, C. "'Wall of Silence.' After Freshman's Death, Some Black Fraternities Question Effectiveness of Anti-Hazing Efforts." *Chronicle of Higher Education*, 22 June 1994, A25–26.

Discussion of persistent hazing, with emphasis on four Black Greek hazings since the death of Michael Davis at SEMO. Includes incidents involving other fraternities (one white, one Latino), attempted changes in pledging, the defense of pledging by undergrads for bonding, and the division between undergrad and grad members. Interviews include Michael Gordon (NPHC).

Shea, C. "Brutal Hazing Death Shocks Missouri Campus. Students Say Rituals Are Still Common Despite Crackdown." *Chronicle of Higher Education* 40 (26), 2 March 1994, A37–38.

Discusses the death of Michael Davis at SEMO pledging Kappa Alpha Psi, with some history on that chapter. Discusses other recent hazing or fraternity-related deaths, especially associated with White groups.

Shea, C. "U. of Maryland Fraternity Chapter Is Suspended for Abusive Hazing." *Chronicle of Higher Education*, 3 November 1993, A38.

Reports on the suspension of the Omega Psi Phi fraternity following an investigation of hazing. Details specific hazing incidents, which resulted in cracked ribs and a ruptured eardrum for one student; one with a rupture spleen, collapsed lung, and blood clot; and a third with a broken ankle. The chapter was suspended for five years. Indicated a pledge wrote a letter to alert police. Interviews include Jason DeSousa (NPHC).

Snider, D. "Brotherhood Branding Tradition Continues at Some African-American Frats." *Indiana Daily Student*, 20 April 1999.

Discusses branding by Black Greeks at Indiana University, including sorority members.

Spangler, T. "Maryland Police Probe Alleged Hazing." *Associated Press*, 13 April 1998.

Five students at the University of Maryland-Eastern Shore were hospitalized from paddlings while attempting to join Kappa Alpha Psi. They underwent surgery for cuts and infections on their buttocks.

Stains, L. "Black Like Me." *Rolling Stone*, 24 March 1994, 69–72.

Discusses the experiences of a White male student who joins Phi Beta Sigma Fraternity at the University of Alabama.

Stanford, D. D. "3 Men Are Charged in Alleged Hazing." *Atlanta Journal-Constitution*, 27 September 1996, B1.

Reports three men ordered to jail due to hazing of UGA football player and fraternity pledge.

Stanford, D. D. "Frat Pledges Describe UGA Player's Paddling." *Atlanta Journal-Constitution*, 27 September 1996, B2.

Reports the testimony given at the magistrate's hearing on the paddling of a UGA football player. Describes, in detail, the events of the evening, including how the paddling took place.

Stanford, D. D. "UGA Cites Students in Hazing." *Atlanta Journal-Constitution*, 25 September 1996, B1.

Reports two students and adviser as well as fraternity received charges from school.

Stanford, D. D. & Cumming, D. "Police Probe UGA Hazing." *Atlanta Journal-Constitution*, 12 September 1996, B1.

Reports that football player Roderick Perrymond went to emergency room for deep bruises and broken blood vessels in his buttocks. He implicated Phi Beta Sigma Fraternity, prompting university police investigations.

Stombler, M., and Padavic, I. "Sister Acts: Resisting Men's Domination in Black and White Fraternity Little Sister Programs." *Social Problems* 44, no. 2 (1997): 257–75.

Discusses the impact of fraternity little sister programs in relation to gender inequality. Compared resistance by both groups, finding that Black little sisters were more successful in their resistance and that there were structural and cultural differences in little sister programs which account for the differences.

Suggs, E. "The Rise of the Black Greek Empire." *The Herald-Sun* [website]. Available from www.herald-sun.com/hbcu/docs/whyhbcu_3.html.

Special report on Black Greek organizations that discusses the organizations with reference to their programs, traditions, pledging, initiation, hazing, and stepping. The special was done as a part of a report on HBCUs. Interviews include Ralph Johnson (interim executive director of Alpha Phi Alpha), Daisy Wood (NPHC), and Alan Colon (history professor, Hampton).

Taylor, C. M., & Howard-Hamilton, M. F. "Student Involvement and Racial Attitudes Among African American Males." *Journal of College Student Development* 36, no. 4 (1995): 330–35.

The relationship between student involvement and racial identity attitudes among African-American males was examined. The Student Involvement Survey (SIS) and the Racial Identity Attitude Scale (RIAS-B) were administered to 117 African-American males at ten predominantly White universities. A significant relationship was found among the four subscales of the RIAS-B and the SIS total. Indicated that those who participated in Greek-letter organizations tend to embrace a stronger, more positive sense of self-esteem and racial identity than their non-Greek counterparts. Recommendations for student affairs practitioners working with African-American students are presented.

Thompson, C. "Fraternity Members Face Hazing Charges." *The Purdue Exponent*, 4 August 1995, 1.

Reports on criminal charges facing twelve members of Alpha Phi Alpha Fraternity at the university. Described hazing activities between February 6 and 11, including calisthenics, beating, and a game of football. Paddling caused one pledge to pass blood in his urine.

"Three Grambling Students Criminally Charged with Hazing" *Black Issues In Higher Education* 15, no. 25 (4 February 1999): 11.

Students arrested for hazing a prospective member of Kappa Alpha Psi. The victim was treated at the infirmary for bruises and swelling from two days of paddling.

Townsend, A. "Group Served 3-Year Probation after 1989 Hazing during Initiation." *The Indianapolis Journal and Courier*, 3 August 1995, A1.

Provides a historical profile of the Alpha Phi Alpha chapter charged with hazing at Purdue University. The chapter was closed from 1989 to 1992.

Tyler, M. "Role Expectations for Black and White Greeks at a Predominantly White Institution" (Doctoral dissertation, University of Missouri-Columbia, 1990). *Dissertation Abstracts International* 51, no. 8 (1991): 2658.

Dissertation to examine the role expectations university administrators, Black Greeks and White Greeks hold for Black and White Greeks. The administrators had greater role expectations for members of Black Greek organizations in the areas of Social and Mentor/Resource. Administrators reported no difference in role expectations for members of Black and White Greek organizations for the categories of Student, Leader, Community Servant, Disciplinarian, or Campus supporter. Members of both Black and White Greek organizations reported greater expectations for themselves in the categories of Student, Leader, Social, Mentor/Resource, and Community Servant than they did for members of the opposite-race Greek organization, and perceived members of the opposite-race Greek organization as having greater expectations in the area of Disciplinarian than they had for themselves. Concluded that administrators have some unrealistic expectations for Black Greeks.

"University Softens on Some Aspects of Hazing Policy" *New York Times*, Campus Life, section I, 4 March 1990, 37.

Discusses a change in the stance of Rutgers University, which banned many traditional activities associated with Black Greek pledging, including walking in line and dressing alike. Interviews include Teresa Loser (Rutgers dean of fraternity and sorority affairs) and Nicole Webb (student-president of Minority Greek Council).

Usdansky, M. L. "Frat Brothers Remorseful, Frustrated. Charged with Hazing, Three Give 1st Interview Since Death." *Atlanta Journal-Constitution*, 5 November 1989, D1, D6.

Provides the details of the events surrounding the death of Joel Harris at Morehouse College on 17 October 1989 as provided by three undergraduate members who gave a public interview concerning the matter.

Walzer, P. "Judge Lets Stand NSU Expulsions over Hazing." *Virginian-Pilot*, 4 May 1999, B1, B4.

Details expulsion of nine members of Delta Sigma Theta for hazing of a student at Norfolk State University, which caused the student to be hospitalized in intensive care. Interviews include a lawyer for those suspended, and the university president (also a member of the sorority).

Watkins, R. T. "Black Social Orders. Expanding Their Goals to Fit the Needs of the Community at Large." *Black Enterprise*, July 1975, 26–28.

Analysis of the reemergence of Black social orders as organizations of social consciousness. Includes discussions of Masons as well as Black fraternal organizations. Concludes with a short digest of some of the organizations' community efforts.

Welsh-Huggins, A. "IU Student Talks about Alleged Fraternity Hazing." *Bloomington Herald-Times,* 5 March 1994, A1.

Report from an hour-long news conference held by an Indiana University student who was allegedly hazed by members of Omega Psi Phi Fraternity. He described, in detail, hazing which included beatings and paddlings. The fraternity's chapter adviser, an IU law student, was also implicated in the events.

Wesley, C. H. *The History of Alpha Phi Alpha: A Development In College Life*. Chicago: Foundation Publishers, 1961.

House history of Alpha Phi Alpha.

Wesley, C. H. *History of Sigma Pi Phi. First of the Negro-American Greek-Letter Fraternities*. New York: Sigma Pi Phi Fraternity, 1954.

House history of Sigma Pi Phi.

Wessel, K. "Hazing Victim to Get $1 Million." *Louisville Courier-Journal*, 7 April 2000.

Discusses Omega Psi Phi dropping its appeal from a court decision requiring the organization to pay $1 million for a hazing incident at the University of Louisville in 1997. The organization did not want to risk the 12 percent annual interest added if they lost the appeal, which could have reached another $1 million.

Wharton, G. "Forging Ties that Can Last a Lifetime." *Boston Globe*, 28 August 1988, B19–B21.

Provides a general overview of Black Greek life. Discusses some of the cultural artifacts, the graduate experience, and community service. Lists persons in Boston who are members. Provides some historical reference for the founding of the organizations. Ends with discussion of the pledge process and general opinions by nonmembers.

Whipple, E. G., Baier, J. L., & Grady, D. L. "A Comparison of Black and White Greeks at a Predominantly White University." *NASPA Journal* 28, no. 2 (1991): 140–48.

The authors present results of a study that assessed the academic attitudes, intellectual values, family socioeconomic status, and financial concerns of Black and White Greeks. A subsample of 620 fraternity and sorority members, part of a total sample of 1,540 students surveyed at the University of Alabama. Conclusions indicated that Black Greeks generally come from lower SES, are more academically motivated, more liberal, more socially conscious, and more peer independent than White Greeks.

White, P. S. *Behind These Doors—A Legacy: The History of Sigma Gamma Rho Sorority.* Chicago: Sigma Gamma Rho Sorority, Inc., 1974.

House history of Sigma Gamma Rho.

Wilcots, K. D. "The Relationship between Level of African-American Acculturation and Affiliation with Fraternities and Sororities" (Master's thesis, University of North Texas, 1998). *Masters Abstracts International* 36, no. 6 (1998): 1700.

Ninety-nine African-American undergraduates, at a historically Black college, completed the African American Acculturation Scale to compare fraternity/sorority members with independents' participation in Black cultural traditions versus dominant White society. Greek members were hypothesized to be more traditional. Findings did not support this, but reasons for joining did. They were more superstitious in their beliefs than nonmembers, likely related to pledgeship and initiation rituals. Why participants join fraternities, why they like/dislike them, and what purposes they serve were also examined.

Wiley, E., and Clarke, A. "Recent Death Rekindles Concern about Fraternity Hazing." *Black Issues in Higher Education* 6 (9 November 1989): 13.

Recaps the death of Joel Harris at Morehouse College and discusses the possible outcomes of the incident. Interviews include James Rogers (California State University professor), who discusses similarities with gang initiations.

Wilkerson, I. "Black Fraternities Thrive, Often on Adversity." *New York Times*, 2 October 1989, A1, B11.

Reports that while the groups were formed with noble intentions, they are criticized mainly due to the perpetuation of the pledge process. Also mentions that groups are criticized due to the large crowds drawn to step shows. Discusses the racial climate when the groups were founded, and continued racial separation in fraternal organizations. Also discusses the service and philanthropic activities of the groups, along with famous members and networking opportunities. Finally discusses the activities associated with pledging, the potential of changing the process, and the expected resistance from members and those seeking membership who want to prove worthiness.

Williams, J. A. *Hazing in Black Fraternities* [website]. Available from http://www. stophazing.org/fraternity_hazing/blackfrat.htm.

Short article about the mind-set of persons who participate in hazing within Black fraternities.

Williams, J. A. "Perceptions of the No-Pledge Policy for New Member Intake by Undergraduate Members of Predominantly Black Fraternities and Sororities" (Doctoral dissertation, Kansas State University, 1992). *Dissertation Abstracts International* 53, no. 9 (1993): 3111.

Dissertation to describe the perceptions of undergraduate members of predominantly black fraternities and sororities on the no-pledge policy for new member intake. Three scales used. No significant differences between fraternity and sorority members were found on the Policy Awareness Scale. Hazing Tolerance Scale and Policy Endorsement Scale showed significant differences in scores from expected outcomes. Content analysis of the optional item indicated undergraduates felt: (a) No-pledge policy enacted too quickly without their input, (b) hazing definitions were too broad, (c) new policy left insufficient time to teach history, (d) bonding was lost,

(e) lifelong commitment is jeopardized, (f) the policy promotes disunity in chapter ranks, and (g) new members feel they get no respect from older members.

Wilson, P. "Credibility Battle Led To Fraternity Suspension." *Maneater* 65, no. 52 (13 April 1991): 1.

Details the hearing for Kappa Alpha Psi at the University of Missouri, Columbia. The chapter was found guilty of hazing after a student came forward, and later retracted his allegations. The chapter was suspended for four years.

Index